THE

GREAT RESET

JOE BIDEN

AND THE

RISE OF 21ST

CENTURY

FASCISM

WRITTEN & EDITED BY

GLENN BECK

WITH JUSTIN HASKINS

CONTRIBUTOR
DONALD KENDAL

Forefront
BOOKS

MERCURY
INK

The Great Reset
Joe Biden and the Rise of Twenty-First Century Fascism

©2022 Mercury Radio Arts, Inc.
Mercury Ink is a trademark of Mercury Radio Arts, Inc.

Published by Forefront Books and Mercury Ink.

Cover Design by Alexander Somoskey
Interior Design by Bill Kersey, KerseyGraphics

ISBN: 978-1-63763-059-4 print
ISBN: 978-1-63763-060-0 e-book

ALSO BY GLENN BECK

DEDICATION

To all those who still believe that men are born to be free.

CONTENTS

PREFACE

IN AUGUST 1787, THOMAS JEFFERSON AUTHORED A LETTER TO his nephew Peter Carr, who had lived with Jefferson at Monticello. At the time, Jefferson was living in Paris while serving as a vital diplomat for the emerging American nation. In the letter, Jefferson advised Carr about various topics, including religion.

"Fix reason firmly in her seat, and call to her tribunal every fact, every opinion," Jefferson wrote. "Question with boldness even the existence of a god; because, if there be one, he must more approve the homage of reason, than that of blindfolded fear."[1]

Question with boldness. Those words instantly captured me. It's as though they were embedded in my soul. And since reading them, many years ago, I have tried to the best of my ability to live by them. I think it's one of the reasons so many in my audience respect the work my team and I have accomplished over the past couple of decades.

Of course, questioning with boldness can also be a dangerous business. There are many people in power who wish I and tens of millions of other Americans would just shut the heck up and do what we're told. That would, after all, make it a whole lot easier for the ruling class to achieve its goal of further consolidating its wealth and authority over the rest of society. Asking questions is one of the most important things any American can do today, because the roots of so many of the world's problems have been concealed from the public. Only by asking questions can we discover the truth and chart a new course for the United States.

Throughout this book, you are going to discover many concepts very few people today understand or have even heard of. Some of this material will shock you, as it did me—and I'm not easily shocked. You will at times be skeptical, and that's a good thing. I don't want you to take my word for anything that's in this book, which is why I have included several hundred citations and mountains of direct quotes from important sources.

I do have one request for you, however. Before we start our journey together, I would like you to take a moment to think about how much the world you live in today has become a fun house mirror distortion of the world you used to know and understand. Then I'd like you to ask yourself the following questions.

Why are large corporations becoming the champions of "woke" causes and engaging in political debates about things like voter identification laws?

Why did the stock market grow substantially throughout 2020 and 2021, despite one of the biggest global economic collapses in history?

Why did housing prices skyrocket in 2020 and 2021?

Why are politicians in both the Democratic and the Republican Parties now spending trillions of dollars more than the government takes in, and why aren't they afraid of runaway inflation?

Why are central banks all over the world talking about creating their own digital currencies?

Why are people who claim that climate change is an existential threat to human life building mansions on islands and beaches, despite alleged fears of rising sea levels, and flying around the world in private jets that spew carbon dioxide into the atmosphere?

Why are social media giants scrambling to stifle speech at every turn?

Why are web hosting companies shutting down massive platforms that advocate free speech, silencing millions of people?

Why are the heads of numerous Western countries—including Canada, France, the United Kingdom, and America—all using the exact same "Build Back Better" slogan?

Why are leading figures on the left, including President Joe Biden, calling for "stakeholder capitalism," and what is the difference between stakeholder capitalism and a free market economic model?

Why do the American people no longer trust many of our society's most important institutions?

Why does the media pay more attention to a tweet from Donald Trump than to a mob burning down a police station or to rioters taking over whole city blocks for days at a time?

Why can't we have an honest dialogue anymore? Why has the political discourse become so vitriolic?

Why are people on the ideological right and left being "canceled" over the slightest societal misstep?

Why were the size and scope of the coronavirus-related stimulus programs so large? Why did government officials distribute thousands of dollars to families who never lost their jobs or suffered from any economic hardships during the pandemic?

Why were massive corporations allowed to stay open during the COVID-19 pandemic while many small businesses were forced to close?

Why has President Joe Biden worked so hard to impose coronavirus vaccine mandates on Americans, regardless of whether they have already developed natural immunity?

Why are people who have been vaccinated forced in many states to wear masks in public places, even when there are very few people present?

If you don't know the answer to all of these questions, it is because you have yet to fully understand the Great Reset—the single most important topic I have covered in my career, and the movement that could finally snuff out the flame of liberty in America.

I do not expect you to agree with everything I have written in this book, but I firmly believe that if you approach this material with an open mind and a commitment to pursuing the truth, you will agree that the United States—and indeed the entirety of Western civilization—is in grave peril because of the Great Reset. Only strong resistance from those who believe in democratic principles and individual liberty can stop it.

1
A ~~BRAVE~~ TERRIFYING NEW WORLD

*To achieve a better outcome, the world must act jointly
and swiftly to revamp all aspects of our societies and
economies, from education to social contracts and working
conditions.... In short, we need a "Great Reset" of capitalism.*

—Klaus Schwab, executive chairman of the
World Economic Forum, June 3, 2020

*Yes, it will happen. And I think it will happen with greater speed
and with greater intensity than a lot of people might imagine.*

—John Kerry, special climate envoy for President Joe
Biden, discussing the Great Reset at a November 2020
event hosted by the World Economic Forum

THE DATE IS AUGUST 29, 2040. TWO DECADES AFTER WORLD leaders gathered at the World Economic Forum's 2020 event to formulate a plan for imposing a Great Reset of the global economic system, life in America has dramatically changed. The rules, social norms, and market economic principles that used to define the American experience have been permanently rewritten.

The economy, once driven by the wants and needs of the individual consumer, is now guided by an agenda crafted by a cabal of international elites. Despite having been marketed as a solution to all of society's ills, the Great Reset agenda has left everyday Americans worse off than ever before and increasingly dependent on the government and wealthy global corporations that serve as the foundation of this brave and terrifying new world.

After committing to the principles of the Great Reset, Congress passed a version of the Green New Deal. The legislation has wiped out more than ten million jobs supported by the oil and gas industry, devastating the economies of Colorado, North Dakota, Pennsylvania, Texas, and other states that once benefited from fracking and other forms of conventional energy development.[2]

A billion solar panels and more than a million wind turbines have been constructed across the United States, destroying tens of millions of acres of land.[3] Hundreds of thousands of additional acres have been decimated by the thousands of miles of new power lines and extensive mining operations needed to obtain the natural resources used to build America's expansive wind and solar facilities.[4]

Millions of birds and bats, including endangered species, are killed every year by the massive spinning blades of America's vast wind farms. Millions of other animals have been displaced following the collapse of countless ecosystems resulting from the destruction caused by developers building new renewable energy facilities.

Energy prices have more than tripled in many parts of the country. In places with less sunshine and wind, energy prices are five times higher. Blackouts are common, especially in regions with frigid winters.

The widespread construction that occurred under the Reset's rapid transformation of America's energy sector has replaced *some* of the jobs lost in the oil and gas industry, but millions of additional jobs—many of which were once located in America's heartland—have been shipped overseas, as manufacturers and other energy-intensive industries have fled in droves to nations with lower prices for electricity and other forms of energy. As a result, hundreds of cities and towns across the United States have become economically depressed.

Restaurants, food vendors, and grocery stores limit meat sales to help battle climate change. High-fat and sugary foods are restricted or banned outright.

Gasoline-powered cars have been outlawed or rendered useless by the elimination of fossil fuels. Air travel has decreased dramatically as prices have increased because of harsh regulations on carbon dioxide emissions. Americans have been promised a new national network of high-speed rail, but more than ten years into its construction, little progress has been made, as environmentalists, concerned communities, and politicians continue to fight over the location of the rail lines.[5]

Taxes on businesses have doubled, and a slew of new sales, wealth, and real estate levies have been created by government officials in an attempt to create greater economic "equity." America's wealthiest business owners and innovators have left the country and moved to competitor nations that refused to go along with the Great Reset, flooding those nations with hundreds of billions of dollars in new wealth. The groups of Americans hit hardest by the economic exodus are lower-income and working-class families.

Nearly three-quarters of Americans now depend on the federal government for many basic goods and services. Tens of millions of working-age adults refuse to find a job and instead live off the government's basic income system. Millions of others are employed by federal or state government agencies through the national government's "job guarantee" program.

The federal government routinely runs deficits of $10 trillion or more. The national debt has surpassed $100 trillion. International unease about the strength of the U.S. dollar galvanized the world's largest economies to develop a new currency for international transactions, causing investors and foreign banks to flood American markets with their cash. Historically high levels of inflation in key industries followed, pushing the United States into a second Great Depression. National GDP has been sluggish, at best, for more than a decade.[6]

A new federal agency—the U.S. Department of Environmental, Social, and Governance (ESG) Compliance—has been created to develop and maintain an ever-shifting series of standards that determine which American businesses are permitted to trade in the country's largest stock exchanges, as well as who can receive the hundreds of billions of dollars pumped into corporations every year by government officials desperate to keep more companies from heading overseas.[7]

Many businesses spend hundreds of thousands or even millions of dollars every year attempting to meet ESG standards, and every corporation is required to have an ESG compliance officer on its board of directors, matching standards that had already been in place for decades in China.[8]

In line with the standards created by the U.S. Department of Environmental, Social, and Governance Compliance, businesses shift their product development toward causes endorsed by and favoring elites in government and business. Every American corporation is forced to report the racial and gender demographics of its staff and management and to justify every hiring decision made over the past year.

Gun and ammunition manufacturers and sellers, frequent targets of government bureaucrats, are effectively forced to close their doors due to overwhelming regulatory compliance costs.

Individual investors, large and small, are given specialized ratings for their investments. Investors who attempt to earn money in those businesses that the ruling class considers to be undesirable for society—like candy stores, vape shops, and ranches—are punished with financial penalties.

Newly structured, ESG-compliant corporations wield more influence than ever over society. Private ownership of most products is a thing of the past. Housing, automobiles, and many other key goods are now available only as services offered by corporations. Most consumers rent products instead of buying, not because they want to but because they can't afford to own property anymore.[9]

Everyday Americans' credit scores—the ratings used by financial institutions to determine creditworthiness for credit cards, car loans, and mortgages, among other things—are no longer based on traditional financial metrics. Instead, financial institutions use consumers' browser history, social media activity, and other previously private user information from tech devices to craft credit scores for the Americans still wealthy enough to own high-priced property. Individuals and business owners with a history of browsing "dangerous" websites that dare to challenge the government's official narrative or of searching for concerning topics online are deemed too untrustworthy for many lenders and credit service companies.[10]

A national free college tuition plan has put, directly or indirectly, the federal government in charge of virtually every higher education institution in America. Most private colleges, including the vast majority of religious schools, have shut their doors forever or have agreed to become secular public institutions in order to take part in the free tuition plan, which is available only to students attending government-run colleges.[11]

Nearly all K–12 school choice programs across the United States have been defunded, pushing thousands of parents to send their children back to their local government-run school district, no matter how dangerous or dysfunctional it is.[12] Parents have virtually no control over curriculum standards. Children spend less time learning about math and science and much more time learning about critical race theory and other social justice topics, causing them to fall even further behind their peers in other developed nations.

Using ESG standards as their excuse, social media companies like Facebook and Twitter, and search engines such as Google, have expanded their content restrictions, banning from their platforms many types of speech, including political and religious speech, which have been labeled "offensive," "misleading," or "misinformation." As a result, tens of millions of voices across the country have been silenced.

China, India, and Russia have refused to comply with the Great Reset reforms mandated by newly created climate accords and several international meetings of government and business officials. This has allowed these countries to keep their energy costs down, which in turn provides them with substantial leverage in trade agreements.

China and India are now the world's most influential and powerful nations. They use their vast wealth to continue buying large amounts of land and natural resources from developing nations in Asia and Africa, setting the stage for their global dominance over the next one hundred years.

This is what life looks like in a post–Great Reset world. This is the potential future we must do everything in our power to stop.

THE AMERICA WE REMEMBER

For the past two decades, I have been warning my audience that the country millions of us grew up in—a nation built on hard work, honor, kindness toward neighbors, and unashamed, flag-waving love of freedom—is on the verge of vanishing, and that the day in which we would no longer recognize our country would soon be upon us. Unfortunately, the events of the past year have proven, beyond any doubt, that the moment I have long feared has come.

The America we remember, the America of carefree summers, Saturday night trips to movie theaters, warm family holiday gatherings, and mom-and-pop restaurants, has been replaced with a culture driven by suspicion, rampant fear, and ideological and political tribalism and dominated by massive, multinational corporations.

Sure, Grandma can still bake apple pies while the family watches a good, ol'-fashioned baseball game, but whatever elements of American culture remain are now superficial. Beneath the glowing stars-and-stripes veneer is a terminally ill superpower teetering on the edge. And the worst part is, our most disruptive, dangerous days still lie ahead.

At lavish cocktail parties in European resort towns and in the boardrooms of the world's largest corporations, powerful and influential leaders are putting the finishing touches on the vast infrastructure needed to alter our communities forever. These changes—some enormous, some barely noticeable—are all part of a sweeping proposal to transform the global economy, a plan ominously named the Great Reset.

The final result of the Great Reset would be the disturbing vision of the future I laid out earlier in this chapter—societies with fewer personal freedoms and even more cronyism and political and economic centralization. And these are just the *features* of their program, not its unintended consequences.

But you don't need to take my word for it—and you shouldn't. There is a seemingly endless sea of downright disturbing quotes from those involved in the Great Reset that clearly articulate their plans for the future of America. Throughout the remainder of the book, you're going to encounter many of these quotes, which are occasionally quite long and sometimes featured more than once. This is by design. I want you to hear what the Great Reset is directly from the globalist horse's mouth, so that the next time someone says, "The Great Reset is nothing but a right-wing conspiracy theory," you'll know with certainty who is telling the truth and who is looking to make big banks and corporations happy.

UNMASKING THE RESET

The Great Reset is a proposal that is breathtaking in its scope. Its backers support altering nearly every part of society, from the cars we drive to the food we eat to the news reports we watch on television. Its core foundation was shaped almost entirely by a small, extremely wealthy and well-connected group of people, one that includes highly influential business leaders, environmentalists, government officials, and bankers.

The goal of the Great Reset is both shocking and wildly ambitious: to transform the global economy, eliminate free markets, impose a new, more easily controllable and malleable economic system, and change the way people think about private property and corporations. The reset part of the Great Reset is an allusion to "pushing the reset button" on the global economy—and boy, do they want to push that sucker hard.

Who is behind this radical plan? In early June 2020, the World Economic Forum (WEF), a large nonprofit based in Switzerland, held a virtual meeting featuring many of the most powerful people on the face of the planet. The purpose of the meeting was to launch a new campaign for a Great Reset of the global economy, using the COVID-19 pandemic and climate change as justifications for their proposed reforms to society.

Although you may not realize it, you have almost certainly heard about the World Economic Forum in media reports, likely in news or opinion stories about WEF's annual meeting. Gathering in the posh resort mountain town of Davos, international elites pamper themselves in luxurious hotels and enjoy extravagant meals between high-level meetings among titans of industry, finance, and government.

The Davos crowd often gets a bad rap for hosting lavish parties after spending long days lamenting about the plight of the common man, but I think we should give them a break. After all, scheming about the best ways to lord over the entire world in between ski trips is hard work.

In an article published on the World Economic Forum's website, WEF executive chairman and cofounder Klaus Schwab explained in detail some the most important goals of the Reset. "COVID-19 lockdowns may be gradually easing, but anxiety about the world's social and economic prospects is only intensifying," Schwab wrote.[13]

"To achieve a better outcome," Schwab wrote later in the article, "the world must act jointly and swiftly to revamp all aspects of our societies and economies, from education to social contracts and working conditions....Every industry, from oil and gas to tech, must be transformed. In short, we need a 'Great Reset' of capitalism."[14]

Changing "all aspects of our societies and economies, from education to social contracts"—what could possibly go wrong?

Schwab and Prince Charles were joined by a long list of important figures in business, economics, and a variety of powerful organizations calling for a Great Reset, including António Guterres, the U.N. secretary-general; Jennifer Morgan, the executive director of

Greenpeace International; Gita Gopinath, the lead economist at the International Monetary Fund; and Bernard Looney, CEO of BP.[15]

In a speech, Greenpeace's Jennifer Morgan explained that the COVID-19 pandemic offers an opportunity to reshape the world in a way that is reminiscent of the "new world order" established after World War II ended.

"We set up a new world order after World War II," Morgan said. "We're now in a different world than we were then. We need to ask, what can we be doing differently? The World Economic Forum has a big responsibility in that as well—to be pushing the reset button and looking at how to create well-being for people and for the Earth."[16]

Sharan Burrow, the general secretary of the International Trade Union Confederation, explained during an interview about the Great Reset that one of those things we can be doing differently is "design a better world" based on "solidarity" and "sharing."[17]

"Solidarity and sharing and deciding on how you protect people—both within nations and globally—is absolutely critical at the moment," she added.[18]

"We need to design policies to align with investment in people and the environment. *But above all, the longer-term perspective is about rebalancing economies*," Burrow later said.[19]

One of the ways in which Great Reset supporters like Burrow want to design a better world is by engaging in massive wealth redistribution schemes, ones that would promote economic "equality," not only among citizens within individual nations but also between countries.

Influential CEOs and presidents from major U.S. corporations have also participated in WEF meetings about the Great Reset, including Ajay Banga, the chief executive officer of Mastercard, and Bradford Smith, president of Microsoft.[20] (I think even the Monopoly guy and Scrooge McDuck threw in their support for the plan, but my research staff is still waiting for confirmation from McDuck's communications director.)

Additionally, several establishment American political figures promoted the Great Reset in the weeks following the June 2020 meeting. The king of climate change himself, Al Gore, called for the Great Reset in a June 19 interview with NBC's *TODAY* television show.

"So, I think this is a time for a 'Great Reset,'" Gore said, after arguing that electric cars and renewable energy sources like wind and solar can provide lucrative economic benefits. "We've got to fix a lot of these problems that have been allowed to fester for way too long. And the climate crisis is an opportunity to create tens of millions of new jobs, clean up the air, and reduce the death rate from pandemics, by the way, because the air pollution from burning fossil fuels heightens the death rates from coronavirus."[21]

John Kerry also promoted the Great Reset in a lengthy June 2020 interview with the World Economic Forum, during which he reportedly said, "This is a big moment. The World Economic Forum—the CEO capacity of the Forum—is really going to have to play a front and center role in refining the Great Reset to deal with climate change and inequity—all of which is being laid bare as a consequence of COVID-19."[22]

Kerry, in particular, has positioned himself as one of the leading voices in the U.S. government for the Great Reset, thanks almost entirely to his close relationship with President Biden.

In the wake of the November 2020 election, Biden announced that Kerry would serve as his administration's special climate envoy—a cabinet-level position, if you can believe it. In that role, Kerry has been given a tremendous amount of authority over one of the most important parts of the Great Reset plan in the United States, the climate and energy policies of the Biden-Harris administration.

Speaking of President Biden, he, too, is a staunch supporter of the Reset and fully committed to enacting its agenda, both in the United States and around the world. President Biden's role in this movement cannot be understated. The moment he became president, the U.S. government's unofficial platform immediately and dramatically shifted from President Trump's "America First" agenda to the globalist Great Reset. But you will have to wait until chapter 6 to see the ironclad evidence that my research team and I have gathered uncovering the fact—not opinion—that President Biden is working toward implementing this far-reaching reset of the global economy. (You didn't think I'd let you in on everything in the first chapter, did you?)

For now, it is vital that you keep in mind that the plan for a Great Reset is not some far-off, left-wing European fantasy that has little or nothing to do with America. Many of the most important figures tied to the Great Reset are, in fact, American. And most of the large corporations, banks, and financial institutions that have backed the plan are also from the United States or have significant financial ties to the country.

Everything we have discussed to this point about the Great Reset is just the tip of the iceberg. The Great Reset is so much more than utopian promises from ruling-class elites and scary quotes about resetting the global economy. And the World Economic Forum and its allies have made it clear that they are planning to expand the Great Reset agenda—which they are now trying to rebrand—at key meetings in the years to come, so it is possible that as spectacularly radical as the movement looks today, it could get even worse.[23]

I can hear the skeptics already: "There goes that nutjob Glenn Beck again! What's next, Glenn? You going to tell us the earth is really flat and that ancient aliens built the pyramids?"

Look, I get it. When I first heard about the Great Reset, it sounded like a poorly written movie plot some struggling thirtysomething in

Los Angeles cooked up in his mom's basement between shifts at the Cheesecake Factory. But then I started to dig into the details about the Great Reset and what its most passionate supporters were saying, not just in private but publicly, on the record. And the more I learned, the more obvious it became that although the Great Reset is indeed a wild, crazy, completely out-there conspiracy, it is a very real one—and it has the potential to dramatically alter our world forever.

TWENTY-FIRST CENTURY FASCISM

I'll discuss much more in chapter 5 about the Great Reset and the specific policies its adherents want to impose. But fully grasping the extent of the Great Reset and the impact it would have on the global economy will require rethinking numerous ideas about society and the roles technology and emerging economic theories have had on our world, especially in the wake of the COVID-19 pandemic.

The Great Reset's biggest advocates never use the words *fascism* or *authoritarianism* to describe the Reset or their agenda. They have worked very hard to integrate capitalistic language like *markets* and *investments* into their plans, and many have even tried to frame the Great Reset's provisions as creating a new kind of capitalism—so-called stakeholder capitalism—while simultaneously talking about ending many of the world's markets.

Do not be fooled into thinking that the Great Reset's use of capitalist-sounding language is anything other than a smartly designed marketing trick. The Reset would create a system that is, in nearly every way, a complete rejection of market economics. And this would happen not just in a handful of European or African countries either but virtually everywhere.

As the head of WEF wrote in a June 2020 article promoting the Great Reset, "Every country, from the United States to China, must participate, and every industry, from oil and gas to tech, must be transformed. In short, we need a 'Great Reset' of capitalism."[24]

Before moving on, take note of the important and overtly fascistic use of the word *must* in the WEF leader's statement. It is not enough to say that the global economy could, should, or ought to change. No, it *must* change. And "every country ... must participate" and "every industry ... must be transformed." (Don't you just love being told what to do by people who spend more money on suits than you earn in a year?)

The mechanisms that Great Reset world leaders would use to create their brave new world are, by design, complex and in some cases require concepts and strategies most people around the world have never heard of, like "modern monetary theory" and "environmental, social, and governance standards." On the surface, many of these ideas can seem agonizingly tedious and even downright boring, especially when you look at them on their own. But once you realize that each of these ideas is a puzzle piece that connects to form a much larger, more transformative and radical scheme, it is easy to see why powerful people around the world are pushing so hard to promote the Great Reset, and why I'm working so hard to fight against it.

Unlike many other troubling plans promoted in the past by elites in government and business, the Great Reset is not dangerous because it *could* lead to soft authoritarianism or a form of fascism at some distant moment in the future. It is dangerous because it *is* soft authoritarianism and it *is* a new kind of fascism. It has merely been carefully rebranded as a variation of capitalism, an "inclusive capitalism," in order to fool well-meaning people—on the political left and right—who otherwise would never want the United States to adopt Great Reset ideas.

It is true that the Great Reset does not look identical to many of the authoritarian movements of the past, and there are some important differences that we will need to dive into later in this book, but I believe that if fascism is ever to take hold in the United States, the Great Reset—or some similar, renamed version of it—is the way in which it will happen.

The Great Reset will not necessarily require the mass imprisonment of dissenters, nationwide confiscation of businesses, or a bloody revolution. It can achieve authoritarian goals without jackbooted storm troopers or gulags, and it includes just enough elements of cronyism and payouts to global elites to make the system palatable to the world's wealthiest and most well-connected people. It is a kind of authoritarian, international, socialistic fascism, yes, but it's not Marx's socialism or the fascistic models embraced by Benito Mussolini. It is authoritarianism for our brand-new technology-rich, corrupt era. It is twenty-first century fascism.

In the twentieth century, communist, fascist, and Marxist revolutions—whether they occurred through democratic reforms, as they did in Sweden, or through bloody revolutions, as they did in the Soviet Union and China—ultimately proved to be wildly unsuccessful. (That is the understatement of the century, I know.) But this long track record of failure has not been enough to convince many people, including millions of Americans, that authoritarian schemes do not work, only that previous methods and models for imposing authoritarianism were unsuccessful. So instead of giving up on literally some of the worst ideas human beings have ever come up with, elites and their political allies continuously work to find new ways to promote policies that have failed for centuries.

That is where the Great Reset comes in. The Great Reset does not reflect an expectation for a global revolution of the working class, contrary to the views of Karl Marx. It also is not attempting to usher in that Marxist revolution using all of Lenin's blood-soaked tactics. The Great Reset's supporters are not interested in mandating the same kind of mass migrations of people we saw under the Khmer Rouge in Cambodia or Stalin in Russia. And perhaps most surprisingly, the Great Reset does not demonize large private businesses and corporations in the same way that others have in the past, including leftists like Bernie Sanders (much more on this in chapter 5).

Under a twenty-first century fascist model, there will likely be, at least at first, much less violence and property confiscation than what the world has witnessed under previous versions of authoritarianism. Instead the Great Reset program is designed to move the world toward collectivism and soft authoritarianism through a combination of new monetary policies, tax regimes designed to punish "undesirable" industries, huge new "green" infrastructure plans, and sweeping social programs that seek to make the vast majority of people, including many in the middle class, dependent on collective institutions and government programs. And rather than confiscate businesses on behalf of the collective or mandate that they become socialist enterprises, the Great Reset's twenty-first century fascist policies would use the power of money printing to coerce and control the world's most influential and powerful businesses, allowing governments to manipulate society and economic activity in unprecedented ways.

DEFINING THE GREAT RESET

The more I have learned about the Great Reset, the harder it has become to define it. The Great Reset is not socialism, even though it does include some socialistic government programs. It isn't free market economics, because elites, governments, and central banks control and even micromanage economic decision making. The Great Reset is full of corporatism, but it is so much more than big bailouts and sweetheart deals between businesses and corrupt politicians. Technology is a huge part of the Reset, but calling it a technocracy fails to capture the full weight of the Reset's transformation of economic and societal activity. The Great Reset is highly fascistic but not violent or nationalistic, like many of the fascist systems of Europe in the twentieth century.

The reason the Great Reset is so hard to define is because nothing quite like it has ever been tried before, at least not on this scale. The most accurate name for the Reset is probably something like "modern corporate cronyist techno socialistic international fascism," but that doesn't exactly roll off the tongue. So after much consideration and debate, I have decided to call it twenty-first century fascism—in large part because of the plan's similarities to Nazi-era controls on businesses in Germany.

However, you will probably notice throughout this book the Great Reset's parallels to the Chinese "capitalist" economic model, which has for decades attempted to blend corruption, technology, despotism, and corporatism together into a soft-authoritarian smoothie that tastes a lot like the delectable poison being peddled under the Great Reset brand today.

This is not a coincidence. For many years, elites in the West have watched with deep admiration the Chinese government achieve an economic transformation at breakneck speed. And on more than several hundred occasions, they have openly remarked with amazement about China's ability to get the job done, while also quietly muttering concerns about China's record of abusing human rights.

The Great Reset is, in a very real sense, Western elites' attempt at improving upon the China model, which probably explains why the World Economic Forum—which, remember, is one of the key players in the promotion of the Great Reset—has numerous close ties with important figures in China, including Chinese leaders who have served on WEF's board of trustees.[25]

Now, some who read this book might be tempted to think that the grand promises of "equality" and "ending poverty" promoted by advocates of the Great Reset sound pretty good. But before you consume one too many drinks at the bar and jump into bed with Davos Man, please take some time to carefully investigate *every* aspect of the Great Reset—not just the smiley face stuff they put in the brochures.

The Great Reset is not really about helping the poor or saving the planet. It is about making the rich richer and expanding the power of the ruling class—goals that many elites have shared across cultures, historical eras, and geographies.

It is tempting to fall into the trap of seeing controversy over the Great Reset as yet another left-versus-right debate. And yes, undoubtedly there are included in the Reset some progressive and even socialistic elements that I believe would be exceptionally harmful to American families—an issue I'll deal with throughout this book. But for the most part, these elements are merely distractions from the Great Reset's most important and transformative components, the ones that would hand over unprecedented amounts of authority to a small collection of elites and their friends.

And as strange as it might sound to some readers, I, along with many in my audience, could soon find myself fighting alongside supporters of Alexandria Ocasio-Cortez and Bernie Sanders, who have repeatedly signaled their skepticism of elite groups like those working at Davos to produce the Great Reset.

Those who support the Reset want Main Street Americans to be divided. They want us to spend all our time yelling at each other about Dr. Seuss book bans and COVID-19 mask mandates so we do not see the bigger, much more important forces at work.

The truth is, the fight against the Great Reset is not a struggle between liberals and conservatives; it is a fight between the ruling-class elites of Wall Street, Davos, and Washington, D.C. and everyone else. And if the American people lose sight of that vital point, there will be no stopping the grand alterations of society that Reset elites have long yearned for.

WHERE WE GO FROM HERE

The rest of this book will be dedicated to outlining exactly how the Great Reset would work, how global elites are planning to use it to solidify their power, what strategies are being employed to push the world toward this new fascistic model, and, finally, what those of us who support individual rights can do to stop it.

Fake news conspiracy theorists on the left and right are creating immense divisions that have the potential to rip apart this country, which I deeply love, so I am the last person you will find wearing a tinfoil hat and supporting crazy, unsubstantiated conspiracy theories. (Also, tinfoil hats make my head look big.) But just because something sounds too crazy to be true does not mean it is false. Conspiracy *facts* are real, and the Great Reset might be the most important conspiracy fact in modern history. It's something the ruling class has been putting into place for more than one hundred years, although their most recent attempt is, I believe, the most dangerous.

Over the past two decades, I have been trying to warn the American people about our country's march toward authoritarianism and government control, and throughout those years, I and many of those people who stood up with me—some of whom are probably reading this book now—were continuously and unfairly labeled "crazy" or "right-wing extremists." But anyone who fairly looks back on the mountain of work my team and I accomplished over those years would find that, on the vast majority of the important topics we covered, we were spot-on.

When we warned you about the radicalism of Far-Left groups like Antifa, we were right. When we told you that we were heading toward race riots fueled by socialists seeking to upend our society, we were right.

When we showed you that the dangerous money printing policies of the George W. Bush and Obama administrations would only get worse and eventually push the country in the direction of even greater government control and economic calamity, we were correct again.

When we told you that the differences between the establishment wings of the Democratic and Republican Parties were rapidly shrinking and that neither group was truly interested in doing what was right for the country, we were right.

When we warned in 2010 about the threats posed by the Arab Spring, and how revolutionaries in the extremist wing of Islamism were attempting to usher in a new caliphate, we were right.

When we predicted that the tragic events of September 11, 2001, would be used to justify draconian restrictions on innocent Americans' privacy rights, we were dead-on.

When we warned you years ago that Big Tech companies like Google, Facebook, Twitter, and Amazon were working to stifle speech and that they would soon start erasing and revising American history and the writings of thinkers who oppose their views, we were right.[26]

And when we showed you how movements like Occupy Wall Street and Agenda 21 were just the beginning stages of a larger, more spectacularly troublesome transformation of our society, we were, as you will see throughout the rest of this book, way ahead of the curve.

As much as it pains certain unnamed, dishonest critics of mine, I have been right a lot over the years. But there is one threat that I have repeatedly missed, dismissed, and even mocked at times, and now it is coming back to haunt me—and not in a fun, Casper the Friendly Ghost kind of way. We are talking a full-blown nightmare straight out of *The Shining.* Throughout my career, I have never taken the danger to liberty posed by powerful, crony, corrupt corporations as seriously as I should have.

In my 2020 book *Arguing with Socialists,* I wrote, "What's the worst Jeff Bezos can do to you, anyway? Cancel your Amazon Prime subscription?"

Boy, that joke did *not* age well. What's the worst thing Jeff Bezos can do? How about destroying Parler, a rapidly growing social media company, on a whim, silencing more than ten million people at the drop of a hat?[27] How about banning books from the world's largest book marketplace, Amazon.com?[28] How about greatly influencing election outcomes through his ownership of the *Washington Post?* It turns out, corporate elites like Jeff Bezos can do a whole lot more damage than I thought, and they are just getting warmed up.

The centralization of power is almost never a good thing. In the long run, too much power breeds corruption, tyranny, and, in our modern world, radical corporatism. Conservatives like myself have long recognized the inherent danger of centralizing political, military, and societal power in the hands of government officials. However, we have woefully neglected how many large corporations have used corrupt elements in government to seize unprecedented amounts of influence for themselves too.

Not all, but many—perhaps even most—of the biggest players on Wall Street and in the halls of power in the nation's capital are not friends of the pro-liberty movement or even of democratic principles, properly understood. Instead they are primarily interested in expanding their own influence and authority. In some cases, I am sure that lust for power is fueled by an altruistic savior complex. In other instances, it is nothing more than a desire to get filthy, stinking, swim-in-a-pool-full-of-gold-coins rich. Whatever their motivation, the result is the same: you end up with no power to control your own life, chart your own destiny, or pursue your dreams—unless, of course, that dream involves working as a cog in the Great Reset machine.

Look, I hope I am wrong about the Great Reset—and I really do mean that. Because if I am right, it means fundamental, damaging, and radical changes to the United States are not just on the horizon; they are here now.

The Great Reset is the culmination of all that globalist elites—not your average Joe and Jane Liberal—have been striving to achieve over the past century, going all the way back to America's Progressive Era and the internationalism of racist, power-hungry men like Woodrow Wilson.

If supporters of this proposal achieve even half of what they are setting out to accomplish, the United States, and indeed the whole world, will never be the same. The Great Reset is not just about revamping the economy; it is also about totally transforming the American way of life. It is an attack on virtually every part of our society, including the basic freedoms generation after generation of men and women in the United States have fought so hard to protect.

The ending of the story is not set in stone, however. Once again, it is up to us—to you, me, and other defenders of freedom—to rise up against the forces of tyranny so that our children and grandchildren can inherit the promise of liberty. The battle is going to be ugly. You will be called radical, racist, bigoted, hateful, ignorant, and greedy, among many other horrible things. Your way of life will be attacked at every turn. You might lose access to financial opportunities and be silenced on social media. You could lose friends. Some of your family members might refuse to talk to you. It is not going to be an easy fight. It never has been. But it is a fight we must endure, and one we must win.

I know there is going to be a lot of material in this book that is going to sound at first, well, crazy. And I know much of what I present here will make you want to ask a lot of questions. Good. As

I encouraged you in this book's preface, ask questions with bold-ness and do your own homework. Do not take anything I say as gospel truth. If you make that effort, I am confident America will once again beat back those forces that would have our country abandon liberty in the pursuit of empty promises from the world's ruling class.

If we fail, the bright light of freedom emanating from America's shores, a light that has long illuminated the rest of the world, espe-cially in its darkest moments, will be extinguished. So the stakes could not be higher. We must rise to the challenge of this moment or risk losing our nation and freedom—perhaps forever.

— 2 —

NEVER LET A GLOBAL PANDEMIC GO TO WASTE

You never want a serious crisis to go to waste.

—RAHM EMANUEL, SPEAKING AT A CONFERENCE HOSTED
BY THE *WALL STREET JOURNAL*, NOVEMBER 19, 2008

YEAH, I KNOW, YOU HAVE HEARD THIS INFAMOUS "NEVER LET
a crisis go to waste" quote from Rahm Emanuel before, and
if you are a conservative, you've probably heard it a lot over the
years from Republican politicians, writers, and others trying to
illustrate how establishment politicians like Emanuel—the former
chief of staff for President Barack Obama and former mayor of

Chicago—try to use disasters as opportunities to achieve liberal, progressive, or socialist goals.

I know I have talked about the quote dozens of times on the air, and I have heard other conservatives and politicians do the same more times than I can count—which is a lot, by the way; I'm a pretty good counter. However, rarely have I taken the time to read the full quote during my radio or television shows.

When I sat down to write this chapter, I went back through my notes, read the Emanuel quote in its entirety, and realized that not only have many conservatives slightly changed the quote over the years, but they have also been neglecting a key detail, one that makes Emanuel's statement more relevant and powerful today than ever before.

Emanuel made the "crisis" comment way back in November 2008, just after Barack Obama won the presidential election. The United States was still in the midst of what was at that time the most significant economic crash in modern American history— although, by today's chaotic standards, it seems like your average Wednesday. Speaking at a conference hosted by the *Wall Street Journal*, Emanuel said,

> You never want a serious crisis to go to waste. And what I mean by that is an opportunity to do things that you think you could not do before. I think America as a whole in 1973 and 1974, and not just my view but obviously the administration's, missed the opportunity to deal with the energy crisis that was before us. For a long time our entire energy policy came down to cheap oil. This is an opportunity, what used to be long-term problems, be they in the health care area, energy area, education area, fiscal area, tax area, regulatory reform area, things that we have postponed for too long, that were long-term, are now immediate and must be dealt with. This crisis provides the opportunity, for us,

as I would say, the opportunity to do things that you could not do before. The good news, I suppose, if you want to see a silver lining, is the problems are big enough that they lend themselves to ideas from both parties for the solution.[29]

You might not have picked up on it, but there are a few important parts of Emanuel's statement that often get overlooked. First, Emanuel does not say, "Never let a crisis go to waste." He says, "You never want a serious crisis to go to waste." That might seem like a small difference, but the "serious" part of the statement is important. Small crises happen all the time. That is how most of the news industry makes it money. But it is the *serious* crises that present real opportunities for radical change.

Emanuel reiterates this point later in his statement, when he says, "The good news, I suppose, if you want to see a silver lining, is the problems are big enough that they lend themselves to ideas from both parties for the solution." See, Emanuel's argument is not that any small problem can be transformed into a larger issue that leads to change but rather that big alterations to our existing system— the kinds of radical things Barack Obama and Emanuel wanted to achieve—are not normally possible without serious crises.

There is also another important part of the statement worth thinking about more carefully. Emanuel does *not* say that the 2008 financial crisis provided *Democrats* with a chance to enact their own reforms, but rather he says that the crisis allowed both parties to provide the solution. Now, you might be tempted to dismiss that part of his statement as pandering, but if the coronavirus pandemic has taught us anything, it is that many Republicans are just as eager to find ways to expand the power of government and their corporate friends as their more left-wing rivals on the other side of the aisle.

The only difference between many Republicans and Democrats in Congress is no longer *whether* government should be intricately involved in economic and societal decision making but rather *the extent to which* this should occur. A party deeply devoted to many traditionally conservative ideas—including "crazy" policies like "don't spend more money than you take in"—no longer exists in Washington, D.C.

Although millions of Americans have been complaining about the gradual shift toward soft authoritarianism that has occurred in both major U.S. political parties over the past couple of decades, the problem has never been more serious than it is now. Those of us who believe in free markets and individual liberty have few champions in government, and the problem appears to be getting worse. It seems that just about everyone in Washington is now looking for ways to use "serious crises" to expand their power and make American families increasingly dependent on government—just as Rahm Emanuel suggested.

This destructive tendency has been perfectly illustrated by governments' reaction to the coronavirus pandemic, which will play a central role in how supporters of the Great Reset plan to implement their radical reforms over the next decade and beyond. Understanding how policymakers have reacted to COVID-19 and taken advantage of this important "opportunity" for creating change provide a vital road map we must understand if we are going to fight back against the Great Reset and other attempts to centralize power in the hands of the ruling class.

TYRANNY GOES VIRAL

When most of the mainstream media and political establishment heard about the possibility of a COVID-19 pandemic, they did not take it seriously. Many mocked people like me for sounding the alarm. I guess stories of Chinese government officials locking people in their own homes by installing bars on their windows, and reports of fearful villagers armed with spears tearing up roads so travelers from Wuhan couldn't infect their families, were not enough to grab the attention of the press.[30] Reporters were still too busy drooling uncontrollably over the now mostly forgotten Ukraine-related Trump impeachment hearings.

As late as February 2020, some pundits and even global health organizations were heavily criticizing the Trump administration for limiting travel from China to the United States. Many suggested it was racist and xenophobic, even though the stated purpose of the travel limitations was clearly to prevent the spread of COVID-19, not to restrict immigration.

Politico warned, "Coronavirus Quarantine, Travel Ban Could Backfire, Experts Fear."[31] The *New York Times* published an article titled "Who Says It's Not Safe to Travel to China?" in which the author, Rosie Spinks, referred to the "political moment" as having been "dominated by xenophobic rhetoric and the building of walls."[32]

Incredibly, the World Health Organization, in an attempt to shield China from criticism, advised that countries like the United States avoid imposing travel bans. "Although travel restrictions may intuitively seem like the right thing to do, this is not something that WHO usually recommends," WHO spokesperson Tarik Jasarevic said. "This is because of the social disruption they cause and the intensive use of resources required."[33]

But by March 2020, everything had changed. Instead of mocking President Trump over his decision to reduce travel from China to slow the spread of COVID-19, conservative and liberal pundits alike were demanding that politicians begin to shut down state economies across the country in line with federal government guidelines, even in places where the presence of the virus was virtually nonexistent. And unsurprisingly, most government officials were happy to comply.

The lockdown orders that followed became so draconian, it inspired me to launch the first-ever Chairman Mao Corona Dictator Awards show, complete with Oscars-style Mao'y statuettes for those engaging in the most tyrannical behavior. (And in case you were wondering, no, I'm not joking. I take the Mao'y Awards very seriously.) My staff and I selected nominees based on viewer-submitted news stories and then sent Mao'y Awards to the winners. I wonder if any of them display the award on their mantel. If not, they should. It's a really nice-looking award.

At the first (and hopefully last) Mao'y Awards, New York City mayor Bill de Blasio took home the Mao'y for Best Achievement in Mayoral Power-Tripping, for his government's decision to restrict church services. Churches that refused to stop worshiping in person were warned that they could be *permanently* shut down if they disobeyed his decree.[34]

Of course, de Blasio was not the only one on a power trip. Oregon governor Kate Brown issued a stay-at-home order that closed most businesses in the state and threatened to punish violators with a $1,250 fine or up to thirty days in jail.[35]

Washington governor Jay Inslee, fresh off his failed campaign to be the Democratic Party's presidential nominee, also closed most businesses in his state and banned nearly all social and recreational gatherings, including funerals and weddings.[36]

From March to April 2020, California state and county officials closed much of the Golden State's economy, mandated stay-at-home orders, released more than thirty-five hundred California state prison inmates, and reduced bail to zero dollars for those charged with misdemeanors and some lower-level felonies—all in an attempt to slow the spread of the virus.[37] [38]

Governor Gretchen Whitmer, Mao'y winner in the category of Best Gubernatorial Beatdown, issued arguably the most extensive lockdown orders. Whitmer's executive order not only shut down economic activity across Michigan and outlawed religious gatherings—which sounds like a pretty obvious violation of the whole First Amendment ban on "prohibiting the free exercise of religion" thing—but also imposed thousand-dollar fines on violators and promised to put those who refused to comply with the order in jail for as many as three months.[39]

A close runner-up in the same category, former Rhode Island governor Gina Raimondo, who now serves as commerce secretary in the Biden White House, called in the state's National Guard to conduct a door-to-door search looking for New Yorkers who crossed Rhode Island's southern border without a government permission slip. Any New Yorkers found were warned about the state's requirement to quarantine for fourteen days.[40]

By the end of April, more than forty states, most of which were led by Republicans, had enacted partial or total shutdowns, with many imposing stay-at-home orders with harsh penalties for those who chose not to follow state or local mandates. Then, in a supreme twist of irony, some of the same critics who had previously attacked Trump for issuing his supposedly racist and unnecessary travel ban endlessly criticized the president for seeming too eager to move the country back toward reopening throughout the remainder of the spring and summer.

At first, the shutdowns were supposed to last for only *two weeks*, and Americans were told that the primary purpose was to limit spikes in coronavirus cases—commonly called "flattening the curve"—so that hospitals throughout the country would not be overflowing with patients. Numerous health experts, relying on models predicting a million deaths or more, feared that if the virus were to get out of control, there would not be enough hospital beds and essential medical equipment like ventilator machines to handle the increased demand.

One faulty model had an especially large impact on public policy. A team of researchers led by Dr. Neil Ferguson at the Imperial

College London predicted that within just one year, more than 80 percent of the U.S. population could get infected with COVID-19, leading to as many as 2.2 million deaths in the United States alone.[41] (At the time of this writing, on September 22, 2021, there have been fewer than seven hundred thousand COVID-19 deaths reported in the United States.)[42]

Future generations of Americans will struggle to comprehend just how much fear resulted from studies like those put forward by Ferguson. The panic, which was amplified by a continuous stream of dire reports from the media, provided policymakers with the justification they needed to enact just about any dictate they pleased, including a number of mandates that they knew would have little or no impact on the spread of the coronavirus.

In Michigan, Mao'y Award winner Governor Whitmer banned "residents from traveling between homes they own in the state or to vacation rentals," according to the *Detroit News*. It was further reported that Whitmer's executive order required "large retail stores . . . [to] cordon off areas dedicated to furniture, gardening and paint," preventing stores that were allowed by the state to be open from selling many of their "nonessential" products.[43]

New York pastor Samson Ryman, who leads Central Bible Baptist Church, was threatened in May 2020 with a thousand-dollar fine for holding a drive-in church service with forty members of his congregation.[44] Greenville, Mississippi, congregants attending a similar drive-in church service were fined five hundred dollars each for refusing to comply with a curfew order issued by the city's mayor.[45]

In Kentucky, officials placed a couple under house arrest—electronic ankle bracelets and all—after a woman, Elizabeth Linscott, tested positive for COVID-19. Incredibly, Linscott had taken the test voluntarily as a precautionary measure prior to visiting her grandparents.[46]

After she tested positive, health officials told Linscott she needed to sign papers that would require her to ask the local health department for permission prior to leaving her house for *any* reason. Linscott agreed to self-quarantine, but she refused to sign the papers, which she said went too far. According to Linscott, they would have prevented her, for instance, from going to the hospital in a medical emergency without first begging for permission from the government.

Soon after Linscott's refusal, the local sheriff's department arrived at her door, demanding she sign the health department's mandate.

"I open up the door, and there's like eight different people, five different cars, and I'm like, 'What the heck's going on?'" said Isaiah Linscott, Elizabeth's husband. "This guy's in a suit with a mask. It's the health department guy and they have three papers for us. For me, her, and my daughter."[47]

The officials forced the couple to wear ankle monitors and to notify them if they needed to travel more than two hundred feet from their home.

"We didn't rob a store. We didn't steal something. We didn't hit and run. We didn't do anything wrong," Elizabeth Linscott said.[48]

Is it just me, or do you also imagine that the government officials at Linscott's door looked like a group of KGB agents demanding, "Papers, please"?

A SELF-IMPOSED ECONOMIC DEPRESSION

By issuing stay-at-home orders and their other wildly authoritarian mandates, governments did not merely *harm* America's economy; they shot the economy in the head and callously dumped its body in the East River, *Godfather*-style.

Prior to the lockdowns going into effect, the U.S. economy had been booming for three years. Unemployment for African Americans, Asians, Hispanics, women, and just about everyone else was at or near an all-time low.[49] In late 2019 and early 2020, the Dow Jones Industrial Average and other key stock market indexes hit record highs, boosting millions of Americans' retirement accounts.[50] Median home prices in the fourth quarter of 2019 were also nearing their all-time high.[51]

But just a few months after the world learned about COVID-19 and ruling-class elites locked down states, the U.S. economy experienced an unprecedented collapse. The number of Americans usually working full time dropped by more than 16.7 million from January 2020 to April 2020.[52] The unemployment rate for all workers rose from 3.5 percent in February to 14.7 percent in April, an increase of 320 percent in just two months.[53] By the end of May 2020, more than 40 million Americans had filed for unemployment.[54]

African Americans were hit especially hard. In the fourth quarter of 2019, Black unemployment had reached its lowest recorded quarterly level in U.S. history, averaging 5.6 percent. By the end of April, it had skyrocketed to 16.7 percent, a level that had not been seen since the height of the Obama-era Great Recession, in 2010 and 2011.[55]

Millions of businesses either closed or were forced to apply for the federal government's Paycheck Protection Program (PPP), which provided hundreds of billions of dollars to businesses to keep unemployment from continuing to spiral out of control.[56]

Not since the Great Depression has an economic collapse of this magnitude occurred. But unlike the Great Depression, the coronavirus crash was *deliberately* created by government, with widespread support from large corporations. It is almost certainly the first time in world history that a country as powerful as the United States consciously chose to decimate its own economy.

"A TREMENDOUS OPPORTUNITY"

There is no denying that for many—although not necessarily all—the initial motivation behind the decision to close the U.S. economy was fear. Some policymakers truly believed that millions of people would soon be dead from an unstoppable global pandemic and that the only hope the country had of saving those lives was forcing Americans to stay in their homes, no matter the cost. Regardless of whether you think that was the right decision, it is not an unreasonable position to take. No one wants to be remembered as the callous monster who voted in favor of millions of people dying.

However, within the first thirty days of the lockdown, it became clear that the models which health experts told us were the world's most accurate would, in some cases, be off by more than a *million* deaths and that the death rates for those infected by the virus were significantly lower than what originally had been estimated. And outside of a relatively small number of urban areas, hospitals were not overflowing—which, again, was the primary concern of health officials in the earliest days of the pandemic.

Health officials were initially so concerned about hospital capacity that in late March 2020, the U.S. Navy sent a massive hospital ship, the U.S.N.S. *Comfort*, from Norfolk, Virginia, to New York Harbor. But shortly after the ship arrived, its crew reduced its hospital bed capacity from one thousand to five hundred because of lower-than-expected demand, and by mid-April about 90 percent of the ship's beds remained unused.[57]

Yet the lockdowns continued in nearly every state. Why? Some public health experts—including many of the same people who had previously overestimated the danger of the virus—said that extending the lockdowns was important for protecting public health. This was despite the fact that there was virtually no danger of reaching bed capacity limits in the vast majority of U.S. hospitals. These same "experts" further argued that the government now had a responsibility to save as many lives as possible from being harmed by COVID-19, regardless of the damage that would be caused to society, to the economy, or even to public health.

The narrative from public health officials shifted from "flatten the curve" to "save lives by staying home," and some pundits and activists suddenly realized that the self-inflicted economic crisis caused by the coronavirus pandemic opened the window to radical changes that had previously seemed politically impossible. (They couldn't let this once-in-a-lifetime crisis go to waste, right?) Others, however, had already been planning to take advantage of a scenario *like* the coronavirus pandemic well before anyone had ever heard of COVID-19.

In October 2019, public health experts and policy wonks from a number of institutions, including Johns Hopkins University, the Bill and Melinda Gates Foundation, and the World Economic Forum—one of the most prominent supporters of the Great Reset—met at The Pierre hotel in New York City. The goal of this meeting was to conduct a "simulation" that presented attendees with "a series of dramatic, scenario-based facilitated discussions, confronting difficult, true-to-life dilemmas associated with response to a hypothetical, but scientifically plausible, pandemic."[58]

The primary purpose of the pandemic exercise—which was creepily named Event 201—was to develop recommended actions for government officials, international organizations, and private businesses to take in order to achieve "unprecedented levels of collaboration" during the next pandemic, providing a partial foundation for what would become the Great Reset.

The Event 201 meeting was simply a thought experiment. But by mid-March 2020, public fear of COVID-19 had given politicians the chance to play these war games for real, as Democrats started quietly discussing how they could take advantage of the pandemic. On March 19, the *Hill* reported that during an important "conference call featuring more than 200 members of the House Democratic caucus, lawmakers one by one laid out a sweeping wish list of provisions they want to see" in Congress's initial COVID-19 relief package, "including a boost in infrastructure spending, an expansion of Social Security benefits and funding for states to set up an all-mail voting system in the event the pandemic extends into November's elections."[59]

James Clyburn, a Democrat from South Carolina who was then serving as the House majority whip and had become a key political ally of Joe Biden, said during the call that the pandemic was "a tremendous opportunity to *restructure things to fit our vision*."[60]

That vision included a wide range of proposed government programs and pet projects, including "cash payments to individuals, low-cost loans for small businesses, new funding to boost the health care system, and a financial lifeline for the hardest hit industries, like aviation and cruise lines,"[61] as well as "$300 million for refugees and migrants, $35 million in funding for the Kennedy Center for the performing arts, new fuel emission standards, and a climate change study."[62]

Of course, establishment congressional Republicans were not going to allow this "tremendous opportunity" to pass them by either. In July 2020, Senate Republicans hosted a caucus meeting to discuss their strategy for negotiating another round of coronavirus relief. After the meeting finished, Rand Paul, one of the few voices of reason left in the Senate, lambasted members of his own party for their rampant hypocrisy.[63]

"They [congressional Republicans] said that President Obama is for borrowing and spending—they're talking about spending another trillion dollars. There should be a law that they are no longer allowed to talk about the debt," said Paul, who later called government's lack of fiscal restraint "an abomination" and said, "There is no difference now between the two parties in spending."[64]

A whole book could be dedicated entirely to talking about the thousands of provisions contained in the coronavirus relief packages passed in 2020 and early 2021, but the following three best illustrate the absolutely mind-exploding insanity that government passed into law after choosing to shut down the economy.

I. "STIMULUS" CHECKS

Perhaps the most notable and far-reaching coronavirus relief program involved sending most adults in the United States $1,200 in "stimulus" money resulting from a provision contained in the Coronavirus Aid, Relief, and Economic Security Act, commonly called the CARES Act. Under the program, individuals earning $75,000 or less received $1,200, plus $500 for every qualifying child age seventeen or younger, up to a specified limit. Married couples earning $150,000 or less received $2,400.[65, 66]

By early June 2020, the federal government had sent 159 million payments, amounting to more than $267 billion, plus another $2.5 billion to people living in U.S. territories.[67]

Of all the stupid government programs that have been imposed on the American people, this one takes the cake. These payments were based on income, not need, so tens of millions of people who had not lost their jobs for even a moment during the pandemic received the payments, even though the purpose of the program was supposedly to offer relief to those who required it the most.

Proponents of the program defended the seemingly bizarre decision to send money to people who had *not* lost their employment by saying the payments would also serve as a kind of stimulus for the economy. The idea was that the millions of people who received checks but hadn't lost their jobs would go out and spend the cash, helping the economy recover from the coronavirus crash.

Besides the government's inability to pay for this huge cash giveaway, there was another glaring problem with this ridiculous theory:

the economy had been mostly shut down, so there were very few places people could go, other than to massive corporate retailers, to spend their hot-off-the-press, government-printed money. What's the point of a stimulus plan if there's almost nothing to stimulate—other than Jeff Bezos's bank account, of course?

It is also worth remembering that the program was based on 2019 tax data, not 2020 income levels. That means some people who experienced large drops in income in 2020 did not immediately receive payments, while others who had enjoyed a significant increase in income in 2020 received $1,200 that they did not need.[68]

Even more stunning, a Democrat-led Congress and President Biden passed another gigantic COVID-19 relief law in early 2021, this time with a $1.9 trillion price tag. Among other things, the law sent $1,400 in direct payments to Americans, even though all signs suggested that the coronavirus pandemic was winding down, not getting worse.[69]

2. UNEMPLOYMENT "BONUSES"

In addition to handing out $1,200 payments, government officials in 2020 also sent unemployed workers a $600-per-week unemployment "bonus" that supplemented unemployment payments already received by workers through state programs. The argument behind the $600 payments was that Americans who lost their jobs because of the shutdowns should have their income completely replaced by the government, since it was the government that caused the unemployment in the first place. I guess that makes sense. I mean, if the government were to come to your house and burn down your garage, it's only fair that it should pay for a new one, right?

The unemployment bonuses went much further than that, though. Instead of limiting the payments to the total amount earned while employed, Congress's program—which, we should not forget, had also been approved by President Trump—allowed people to receive *more* in unemployment payments than they earned while working. This destroyed any incentive those people would otherwise have had to find another job. Instead of just replacing the garage it burned down, the government threw in a new gazebo as well!

In May 2020, *FiveThirtyEight* reported, "A new analysis by Peter Ganong, Pascal Noel, and Joseph Vavra, economists at the University of Chicago, uses government data from 2019 to estimate that 68 percent of unemployed workers who can receive benefits are eligible for payments that are greater than their lost earnings."[70]

And government did not merely pay people a little more than their full salaries to stay home either. In many cases, Congress paid recipients *significantly* more. Ganong, Noel, and Vavra "found that the estimated median replacement rate [in 2020]—the share of a worker's original weekly salary that is being replaced by unemployment benefits—is 134 percent, or more than one-third above their original wage. A substantial minority of those workers, particularly in low-wage professions like food service and janitorial work, may end up receiving more than 150 percent of their previous weekly salary."[71]

Although some said the bonuses were meant only to help people get through a short economic shutdown lasting just a month or two, by mid-July thirty million Americans were still receiving the bonuses.[72] And in the 2021 legislation signed into law by President Biden, the bonus payments were extended again, although the maximum amount provided was reduced to $300 per week.[73]

3. MEDICAID MADNESS

In March 2020, Congress passed and President Trump signed the CARES Act and the Families First Coronavirus Response Act (FFCRA). Anticipating additional Medicaid costs, Congress provided in these laws more Medicaid-related funding for states, which share the cost of Medicaid enrollees with the federal government. However, rather than simply offering states additional cash to help them get through the pandemic, Congress tied strings to the money that required states accepting additional funds to keep Medicaid beneficiaries enrolled in the program even after they would ordinarily lose their eligibility.

Researchers at the Foundation for Government Accountability (FGA) noted in a 2020 report that in order to receive the additional funds, "states cannot remove even ineligible enrollees unless those enrollees request a voluntary termination."[74]

"States are also blocked from strengthening eligibility standards, methodologies, or procedures and cannot increase premiums beyond those in effect in January 2020," the authors of the report said. "FFCRA also blocks states from requiring local governments to increase contributions to Medicaid."[75]

This disastrous provision put states in a terrible situation, forcing them to choose between missing out on federal funds or accepting unsustainable terms.

"Ultimately, these restrictions will prevent some states from receiving COVID-19 aid, exacerbate state budget crises stemming from the pandemic, strip states of needed tools to manage Medicaid, rob resources from the truly needy, and bind states' hands for decades to come," the FGA authors wrote.[76]

According to FGA's report, this absurd provision made it possible for Americans in states that expanded Medicaid under the Affordable Care Act of 2010 to lose their job, enroll in Medicaid, get a new job with a larger salary, yet stay enrolled in Medicaid.

Why in the world would Congress force states to continue enrolling Medicaid beneficiaries who have found good-paying jobs—other than, of course, because it wants to get as many people as it can hooked on a costly government program?

A "WAR ON SMALL BUSINESS"

Making matters even worse, many of the COVID-19 lockdown and relief policies disproportionately benefited groups and businesses favored politically. In her remarkable book *The War on Small Business: How the Government Used the Pandemic to Crush the Backbone of America*, Carol Roth, an entrepreneur and former investment banker, outlines in great detail how the coronavirus policies imposed by governments throughout much of 2020 decimated small businesses while allowing many large corporations to remain at least partially open.

Summarizing the war on small business at the height of the pandemic lockdowns, Roth writes,

> Government entities, the same ones that were supposed to protect property rights and all individual rights, told many businesses, primarily small businesses, that they were considered "nonessential" and that they had to shut down, some in whole, some in part.
>
> That was it: millions of businesses across the country received directives to close but nothing else. No compensation for helping the government or "society," no special provisions to safeguard their own or their staffs' livelihoods; just pack it in, shut it down, and go home.[77]

Additionally, Roth notes how even after Congress put coronavirus relief programs into place, small businesses ended up with the short end of the stick.

> With all of those giveaways, you might expect that small businesses would have also been taken care of by the government.
>
> The amount of money required to ensure that small businesses stayed open, appropriately compensate them under an

"eminent domain" scenario, and preserve jobs was probably in the $1 trillion range. Instead, what small businesses received as part of the CARES Act amounted to less than 20 percent of the overall relief package—again, a figure that makes little sense given that small businesses account for around half the economy and are the most vulnerable and most directly affected by the government black swan.

Instead of getting money to small business owners quickly and directly, which would have been the most effective tactic and consistent with the direct payments received by the likes of Congress members' cronies such as the Kennedy Center and universities, Congress cobbled together a shoddy, confusing "forgivable" loan program in the PPP.[78]

On its own, the lack of adequate funding for small businesses caused substantial harm, but when combined with the advantages that larger corporations had but many small businesses did not— like large cash reserves, teams of lawyers and tax experts, and the ability to shift much of their operations online—the disadvantages faced by countless small businesses were crushing.

Why did politicians leave many small business owners out in the cold during the height of the pandemic? And why didn't corporate America suffer the same fate? The answer to these questions will become evident when the Great Reset is discussed in detail in chapter 5, but—spoiler alert!—the short answer is, the reason corporations were preserved and small businesses destroyed is because in the grand new "stakeholder" economy dreamed up by the elites in Davos and Biden's White House, corporations could easily be controlled. Manipulating tens of millions of small business owners would be much more difficult.

I do not believe the coronavirus was released into the public by American officials on purpose, as some wild conspiracy theorists claim, to destroy the economy and dismantle millions of small businesses. But I do believe that undermining small businesses is considered to be a benefit of the pandemic, in the minds of many in the ruling class.

NO CASH? NO PROBLEM

Before the pandemic hit America, the United States added more than $3 trillion to the national debt from 2016 to 2019, and it was on pace to run a $1 trillion deficit in 2020, one of the largest deficits in history. Figures like these used to shock and appall Americans. But in the wake of the federal government's coronavirus spending spree, they really do not seem so bad anymore.

In just the first six months of 2020, the national debt, spurred mostly by the coronavirus lockdowns and related government spending programs, increased by a gargantuan $3 trillion.[79] And that is just the beginning. Analysts predict that the increased spending and debt caused by the federal government's relief legislation could add a total of $6 trillion to the national debt by 2030.[80]

To put that in perspective, during the one-hundred-year period from 1900 to 2000, the national debt increased by $5.62 trillion—and that's after two world wars, the Korean War, the Vietnam War, a decades-long cold war with Russia, countless foreign operations in countries around the world, Franklin Roosevelt's massive expansion of government under the New Deal, Lyndon Johnson's even more expensive "War on Poverty" and "Great Society" reforms, and the seemingly never-ending war in Afghanistan.[81]

But I guess the coronavirus is more important than all that other stuff *combined*, right?

Things have gotten so out of control that President Obama— who added as much money to the national debt as did all the other presidents who came before him combined—seems like a real fiscal conservative by today's standards. At least President Obama on occasion still *pretended* to care about the national debt. Congressional Democrats and Republicans do not even respect the American people enough to fake it anymore. Hey, politicians and bankers: if you are going to saddle my children, grandchildren, and great-grandchildren with an insurmountable amount of debt, the least you could do is lie to me when you do it.

And the national debt is only part of the story. The Federal Reserve balance sheet, a way to track the Fed's assets and liabilities, has been skyrocketing in the wake of the coronavirus response. Increasing the Fed's balance sheet is the real "money printing." When the Fed began its quantitative easing (QE) program, which I cover in more detail in chapter 4, it was directly reflected in the Fed's balance sheet.

In 2008, the balance sheet sat at around $900 billion. By the end of 2014, after several rounds of QE, the balance sheet peaked at $4.5 trillion.[82] This new number is composed of Treasury securities, federal agency debt securities, and a ton of mortgage-backed securities.[83]

The idea behind QE was to use money printing to drag the country out of the 2008 Great Recession but then let the balance sheet gradually unwind after the U.S. economy returned to full strength. Prior to the coronavirus pandemic, this had very slowly started to occur. By September 2019, the Fed's balance sheet dipped below $3.8 trillion.[84] If the economy had continued to hum along, it was possible a further unwinding of this unprecedented QE experiment would have taken place, although it is extremely unlikely that the balance sheet ever would have returned to normal without radical changes to U.S. monetary policy. Of course, all of that is now subject to speculation, because COVID-19 happened.

In response to the government-induced economic downturn, the Fed once again kicked the money printers into high gear. Fueled by purchases of trillions of dollars of treasuries, mortgage-backed securities, and other assets, the Fed balance sheet is spiking again, this time to unprecedented levels. By the time the pandemic is over, the Fed's balance sheet may end up topping $10 trillion—not quite Zimbabwe levels of money printing, but hey, they are just getting warmed up.[85]

The reason President Trump and Congress spent more money than even the most liberal American governments of the past dreamed possible, and the reason the Fed is adding trillions more to its balance sheet with no real long-term strategy for returning things to normal, is because they have all adopted some version of a radical economic idea called modern monetary theory (MMT), even if they won't admit it publicly.

In chapter 4, I discuss modern monetary theory at length and explain the key role it plays in the Great Reset, but for now all you need to know is that supporters of this theory believe that debts and deficits do not really matter. They argue that as long as a government controls its own currency, like we do in the United States, it can print as much money as it needs to—until inflation occurs. Then the government needs to impose new regulations and make reforms to tax and spending policies to "target" inflation.

In some cases, but certainly not all, the folks calling for large increases in spending have adopted MMT without even knowing that the theory exists, and I have no doubt that many Democrats and Republicans fall squarely into that camp. But that does not change the fact that MMT's foundational principle—that debts and deficits really don't mean all that much—has become the new standard operating practice in our brave new Great Reset world.

I am not the only one who noticed this important transition to modern monetary theory. In an August 2020 interview, Robert Hormats, formerly the vice chairman at Goldman Sachs International and an economic and trade policy adviser for five U.S.

presidents, acknowledged that America is now essentially practicing modern monetary theory. "Well," he said during the interview, "now we have a particularly unusual set of circumstances whereby we're in the midst of forced, or involuntary, utilization of modern monetary theory."[86]

"The federal government is issuing and will continue to issue trillions of dollars' worth of bonds," Hormats continued. "And the market is, by and large, buying them up at a very low interest rate. And the Fed, if the market is not going to do it, the Fed has demonstrated its desire and its willingness to buy those assets up and keep interest rates extremely low."[87]

I know this will be hard for some readers to hear, but I think the evidence is clear that President Trump accepted the basic principles of MMT, and not just because he signed into law costly coronavirus relief legislation without any way of paying for it. Throughout his first term, Trump routinely criticized the Federal Reserve whenever it chose to raise interest rates or even seriously considered a rate increase.[88] In October 2019, responding to a quote suggesting the Fed should raise rates, Trump criticized the Fed for considering an interest rate hike, tweeting, "The Fed doesn't have a clue! We have unlimited potential, only held back by the Federal Reserve."[89]

This is right in line with the views of modern monetary theory economists like Stephanie Kelton, a former adviser to Bernie Sanders and professor at Stony Brook University. She and other MMT supporters often dismiss the role of the Fed altering the baseline interest rate. Kelton has argued that "in a slump, cutting interest rates is weak tea against depressed expectations of profits. In a boom, raising interest rates does little to quell new activity."[90]

Do not for one second think I am suggesting that President Trump rigorously studied economics with MMTers like Kelton, who is, as far as I can tell, a socialist. He has probably never even heard of her. But Trump's actions do show that even Republican elected officials can fall for the allure of MMT's siren song.

GREAT RESET "FUEL"

Now, you may be thinking, "Glenn, you're looking at this whole coronavirus crisis thing the wrong way. We should be celebrating! It turns out we really can just print as much money as we want without facing any serious economic consequences. It's not like all that government money printing has us pushing around wheelbarrows full of cash to buy loaves of bread, like we've seen in places such as the Weimar Republic."

Believe me, I can understand the sentiment, but I am sure that nameless guy pushing the wheelbarrow said the same thing before everything went to hell. Economic catastrophes often happen so quickly that most people do not realize a problem exists until it is too late. Rapid inflation is a very real and dangerous possibility. You should not ignore hundreds of years of economic thinking because a few governments have been able to get away with reckless spending over the course of several years or even a decade or two. Eventually, inflation always catches up with big-spending governments, one way or another.

Further, as I will explain more in chapter 4, over the past few decades, the Japanese have essentially been operating under modern monetary theory, and although Japan has not experienced hyperinflation, its citizens have had to endure two decades of virtually no economic growth—the other consequence of a government printing trillions more than it takes in.

But as hard as it might be to put aside the economic effects of debt, deficits, and seemingly endless money printing, that is exactly what I am going to do for the rest of this chapter. You see, as much time as I spend on my radio and television shows talking about the possibility of an economic catastrophe right around the corner, that is *not* the reason I devoted an entire chapter in this book to modern monetary theory. And as much as I care about Congress's expansion of government programs and the authoritarian coronavirus rules imposed by the little tyrants occupying so many of the governors' mansions across the country, I did *not* rehash all of that craziness to simply comment on the harm those policies have caused. Those issues are undoubtedly important, yes, but not nearly as important as the question so many supporters of the Great Reset have been asking since the pandemic began: What comes next?

Modern monetary theory is the extremely powerful fuel needed for the machinery—the Great Reset programs—that elites are trying to use to seize control of the world. Without the MMT fuel, tyrants must turn to less desirable fuels, like outright violence, the confiscation of land, and other, often more overtly authoritarian modes of seizing control. Elites and revolutionaries throughout the West have tried over the past century to build long-lasting, stable societies using more violent models, and it has never worked out, especially in wealthier nations like the United States.

MMT offers a different approach. It gives the Great Reset machine the power it needs to seize control without requiring gulags—or at least without needing so many of them—and it can be put into place without the need for eliminating democracy, an essential part of making any Reset scheme tolerable to Americans.

But before the MMT fuel can be poured into elites' new Great Reset tyranny machine, they first need to get enough government officials, politicians, well-connected activists and special interest groups, and powerful business leaders to believe that the MMT fuel actually works. As everyone who has ever accidently put diesel fuel in a car without a diesel engine knows, the wrong kind of fuel can leave even the best machine stranded on the side of the road.

The reason the coronavirus crisis has been so important for the Great Reset movement is because it has shown not only that modern monetary theory can be used by governments to rapidly expand government power but also that the public in the United States is much more willing to accept modern monetary theory than many previously thought, even though most Americans have never heard of it. In the wake of the expansive quantitative easing policies that were implemented during the Obama and Trump eras, the multibillion-dollar bailouts of banks and businesses that occurred over the past decade, the seemingly always-growing national debt under both Democratic and Republican leadership, and the multi-trillion-dollar government "stimulus" packages of the early 2010s and 2020, most Americans could not care less about the national debt anymore.

Those who have been clamoring for many years now to use modern monetary theory have more "proof" than ever that their theory can work and be tolerated by the public. Do not get me wrong—the "proof" is nothing but fool's gold. But to many of those in power, MMT is just too tempting to ignore. And now that modern monetary theory has been to a large extent normalized by the coronavirus pandemic—which, again, we must continue to remind ourselves was *not* what killed the economy; it was government's *response* to the virus that killed the economy—there's never been a better time to try to push the bounds of MMT as far they will go.

"A GOLDEN OPPORTUNITY"

There are at least two other reasons the pandemic has been so important for the Great Reset movement. First, it has given state and federal government officials in the United States more confidence than ever that they can enact radical, tyrannical, and even arbitrary mandates. Further, it shows not only that many Americans will go along with whatever their masters in government tell them but also that they will work with government to help silence anyone who stands up against these actions. Sounds like the perfect recipe for a disgustingly fascist cocktail to me.

Second, it is virtually impossible to convince people that the global economy needs to be torn down and replaced with a new system when unemployment for African Americans, Hispanics, women, and just about everyone else is historically low, retirement account values are soaring, and the economy seems poised to continue growing for years to come—and that's exactly what was happening prior to the coronavirus pandemic.

After the government lockdowns, though, everything changed. The economy burned to the ground, which means there is a favorable set of circumstances for elites to rebuild—or *reset*—it in an entirely new way.

This is not a theory. The loudest and most prominent voices of the Great Reset have made it abundantly clear that the global pandemic has created an incredibly important, perhaps once-in-a-lifetime "opportunity"—a word they use over and over again—to change society and the world's economy.

On its website, the World Economic Forum stated, "The Covid-19 crisis, and the political, economic and social disruptions it has caused, is fundamentally changing the traditional context for decision-making. The inconsistencies, inadequacies and contradictions of multiple systems—from health and financial to energy and education—are more exposed than ever amidst a global context of concern for lives, livelihoods and the planet. Leaders find themselves at a historic crossroads, managing short-term pressures against medium- and long-term uncertainties."[91]

WEF also wrote, "As we enter a unique window of opportunity to shape the recovery, this initiative [the Great Reset] will offer insights to help inform all those determining the future state of global relations, the direction of national economies, the priorities of societies, the nature of business models and the management of a global commons."[92]

Don't forget, WEF is the same nonprofit organization that in 2019 hosted the Event 201 meeting discussed earlier in this chapter, during which "experts" planned how government officials, international organizations, and private businesses could achieve "unprecedented levels of collaboration" during a future pandemic. It is also the same group that has been leading the Great Reset campaign since 2020.

At a WEF launch event for the Great Reset in June 2020, Prince Charles, one of the leading supporters of the plan, called the coronavirus pandemic "a golden opportunity" because people are now "more receptive to big visions of change."

"We have a golden opportunity to seize something good from this crisis—its unprecedented shockwaves may well make people more receptive to big visions of change," Prince Charles said. "As we move from rescue to recovery, we have a unique but rapidly shrinking window of opportunity to learn lessons and reset ourselves on a more sustainable path."[93]

Klaus Schwab, the executive chairman of the World Economic Forum, said, "COVID-19 has accelerated our transition into the age of the Fourth Industrial Revolution. We have to make sure that the new technologies in the digital, biological and physical world remain human-centered and serve society as a whole, providing everyone with fair access."[94]

Schwab added, "This global pandemic has also demonstrated again how interconnected we are. We have to restore a functioning system of smart global cooperation structured to address the challenges of the next 50 years. The Great Reset will require us to integrate all stakeholders of global society into a community of common interest, purpose and action."[95]

Sharan Burrow, the general secretary of the International Trade Union Confederation, was interviewed by the World Economic Forum in June about the Great Reset. Referring to the COVID-19 pandemic, Burrow said, "I can see how we could use this opportunity to design a better world, but we need both national and multilateral institutions to make it work."[96]

Kristalina Georgieva, the managing director of the International Monetary Fund, said in a statement about the Great Reset, "We know this [COVID-19] pandemic, if left to its own devices, will deepen inequality. But if we were to concentrate in investing in people, in the social fabric of our societies, in access to opportunities and education for all, in expansion of social programs—then we can have a world that is a better world for all. The best memorial to those who lost their lives to pandemic is a greener, smarter, fairer world."[97]

Robert Moritz—the global chairman of Pricewaterhouse-Coopers, one of the world's most powerful accounting firms—has said that the coronavirus pandemic has made the "flaws" in society and the global economy "more apparent."

"In early June, Klaus Schwab—Chairman of the World Economic Forum—called for a 'great reset' following the pandemic," Moritz wrote in an article for the World Economic Forum.[98] "Pressing the case for rapid collective action, Schwab said the response to COVID-19 proved that a reset of our economic and social foundations is possible. He added that now is our best chance to achieve it.

"I agree," Moritz continued. "It is becoming increasingly clear that the global economy is no longer delivering what is needed.... The most obvious symptoms of this breakdown include climate change, inequality and populism. Social progress has become decoupled from economic progress. Put simply, we have a design problem. And now COVID-19 is making the flaws even more apparent."[99]

NEVER LET A SERIOUS CRISIS GO TO WASTE

As the quotes discussed in the previous section of this chapter show—and there are plenty more I left out too—many of the Great Reset's most prolific and influential backers view the coronavirus pandemic as a key opportunity and justification for enacting radical change, one that rarely comes around, as Prince Charles said during the June meeting: "It is an opportunity we have never had before and may never have again."[100]

Prince Charles and his yacht club buddies over at the World Economic Forum are right; the extreme and destructive nature of the policies imposed by governments in response to the pandemic have caused enough economic damage and societal destabilization that ruling elites now have the chance to, in the words of Joe Biden, "build back better" (more on this in chapter 6). And the normalization and widespread use of radical monetary policies, especially those associated with modern monetary theory, have given governments the tools they need to further centralize power and put most economic decision making in the hands of elites in large corporations and government bureaucracies, rather than in the hands of individuals and families.

The Great Reset is a well-designed, serious plan—terrifying, to be sure, but it's one that has a real chance of working out for those who want to run every aspect of society. Rahm Emanuel would be proud.

However, there is one big flaw that needs to be overcome: How can elites justify building an entirely new economy based on economic damage and societal fears linked to a *temporary* crisis like the coronavirus pandemic? The truth is, they cannot—at least not successfully. They might be able to get some of the infrastructure in place, but completely overhauling the world? That is going to take just a little more work.

To formulate a truly long-lasting transformation of the global economy and create, in the words of one Great Reset speaker, another "new world order"[101] like the one that emerged after World War II, elites hell-bent on a Great Reset need another, even more dire and dangerous "crisis" to solve. They need a crisis that will supposedly imperil human life on our planet and pose an "existential threat" to all living things. Luckily for the supporters of the Great Reset, just such a "crisis" exists: climate change.

If Great Reset proponents can convince the world that the only chance the human race has of lasting—not just of enjoying economic equality, social justice, and other left-wing goals but of actual *survival*—is to put most of the global economic power in the hands of the ruling class, well then, now you've got a crisis you can hang your obnoxiously large Russian fur hat on. That's why climate change is so important to understand, and why I have chosen it to be the topic of my next chapter.

— 3 —

CLIMATE CHANGE: THE CATALYST FOR A "NEW WORLD ORDER"

Climate change poses an existential threat to our lives, to our economy, and the threat is here. It's not going to get any better.
—President Joe Biden, September 7, 2021[102]

Times Square in New York City is truly one of the most remarkable locations on earth. It is the very definition of sensory overload, a place that has the potential to captivate, amaze, and disgust visitors—often all at the same time. (If you ever want to eat one of the world's best hot dogs while watching a homeless man fight a guy in a bear suit, Times Square is the place for you.)

Anyone who has ever lived in the city knows that *real* New Yorkers don't go to Times Square, but I admit that when I lived in New York, every now and then I would find myself wandering past its perpetually glowing streets, if for no other reason than to be reminded of how breathtaking and shocking the city can be.

When I would make these little excursions, I was always struck by the continuous presence of doomsayers. No matter what was happening in New York, you were guaranteed to find at least one person, and usually many more, standing on a street corner in Times Square shouting prognostications about the end of the world, often with a crudely written sign made of cardboard that declared, "The end is near!"

Every single day, hundreds of thousands of people pass through Times Square, and almost no one takes these claims seriously, and why would they? A dire warning scribbled on the back of an old pizza box is hardly the most persuasive mode of communication. But that is not the only reason New Yorkers take these predictions of doom and gloom with a grain of salt.

Even if someone were to come along and build elaborate booths featuring the country's most articulate and intelligent persuaders, and even if these folks could convince some passersby that the world really is about to end, eventually no one would take them seriously no matter how much "proof" they claim to have. Why? Because we wake up each morning to find that the world has, in fact, not ended.

Sure, things change, but inevitably the sun rises in the east, sets in the west, and life goes on. The reason people, especially nonreligious people, do not believe the world is on the verge of ending is because no matter how many times those predicting disaster say, "The end is near," the end never comes. Our very existence serves as proof against the claim, and the more these predictions are proven false, the less reliable the sources appear.

Street corner doomsayers are going about fearmongering all wrong. If they really want to fool people into thinking the whole of humanity is staring down the barrel of a gun, they should ditch their cardboard signs and adopt the following four-step guide utilized by radical environmentalists over the past half-century.

Step 1: Establish a Flexible Timeline

Do not tell people the disaster you are predicting is so imminent that they will see whether you are right in the near term, but also don't make your soon-to-be crisis so far into the future that no one walking around today will live to see its effects.

Step 2: Propose Potential Solutions

Do not predict a disaster that cannot be "solved." There is no point in convincing people life on earth is going to end if there's nothing that can be done about it, because even if you convince everyone they are doomed, all they can do is hope you are wrong.

Step 3: Create a "Consensus"

Find real scientists who support *some* part of your claim, and then pretend that they support *all* of it. Do not worry about getting caught in a lie; most people won't bother to check the scientific literature to see if what you have been saying is true. Also, if possible, track down dishonest "scientists" who will back your claim in exchange for funding.

Step 4: Constantly Shift Your Predictions

Before it becomes apparent to everyone that your first prediction is wildly incorrect, make a new prediction, and then repeat steps 1, 2, and 3.

By following this proven four-step process, environmental groups with close ties to ruling-class elites have managed to fool many people for decades, especially young Americans, who have not had the benefit of seeing firsthand just how inaccurate so many predictions of environmental catastrophes have been. But the closer that fair-minded people look at the constant fearmongering of environmental elites, the more obvious it is that many of those claiming "the science is settled" on alleged environmental crises like climate change are nothing more than highly sophisticated street corner doomsayers. They may not be writing their messages on the back of old pizza boxes, but their predictions are often just as inaccurate.

In several of my previous books, I spent a great deal of time showing that the so-called climate crisis we are always hearing about from the mainstream press is not nearly what it has been cracked up to be—you know, somewhere between a postapocalyptic *Mad Max* hellscape and the planet Tatooine in the *Star Wars* universe.[103]

We have not—contrary to the claims of so many elitist environmentalists—experienced substantially more wildfires in recent years. According to the National Interagency Coordination Center, which is responsible for tracking wildfires in the United States, there were *more* wildfires during the 2005–2009 period (406,614) than there were from 2010 to 2014 (324,762). And there were more wildfires from 2010 to 2014 than from 2015 to 2019 (315,953).[104]

We have not experienced any significant increase in the number or severity of hurricanes either. In 2018, a study of hurricane activity published in the *Bulletin of the American Meteorological Society* found that despite some modest warming in the United States, there has been "no significant trends in landfalling hurricanes, major hurricanes, or normalized damage consistent with what has been found in previous studies."[105]

Further, and perhaps most important, crop production has not been in decline. It has been dramatically increasing. The U.N. Food and Agriculture Organization's (FAO) database shows worldwide production of cereals, wheat, coarse grain, and rice are all at or near record highs.[106] And in February 2020, the United Nations reported, "FAO's forecast for world cereal production in 2020 has been revised upward by 9.3 million tonnes this month and now stands at almost 2,790 million tonnes, with the global output set to surpass the record-high reached in 2019 by as much 3.0 percent (81.3 million tonnes). Global wheat production is pegged at 761.5 million tonnes, up 3.2 million tonnes from the previous month and now at par with last year's above-average outturn."[107]

Unfortunately, because of the great influence that elites have over the mainstream press, these facts are lost on most of the American public, which is routinely battered with dire and disturbing reports about famine, fires, and storms that are allegedly linked to climate change. Fueled by shoddy, ideologically motivated reporting and propaganda, tens of millions of Americans now think climate change poses a grave danger to human civilization and all life on earth.

When Senator Elizabeth Warren—an ivory-tower elitist if there ever was one—said that climate change "is the existential threat ... the one that threatens all life on this planet," millions of people believed her.[108]

When Joe Biden—a man who came to Washington *ten presidents* ago—said, "Climate change poses an existential threat to our future, and we are running out of time to address it," millions believed him, and then voted for him to be president.[109]

When well-read publications like the *Washington Post*—a newspaper owned by Amazon's billionaire CEO Jeff Bezos—repeatedly frames climate change as an "emergency" and an "existential threat" and says it is likely to cause an "indescribable catastrophe," millions of people believe it.[110]

This does not mean, of course, that climate has not changed in recent decades, won't change in the future, or isn't changing now. Climate is always changing, and there are some highly respected, well-intentioned scientists who believe that climate change is being driven, at least in part, by human activity. And there are other well-qualified scientists and economists who believe that those changes to the climate are going to create economic problems and some environmental problems. (There are many scientists who disagree with these claims, by the way, but we'll address that later in the chapter.) But here's what virtually no reasonable scientist believes: that humanity is in grave danger because of climate change or that the human race and "all life on this planet," as Elizabeth Warren said, is facing the possibility of extinction.

The constant, false drumbeat that because of global warming, human life could soon be wiped out—the meaning of "existential threat"—has deeply impacted an entire generation of young people worldwide, including in the United States. This has opened the door to the radical changes to society and the global economy that supporters of the Great Reset are now calling for. Without the widespread fear of climate change and its impacts, shifting economic and social power into the hands of elites would be considerably more difficult under the Great Reset's framework.

GENERATION GRETA

Perhaps the single most surprising comment you will read in this book, which is really saying something, since it's a book about a massive conspiracy to reset the global economy, is that I like Greta Thunberg—well, kind of.

In recent years, Greta, a teenager from Stockholm, Sweden, has become one of the world's most beloved and influential young climate activists. Thunberg became famous in 2018 after leading massive student strikes in front of the Swedish parliament building, during which she and thousands of other young people demanded reforms that would reduce carbon dioxide emissions, which they believe to be the cause of deadly climate change.[111] These "climate strikes" soon spread to other countries, and by late 2019, millions of students had participated.[112]

In September 2019, Greta became a household name after traveling to the United Nations' headquarters in New York City to deliver a speech for the U.N. Climate Action Summit. During the speech, Thunberg skewered, to put it mildly, government leaders across the globe for not doing enough to avert a climate catastrophe.

"This is all wrong," Thunberg said. "I shouldn't be up here. I should be back in school, on the other side of the ocean. Yet you all come to us young people for hope. How dare you! You have stolen my dreams and my childhood with your empty words. And yet I'm one of the lucky ones. People are suffering. People are dying."[113]

"Entire ecosystems are collapsing," she continued. "We are in the beginning of a mass extinction, and all you can talk about is money, and fairy tales of eternal economic growth. How dare you! . . . You say you hear us and that you understand the urgency. But no matter how sad and angry I am, I do not want to believe that. Because if you really understood the situation and still kept on failing to act, then you would be evil. And that I refuse to believe."[114]

Thunberg later accused international leaders of being guilty of "betrayal" of young people, warning them that "we will never forgive you" and that "change is coming, whether you like it or not."[115]

You have got to hand it to her—Greta has some serious spunk.

Although I disagree with Thunberg on, well, just about everything, I could not help but feel sympathetic while listening to her

rant about climate change and dysfunctional government bureaucrats and politicians.

Try for just a moment to put yourself in her tiny clog shoes.
You have been told your entire life that the world is on the verge of
total collapse. You believe oceans will soon swallow up whole cities
and possibly even some countries. You believe, as Thunberg said
during her speech, that "people are suffering" and "dying" because
of climate change. You think government officials have stolen the
dreams of children all over the world. You believe that disasters of
biblical proportions are on the horizon—real wrath-of-God type
stuff, fire and brimstone coming down from the skies, rivers and
seas boiling, forty years of darkness, earthquakes, volcanoes, the
dead rising from the graves, human sacrifice, dogs and cats living
together, mass hysteria.[116] (Oops, sorry, I think I just trailed off into
the *Ghostbusters* script. Don't be alarmed. It happens more often
than you might think.)

The point is, if you were not sure that the human race is going
to survive, because you believe climate change truly is an existential threat, and then you look around and see those in power doing
much less than what even many of them say would be required to
save the planet, suddenly every other public policy problem looks
like rearranging deck chairs on the *Titanic*. I'm sure Greta sees
herself as one of the few voices of reason yelling, "What the heck is
wrong with you people? We're about to hit an iceberg!"

"Yeah, yeah, kid. We get it," the crew responds. "But let's get back
to work on this whole deck-chair-crisis thing."

So like I said, I like Greta—sort of. I appreciate that she is at least
consistent with her messaging and passionate about an issue she really
believes is causing a worldwide crisis. Unlike so many people in government and media who spend their time talking about climate change,
Greta is not interested in attaining power for herself; she just wants

to positively impact the planet. I do not share many of her beliefs or proposed "solutions," but I do respect her sincerity.

Climate alarmist politicians, on the other hand, are anything but sincere, which is why you will frequently catch them putting down their climate-doomsday pizza box sign so they can spend more time talking about far less dire public policy problems, like immigration reform, student loan debt, or adding more bike trails. If they really believed the world is about to end, like Greta does, they would not waste one second or dollar worrying about anything else. The inherent contradiction is enough to drive anyone mad— even Swedish teens, apparently.

This is the bizarre world in which Greta Thunberg lives, and she is not alone. A growing share of people believe that human civilization is on the brink of collapse because of climate change.

An extensive 2019 survey of attitudes around the world about climate change found that 40 percent of Americans believe it is "likely" or "very likely" climate change will cause "a new world war." Further, 61 percent of Americans said it is "likely" or "very likely" that cities will be "lost to rising sea levels," and 38 percent said it is "likely" or "very likely" climate change "will cause…the extinction of the human race."[117]

And in many European and Asian countries, these figures are even higher. Forty-five percent of those surveyed in France, 43 percent of those surveyed in Spain, and 70 percent of those polled in the Philippines said they believe climate change will cause the human race to go extinct.[118] That's right, *extinct*, as in the whole human race will cease to exist forever.

Evidence suggests these fears are having a powerful and disturbing impact on millions of people around the world, including many children. In March 2020, Reuters reported that a poll of two thousand kids in Britain aged eight to sixteen, conducted by Savanta

ComRes for BBC's *Newsround*, showed that "one in five children are having nightmares about climate change."[119]

"About 17% of children in Britain said worries about climate change were disturbing their sleep while 19% said these fears were giving them nightmares," Reuters reported.[120]

In an article about "climate grief" published in 2019 by *Kaiser Health News*, Seattle-area therapist Andrew Bryant said that a U.N. report on climate change issued in October 2018 had a profound impact on his patients.

"I remember being in sessions with folks the next day," Bryant said. "They had never mentioned climate change before, and they were like, 'I keep hearing about this report.' Some of them expressed anxious feelings, and we kept talking about it over our next sessions."[121]

According to *Kaiser Health News*, Bryant further said that he "has been seeing patients with anxiety or depression related to climate change and the Earth's future."[122]

"Often these patients want to do something to reduce global warming but are overwhelmed and depressed by the scope of the problem and difficulty in finding solutions," *Kaiser Health News* reported. "And they're anxious about how the Earth will change over the rest of their or their children's lifetimes."[123]

Climate grief has become such a big problem that numerous support groups helping students and even older adults learn how to cope with climate change have developed across the country. In 2019, CBS News reported, "As the planet continues to deal with the effects of climate change, the American Psychological Association says more people are dealing with eco-anxiety, 'a chronic fear of environmental doom.' Two women, Aimee Lewis Reau and Laura Schmidt, have created a 10-step program to help people cope with the psychological fallout associated with climate change."[124]

The name of the organization founded by Reau and Schmidt is the Good Grief Network (GGN). On its website, GGN asks questions such as, "Does species extinction or climate change keep you up at night?" "Do you see collapse on the horizon?" and "Have you ever felt helpless or hopeless about racism, classism, sexism, homophobia, and other systemic issues?" And it promises to help people build "personal resilience while strengthening community ties to help combat despair, inaction, eco-anxiety, and other heavy emotions in the face of daunting systemic predicaments."[125]

"I saw that no government was taking it seriously enough and that caused me a lot of eco-grief and climate anxiety," Schmidt explained to CBS News in an interview. "And so what we did is designed a program that can help other people move from that place of despair and disempowerment to building community. Really feeling the weight of the world, but in a good way, in an empowering way, that allows us to make change once we come together and see we're not the only ones feeling this deep despair."[126]

In March 2017, the American Psychological Association, Climate for Health, and ecoAmerica issued a report outlining many of the psychological impacts of climate change. In the report, the authors noted, "Watching the slow and seemingly irrevocable impacts of climate change unfold, and worrying about the future for oneself, children, and later generations, may be an additional source of stress.... Qualitative research provides evidence that some people are deeply affected by feelings of loss, helplessness, and frustration due to their inability to feel like they are making a difference in stopping climate change.... Some writers stress the possible detrimental impact of their own behavior on future generations."[127]

The issue has become so widespread among younger people that universities have started issuing guidance to students struggling to deal with the perceived danger of climate change.

In an article published by Boston University (BU) titled "Feeling Stressed about the Environment? You're Not Alone," BU environmental activists provide students with advice for dealing with climate catastrophes and climate grief, including, "You have to be kind to yourself and kind to other people, and understand that everyone has a lot on their plate already ... so finding that balance between pushing yourself and also being kind to yourself can be really hard to navigate. When I find myself going down rabbit holes like, *Should I even have kids? Is our planet going to exist that long?*, running is a good, grounding thing.... Being outside has got to be the biggest thing I do to find inspiration and relieve anxiety. I find it's such a good stress reliever and a powerful reminder of why all of this matters."[128]

As the Boston University article suggests, fears of a looming climate change disaster have become so completely out of control that many people are now questioning whether they should even bother bringing children into a warming world. Alexandria Ocasio-Cortez, a congresswoman and the face of the Green New Deal, made headlines in March 2019 when she admitted that extreme worries over climate change have affected her thinking about becoming a mother, as well as the thinking of other young people.

"Basically, there's a scientific consensus that the lives of children are going to be very difficult," Ocasio-Cortez said. "And it does lead, I think, young people to have a legitimate question: Is it okay to still have children?"[129]

Around the same time Ocasio-Cortez made her comments, *Business Insider* conducted a survey which found that "nearly 38% of Americans between the ages of 18 and 29 agreed that climate change should be a factor in a couple's decision about whether to have children. And 34% of Americans between the ages of 30 and 44 agreed."[130]

Additionally, *Business Insider* reported, "Agreement was also linked to the belief that climate change is man-made: 38% of respondents who said 'the earth is getting warmer mostly because of human activity such as burning fossil fuels' said couples should factor in the effect of that warming on their children before having them. Meanwhile, 33% disagreed, and another third were neutral or didn't know."

In 2018, a similar poll by the *New York Times* found that one-third of Americans said they decided to have fewer children than their ideal number because of fears related to the effects of climate change.[131]

Along with depression, anxiety, and general malaise caused by elites' constant scare tactics, climate hysteria has also spawned radical protests. I am not talking about the students-taking-the-opportunity-to-leave-school-early protests either. I am talking about the stopping-trains and spraying-blood-on-government-buildings kind of protests—also called a riot.

One of the leading groups dedicated to climate riots is called Extinction Rebellion, which labels itself "an international movement that uses non-violent civil disobedience in an attempt to halt mass extinction and minimize the risk of societal collapse."[132] These "non-violent" acts of "civil disobedience" include, but are not limited to, using an old fire truck to spray fake blood on the treasury building in central London,[133] disrupting mass transit systems during rush hour,[134] and gluing themselves to the doors of a bank.[135] (You can't make this stuff up.)

These protests might seem asinine—as well as frustrating for Londoners trying to take the train home from work or bank employees forced to spend the morning scraping glue-covered lunatics off the front door—but try to imagine what you would be willing to do if you truly believed the world is about to come to an end.

"GREEN" IS THE NEW "YELLOW" JOURNALISM

It is easy for those of us who do not cry ourselves to sleep at night out of fear the world is ending to dismiss climate grief and climate anxiety as totally insane. However, it is important to remember that these intense feelings are logical if the underlying assumption behind them—that the world is on the edge of climate annihilation—is true. So the real question is not, Why are so many people terrified? It's, Why do they think those fears are justified?

For more than two decades, America's education establishment, both at the K–12 and higher-education levels, as well as Hollywood and even the music industry, have been working to convince Americans all over the country that climate change is imperiling life on earth. But no one has done more to brainwash the masses than the elitist news media. For years, biased reporters have run literally thousands of stories promoting climate change doomsday scenarios that fair-minded scientists on both the left and the right have rejected as extremely unlikely to occur, regardless of whether earth's modest warming trend continues.

In 2017, *New York Magazine* published a shocking and disgustingly alarmist propaganda piece titled "The Uninhabitable Earth." In the article, author David Wallace-Wells told readers,

> It is, I promise, worse than you think. If your anxiety about global warming is dominated by fears of sea-level rise, you are barely scratching the surface of what terrors are possible, even within the lifetime of a teenager today. And yet the swelling seas—and the cities they will drown—have so dominated the picture of global warming, and so overwhelmed our capacity for climate panic, that they have occluded our perception of other threats, many much closer at hand. Rising oceans are bad, in fact very bad; but fleeing the coastline will not be enough.[136]

No matter how well-informed you are, you are surely not alarmed enough. Over the past decades, our culture has gone apocalyptic with zombie movies and *Mad Max* dystopias, perhaps the collective result of displaced climate anxiety, and yet when it comes to contemplating real-world warming dangers, we suffer from an incredible failure of imagination.[137]

So I guess rampant hurricanes and wildfires and cities sinking into the sea like Atlantis aren't enough, then?

Wallace-Wells goes on to provide one of the most shocking lists of climate alarmism you will ever find, broken down by the following categories: "heat deaths," "the end of food," "climate plagues," "unbreathable air," "perpetual war," "permanent economic collapse," and "poisoned oceans."[138] (By the way, I'm still trying to figure out how climate change can cause both "the end of food" and "perpetual war." If everyone has starved to death, who the heck is doing all that fighting?)

Of course, Wallace-Wells is just one writer out of hundreds who regularly promote extreme climate alarmism. CNN reported in January 2019 that "250,000 deaths a year from climate change is a 'conservative estimate,'" citing a ridiculous study predicting that food shortages—which have become *less common* in our warming world—will cause more than five hundred thousand additional adult deaths by 2050.[139] The study also claimed that climate change will push one hundred million more people into "extreme poverty" by 2030, another ludicrous claim in light of the fact that hundreds of millions of people have been lifted out of poverty over the past few decades, despite higher average global temperatures.

In September 2019, *Foreign Affairs* writer Tedros Adhanom Ghebreyesus posted an article titled "Climate Change Is Already Killing Us," in which he said the bubonic plague could once again become a major global catastrophe if global warming continues, and that anthrax—yes, anthrax—could "spread farther as a result of stronger winds." He also wrote that global warming is making cholera "more difficult to control," and that malaria and dengue could become even more widespread.[140]

And Ghebreyesus said that is just the beginning. He also claimed, "Rising sea levels and increased ocean acidification will reduce fishing and aquaculture, aggravating malnutrition and food insecurity. Contamination of aquifers will exacerbate water shortages. Droughts, which already kill and displace more people than any other type of weather catastrophe, are predicted to grow longer and more frequent. The World Bank estimates that by 2050, there could be one billion climate refugees from sub-Saharan Africa, South Asia, and Latin America."[141]

In November 2019, *Wired* published "How the Climate Crisis Is Killing Us, in 9 Alarming Charts." In the article, author Matt Simon presents and comments on one misleading chart after another in an obvious attempt to scare people. Charts include a map titled "Infernos Everywhere" and a graph titled "Here Come the Diseases."[142]

One of my all-time favorite examples of climate alarmism is perhaps the most terrifying. In 2019, *USA Today* published an article titled "Climate Change Could Zap Clouds, Bake the Earth Even More." In the article, writer Doyle Rice reported, "Many of the world's clouds could disappear if the carbon dioxide we keep pumping into our atmosphere soars to extreme levels, a new study suggests." Rice further wrote, "The lack of those cooling clouds would then trigger a spike in global temperatures, potentially as much as 14 degrees, melting polar ice and leaving coastal cities underwater."[143]

The bubonic plague, thousands of cities and towns underwater, one billion climate refugees, and a cloudless, lifeless, baked earth— if you believed, and I mean *really, truly believed*, that this is what the future looks like, then boy, why wouldn't you be screeching, "How dare you!" to the global elites refusing to put an end to this insanity? I know I would.

This climate hysteria has also been driven to new heights in recent years due to the effects of a death spiral of common sense that works a little something like this: Elites and their well-funded allies in environmental groups and, in some cases, academia make increasingly absurd predictions about climate collapse. The news media dutifully reports it as though God had handed the predictions down from heaven on stone tablets. Although an ever-larger group of people, especially children, have started to believe the predictions, most adults still reject them. In an attempt to scare those skeptical Americans into believing "the science" on climate change, the doomsday predictions and rhetoric get more extreme. "Oh, flooding cities won't do it for them. How about a baked earth? That will do it, I bet."

Because climate change has been portrayed as so imminent and potentially cataclysmic, alarmists say there is no time for debate. "The science is settled," they have declared. Anyone who disagrees is labeled a "climate denier"—an obvious attempt to conjure up Holocaust denialism—and pushed out of the public square, which moves the entire national conversation further and further toward insanity. Eventually, the only people allowed to talk about climate change in major media platforms are elites (who stand to benefit financially and/or politically from the hysteria) and their friends.

This is not theoretical. This is exactly the strategy elites in media have been pursuing for many years. In 2014, hundreds of BBC staff and journalists attended BBC Trust seminars, in which they were told to stop giving "climate skeptics" airtime. A report by BBC Trust explains its stance: "The Trust wishes to emphasise the importance of attempting to establish where the weight of scientific agreement may be found and make that clear to audiences."[144]

So now, when someone comes on the air to talk about a dire cloud-pocalypse, no one will be invited on to counter the claim, because, in the subjective opinion of the BBC's editors, that's "where the weight of scientific agreement may be found." And how exactly does BBC know what the "weight of scientific agreement" is? Are they themselves scientists? Of course not, and they are not allowed to have on the air any scientists who do not agree with dire claims (these are the "deniers," remember?), so there's no reason to believe that what you see and read from the BBC is truly reflective of the best available science.

These sentiments have been expressed by many others in the media, too, and not just BBC. CNN made its views clear when it released a video in December 2018 telling viewers not to believe the "climate change lies" spread by prominent Republicans.[145] Chuck Todd, host of NBC's *Meet the Press*, opened his show on December 30, 2018, with a monologue about how he is "not going to give time to climate deniers."[146]

And what makes someone a climate denier, anyway? I have created a short list of things that might get you labeled a denier.

1. You point out facts and statistics that counter alarmist assertions about catastrophic climate change. (And by "catastrophic," I mean humanity-ending.)
2. You do not think the world is going to be put on an unstoppable path toward human extinction in ten years because of climate change.
3. You think wind and solar energy cannot reasonably power the entire world.
4. You are concerned about the immense environmental damage caused by wind and solar facilities.
5. You are worried that switching to more expensive energy sources will raise prices, reduce economic activity, and hurt the poor.

Not only are these decisions by the media to ignore opposing views on climate change prime examples of terrible journalism and overt bias, but they are also, quite ironically, completely opposed to the scientific method. Many of the most important scientific discoveries in human history—from those made by Galileo to the world-changing theories advanced by Einstein—were so remarkable precisely *because* they defied the scientific "consensus" of the time. In real science, carefully cultivated evidence and the scientific method is what matters, not consensus. And even if consensus were the gold standard, there is no scientific consensus suggesting that climate change is an existential threat that could wipe out humanity. Anyone who tells you otherwise is, in a very real sense, a true science denier.

REASONS FOR SKEPTICISM

There are many reasons to reject the hellish vision of the future that elites are always screaming about and to believe it's very unlikely to occur. But I think I can convince you by focusing on only three.

First, many of the dire global warming predictions about hurricanes, wildfires, and other disasters that have been made over the past few decades have already been proven false.

Second, there are thousands of scientists all over the world who believe that a climate change doomsday scenario is not going to happen, contrary to the slew of breathless media reports that consume radio, television, and print and digital publications on a nearly daily basis.

During the same week Greta Thunberg was publicly shaming elites at the United Nations, five hundred scientists and prominent professionals in climate science and related fields sent a letter to the head of the United Nations, warning the world against relying on many of the most popular climate models, calling them "unfit for their purpose."[147] They wrote,

> Therefore, it is cruel as well as imprudent to advocate the squandering of trillions of dollars on the basis of results from such immature models. Current climate policies pointlessly and grievously undermine the economic system, putting lives at risk in countries denied access to affordable, reliable electrical energy. We urge you to follow a climate policy based on sound science, realistic economics and genuine concern for those harmed by costly but unnecessary attempts at mitigation.[148]

The signees also provided a list of arguments they claimed are strongly supported by available science, including:

- "Natural as well as anthropogenic factors cause warming."
- "Warming is far slower than predicted."
- "Climate policy relies on inadequate models."
- "More CO_2 is beneficial for nature, greening the Earth."
- "Global warming has not increased natural disasters."

Ultimately, they declared, "There is no climate emergency" and thus "no cause for panic."[149]

Further, organizations like the Nongovernmental International Panel on Climate Change (NIPCC) have for more than a decade been compiling a mountain of research by scientists skeptical of climate alarmism. Here, too, are good reasons to reject the world-is-going-to-end-in-ten-years arguments of the Far Left. In 2019, NIPCC released the fifth volume of its Climate Change Reconsidered series, which features thousands of pages of peer-reviewed scientific and economic data and analysis showing that the world is not about to experience a climate-change-induced apocalypse.[150]

So much for that whole "the science is settled" slogan many elites in business and government are always parading about.

A third reason fair-minded Americans should not buy "the sky is falling" views on global warming is that, for a half century or longer, establishment environmentalists have been making similarly terrifying yet false predictions about other topics, including population growth, pollution, and global cooling. Why? Of course, it's all to promote far-reaching public policies, many of which promised to provide huge amounts of funding to big businesses willing to play ball. In many cases, the "experts" whom the mainstream press trot out to convince the world that the planet will be an environmental nightmare by 2050 are the *same people* who told us the planet would be an environmental nightmare by 2010.

One of the most famous and influential doomsayers of the past century was Stanford scientist Paul Ehrlich. In the 1960s, media ran wild when he and a whole host of other "experts" from leading U.S. academic institutions claimed humanity was on an unstoppable trajectory toward widespread famine, death, and misery. In a *Los Angeles Times* report published in November 1967 citing Ehrlich's work, reporter George Getze wrote, "It is already too late for the world to avoid a long period of famine."[151]

"Paul Ehrlich said the 'time of famines' is upon us and will be at its worst and most disastrous by 1975," Getze also reported.[152]

"He [Ehrlich] said the population of the United States is already too big, that birth control may have to be accomplished by making it involuntary and by putting sterilizing agents into staple foods and drinking water, and that the Roman Catholic Church should be pressured into going along with routine measures of population control," Getze added.[153]

I am sure glad we did not adopt Ehrlich's plan to stuff birth control pills in every Big Mac in America, because it turns out that whole "time of famines" thing never happened. The opposite occurred. Farmers and food manufacturers are feeding more people today than ever before, and there is still plenty of room for progress.

In December 1972, George Kukla from the Lamont-Doherty Earth Observatory and Robert Matthews, who was then chairman of the Department of Geological Sciences at Brown University, wrote a highly influential letter to President Richard Nixon, claiming that a recent conference of "42 top American and European investigators" examining climate change determined that "a global deterioration of climate, by order of magnitude larger than nay hitherto experienced by civilized mankind, is a very real possibility and indeed may be due very soon."[154]

Those of you reading this who believe earth is headed for a global warming existential crisis are probably tempted to think, "Yeah, see, Glenn, it looks like the scientific consensus on climate change has been around for at least fifty years." But it turns out the warning issued by these "top" climate investigators in the 1970s was not of a global *warming* crisis but rather of a global *cooling* crisis.

"The cooling has natural cause and falls within the rank of processes which produced the last ice age. . . . Existing data still do not allow forecast of the precise timing of the predicted development, nor the assessment of the man's interference with the natural trends," the letter continued. "It could not be excluded however that the cooling now under way in the Northern Hemisphere is the start of the expected shift. The present rate of the cooling seems fast enough to bring glacial temperatures in about a century, if continuing at the present pace."[155]

These climate scientists then went on to warn President Nixon of the "practical consequences" of global cooling, including "substantially lowered food production" and "increased frequency and amplitude of extreme weather anomalies such as those bringing floods, snowstorms, killing frosts."[156] The global ice age scare soon caught on, and for the next several years it seemed to be all the media could talk about.

In January 1974, the *Guardian* reported, "Space Satellites Show New Ice Age Coming Fast."[157]

In June 1974, *Time* reported that "another ice age" could soon be upon the world. "As they review the bizarre and unpredictable weather pattern of the past several years, a growing number of scientists are beginning to suspect that many seemingly contradictory meteorological fluctuations are actually part of a global climatic upheaval," a *Time* reporter wrote, adding later that "the atmosphere has been growing gradually cooler for the past three decades," a trend that "shows no indication of reversing."[158]

Time further reported, "Climatological Cassandras are becoming increasingly apprehensive, for the weather aberrations they are studying may be the harbinger of another ice age."[159]

By the way, it is a really good thing that the "new ice age" so many environmentalists were clamoring about in the 1970s never developed, because even though many elites today make it sound as though a warming planet is the worst thing that could ever happen to humanity, history has repeatedly shown that global cooling events are much, much worse.

Researchers who authored a 2015 article published in the prestigious academic journal the *Lancet* found, after examining more than 74 million deaths occurring in 384 locations worldwide from 1985 to 2012, that "most of the temperature-related mortality burden was attributable to the contribution of cold. The effect of days of extreme temperature was substantially less than that attributable to milder but non-optimum weather."[160] In other words, cold weather is much deadlier than warm or even hot weather.

Of course, eventually fears about a global ice age gave way to fears about global warming, which was then conveniently renamed "climate change" when surface temperature rise slowed dramatically from 1998 to 2012. But the long tradition of failed predictions continued into the 1980s, 1990s, and well into the present period.

In 1989, famed climatologist Jim Hansen, now a professor at Columbia University, predicted that the West Side Highway in New York City would be underwater by 2019 because of rising sea levels caused by global warming.[161] And this is just one of the many false predictions made by Hansen over the years. In 2008, Hansen also alleged that earth had reached its climate change "tipping point" and that within a decade the Arctic would be free of sea ice in the summer.[162] Now some scientists say it could occur within the next fifteen years, while others predict it will not happen until 2050, if at all.

The Associated Press reported in 1989 that Noel Brown, a senior environmental official for the United Nations, predicted that "entire nations could be wiped off the face of the earth by rising sea levels if the global warming trend is not reversed by the year 2000."[163] According to the report, Brown also claimed that governments only had a "10-year window of opportunity" to fix the coming climate crisis. (Wow, that sure sounds familiar. I wonder if the "experts" at big corporations and the World Economic Forum pushing climate change "solutions" spend their free time reading old newspaper articles from the 1980s, like I do.)

"As the warming melts polar icecaps, ocean levels will rise by up to three feet, enough to cover the Maldives and other flat island nations," the Associated Press (AP) reported. AP later added that the U.N. Environment Program and U.S. Environmental Protection Agency predicted, "Coastal regions will be inundated; one-sixth of Bangladesh could be flooded, displacing a fourth of its 90 million people. A fifth of Egypt's arable land in the Nile Delta would be flooded, cutting off its food supply."[164]

In 2004, the *Guardian* published an article covering a report issued by the Pentagon that predicted, "By 2010 the US and Europe will experience a third more days with peak temperatures above 90F." The Pentagon also reportedly predicted that climate would become an "economic nuisance" due to "storms, droughts and hot spells," which would "create havoc for farmers."[165]

The *Guardian* also noted that the Pentagon report claimed that "mega-droughts" would "affect the world's major breadbaskets, including America's Midwest, where strong winds bring soil loss," and that Bangladesh would become "nearly uninhabitable because of a rising sea level."[166]

None of these doom-and-gloom predictions, nor any of the thousands of other promises of existential crisis–level climate catastrophes I have seen over the past few decades, has come even close to occurring. But that has not stopped ruling-class elites and the environmentalists they provide funding to from continuing to promise more and more chaos.

If the mainstream media were even remotely close to being a truly unbiased source of information, they would at the very least point out the abysmal, dumpster-fire-level track record of climate doomsday prognosticators when reporting on their latest and greatest horror show climate change predictions. Of course, they do not, so tens of millions of Americans are fooled every year into believing that just because a newspaper columnist says a catastrophe is right around the corner, that means it must be true.

THE NUCLEAR OPTION

You should always be skeptical of politicians, business leaders, activists, and others who say that the only way to solve a societal problem supposedly being caused by one or more groups having too much power is to vest even more power and authority in the hands of other, supposedly better, wiser, or more knowledgeable groups, especially government. This is true when considering not only environmental issues but also every other topic of importance.

British politician and historian John Dalberg-Acton, today commonly referred to as Lord Acton, famously wrote, "Power tends to corrupt, and absolute power corrupts absolutely." That's a great line, but the rarely quoted sentence that follows it is arguably even better: "Great men are almost always bad men, even when they exercise influence and not authority; still more when you superadd the tendency of the certainty of corruption by authority."[167]

"Great men are almost always bad men" does not mean that the only people who achieve greatness or success in life are bad people, but rather it means that those who are able to succeed in attaining power and influence for themselves tend to be corrupted by it, no matter how good their intentions are at first.

Pundits and politicians on both the left and the right continuously warn us to be wary of granting great power to any person or group. Yet that hesitancy to give power is incompatible with the goals of elite and globalist institutions—all of which, to varying degrees, seek to attain substantial amounts of influence and/or authority in the pursuit of some noble goal.

Elites often say they care a great deal about limiting the dangers associated with the centralization of political and economic power, but that's really true only when it comes to their ideological and political rivals. They don't believe power corrupts *everyone*; they believe *certain kinds* of power corrupt *certain kinds* of people.

This way of thinking has developed into a savior complex that is rampant within the ruling class, especially within organizations like the World Economic Forum, in which nearly everyone believes, "If only we had more authority and control over society, the world would be a much better place." Over time, no matter how altruistic a movement starts, this way of thinking always—not sometimes but *always*—corrupts the minds of those seeking power. They inevitably transform every cause into a movement to gain more authority for themselves and like-minded people and institutions.

Most Americans do not think of environmentalism as having been bastardized in this way. Environmentalists care only about stopping the extinction of the lesser prairie chicken, protecting the sage-grouse hen from annihilation, and saving panda bears, right? And panda bears are cute and cuddly and would never be saved by power-hungry authoritarian monsters.

But the truth is, elitist environmentalists have proven to be one of the best examples of how a well-intentioned cause can evolve into a corrupt movement for societal control. Perhaps the best evidence for this argument is American elites' near-total rejection of nuclear power, which, although expensive relative to existing conventional energy sources like natural gas, provides tremendous environmental benefits. Compared to the "green" energy sources the ruling class is always trying to impose on Americans—primarily wind and solar power—nuclear energy is significantly more reliable, cost-efficient, and environmentally friendly. Plus, it produces almost no carbon dioxide emissions, the very thing environmentalists are always touting as the most important issue when it comes to building energy infrastructure.

Wind and solar power sources are not nearly as reliable as nuclear power because they do not generate any energy when the wind isn't blowing and the sun isn't shining. Believe me, I know from personal experience. I was an early adopter of solar. My ranch in the Rocky Mountains is powered almost entirely by renewable energy. And every time it snows—which, in case you didn't know, is *a lot* in the Rocky Mountains—I have to drag my butt outside to shovel the snow off the panels so they will start generating energy again once the snowstorm passes.

This intermittency problem might merely be a pain for a guy with a ranch in the mountains, but it would be catastrophic for a nation the size of the United States, if that nation were to try to run mostly on these unreliable sources of energy. This is a big reason why in 2019, despite billions of dollars' worth of government subsidies rolled out over many years, wind and solar accounted for only 7.3 percent and 1.8 percent, respectively, of total U.S. utility-scale electricity generation.[168] Nuclear, which receives very little positive attention, produced nearly 20 percent of utility-scale electricity.[169]

Intermittency is such a huge problem for wind and solar that currently it is virtually impossible to run the electric grid on these two forms of energy. "Solar and wind require that natural gas plants, hydro-electric dams, batteries or some other form of reliable power be ready at a moment's notice to start churning out electricity when the wind stops blowing and the sun stops shining," wrote Michael Shellenberger for *Forbes* in 2019. Shellenberger, a leading environmentalist and expert on nuclear energy, also added in the article, "Unreliability requires solar- and/or wind-heavy places like Germany, California, and Denmark to *pay* neighboring nations or states to take their solar and wind energy when they are producing too much of it."[170]

Wind turbines and solar panels also have a much shorter life span than nuclear facilities. The U.S. Office of Nuclear Energy noted in 2020 that even as "the average age of American [nuclear] reactors approaches 40 years old, experts say there are no technical limits to these units churning out clean and reliable energy for an additional 40 years or longer.... Utilities now have the confidence and data they need to apply for a second 20-year operating license with the Nuclear Regulatory Commission (NRC)."[171]

Solar panels and wind farms, on the other hand, last only two to three decades before they must be replaced. "The short useful lifetimes of wind turbines and solar panels are one of the least talked about, but most important, aspects of energy policy," wrote Isaac Orr, an expert on energy policy at the Center of the American Experiment.[172]

"Here today, scrap metal by 2050. That's the rough life of wind turbines and solar panels, which only have useful lifetimes of 20 and 30 years, respectively, according to the National Renewable Energy Laboratory (NREL) and Energy Sage," Orr added.[173]

The short life spans of wind and solar power facilities, coupled with their lack of reliability, make these energy sources much more expensive than nuclear power.

Orr noted, "When the shorter operating lifespans for wind and solar are accounted for…the total cost of rebuilding wind turbines every 20 years brings the cost to $13.5 million per MW [megawatt], and replacing solar on 30-year timescales results in a total cost of $21 million [per megawatt]," compared to less than $7 million per megawatt for nuclear.[174]

"Nuclear is clearly the superior value to consumers," Orr concluded.[175]

Wind and solar are so much more expensive that if America were to get just 80 percent of its electricity from wind, solar, and battery storage, the United States' electricity bill would skyrocket by more than $1 trillion per year—yes, that's *trillion*, with a *t*.[176]

Also, despite the media-contrived depictions to the contrary, nuclear is a lot better for the planet than wind or solar, which is especially important considering that the whole reason Americans are being urged to commit economic suicide with plans like the Green New Deal and Biden's Green New Deal–lite plan—which would impose wind and solar energy on most of the country over just a couple of decades—is that wind and solar facilities are so much greener than other forms of energy production. But nuclear facilities emit four times *less* carbon dioxide into the atmosphere than do solar farms, and wind farms require four hundred times *more* land than do nuclear power plants.[177]

A 2019 Heartland Institute policy study noted the tremendous amount of environmental harm that would be caused by replacing conventional energy sources with wind and solar. Not only would millions of bats and birds, including endangered species, be wiped out by wind and solar facilities, but millions of other animal habitats across the country would need to be destroyed to make way for millions of new wind turbines and billions of new solar panels.

According to Heartland's report, which was based in part on research conducted by environmental groups, "The Fowler Ridge Wind Farm in Indiana covers 68 square miles, an area larger than Washington, D.C. If similar facilities were used to replace all of the country's fossil fuels and nuclear power, it would require 2.12 million turbines on 500,682 square miles of farm, wildlife habitat, and scenic lands. This would require an amount of land as large as the combined total for Arizona, California, Nevada, Oregon, and much of West Virginia."[178]

Heartland further estimated, "If we use the cutting-edge Nellis Air Force Base solar farm as a model of the power such facilities can produce, we find that to generate the more than eight billion [megawatt hours] each year [the energy needed to power the country] with solar would require completely blanketing 57,048 square miles of land—an area equivalent to the size of the states of New York and Vermont—with 18.8 billion solar panels. Obviously, this would wreak much havoc on the environment."[179]

Gee, I wonder how many endangered eagles would be obliterated by all those new wind turbines? And how many sage-grouse hens and lesser prairie chickens would be forced from their habitats in order for us to build billions of solar panels? (By the way, I don't know about you, but suddenly I have a real hankering for Chick-fil-A.)

Bulldozing millions of acres of land and killing millions of animals hardly sounds like green energy to me, but building these poor-performing monstrosities is just the beginning. After a few decades, when all the gigantic turbines and solar panels must be torn down, where do elites plan on putting them? I hate to break it to those of you who still think relying on wind and solar is a good idea, but you cannot just throw decommissioned wind and solar parts into a big blue recycling bin and leave it out on the street for your local garbageman to pick up. Wind turbines and solar panels create huge amounts of waste, much of it toxic, and no one has developed a clean, cost-effective way to deal with that gigantic problem. And remember, this is an issue that would come up every twenty or thirty years, as these facilities wear out.

"The International Renewable Energy Agency (IRENA) in 2016 estimated there was about 250,000 metric tonnes of solar panel waste in the world at the end of that year. IRENA projected that this amount could reach 78 million metric tonnes by 2050," noted Michael Shellenberger in an article for *Forbes* in 2018.[180]

"Solar panels often contain lead, cadmium, and other toxic chemicals that cannot be removed without breaking apart the entire panel," added Shellenberger, writing later that "researchers with the Electric Power Research Institute (EPRI) undertook a study for U.S. solar-owning utilities to plan for end-of-life and concluded that solar panel disposal in 'regular landfills [is] not recommended in case modules break and toxic materials leach into the soil' and so 'disposal is potentially a major issue.'"

Additionally, wind turbines, which are ineffective in many parts of the country, are not good options for the environment. In 2019, NPR reported, "The U.S. will have more than 720,000 tons of [wind turbine] blade material to dispose of over the next 20 years, a figure that doesn't include newer, taller higher-capacity versions."[181]

So it seems clear, beyond a shadow of a doubt, that wind and solar are not nearly as environmentally beneficial as so many seem to think they are. They are environmentally toxic. But what about the big radioactive elephant in the room, nuclear waste? And what about nuclear disasters like Chernobyl? Didn't that one event kill millions of people and thus justify never building another nuclear power plant again?

The biggest roadblock for nuclear power is unquestionably misinformation about it that has been spreading for decades. When most people think of nuclear energy in America, they imagine glowing green sludge, three-eyed fish, and huge radioactive catastrophes. But these images are not even close to reflecting the realities of nuclear power.

"It's reasonable to ask whether nuclear power is safe, and what happens with its waste," wrote Shellenberger in 2019. "It turns out that scientists have studied the health and safety of different energy sources since the 1960s. Every major study, including a recent one by the British medical journal *Lancet*, finds the same thing: nuclear is the safest way to make reliable electricity."[182]

The truth is, as Shellenberger notes, nuclear waste is not nearly the problem so many people claim it is. Homer Simpson isn't actually burying barrels of glowing green sludge under parks for his villainous billionaire boss, Monty Burns. Instead nuclear waste consists of "used nuclear fuel in the shape of rods about 12 feet long" that eventually end up in "15-foot tall canisters known as 'dry casks' that weigh 100 tons or more."[183]

And although many imagine nuclear waste requires huge amounts of land to store, Shellenberger notes, "If all the nuclear waste from U.S. power plants were put on a football field, it would stack up just 50 feet high. In comparison to the waste produced by every other kind of electricity production, that quantity is close to zero."[184]

It is also not true that millions of people have died from nuclear disasters like Chernobyl—which occurred more than three decades ago, in 1986—or the 2011 Fukushima crisis in Japan, when an earthquake and subsequent tsunami hit a nuclear plant. Although the Chernobyl event was the worst nuclear disaster in history, World Health Organization estimates show that only about nine thousand people have died or will die as a result of it, including cancer-related deaths. Only thirty-one individuals died as a direct result of the incident.[185]

Further, as of 2018, only one person had died from radiation exposure coming from the Fukushima site, and about 573 died from the stress of related evacuations. For context, about twenty-five times more people (15,893) died in the tsunami that caused the nuclear disaster in the first place.[186]

Obviously, any loss of life is tragic, but these extremely rare instances hardly serve as proof that nuclear energy is comparatively dangerous. History has shown that the exact opposite is true. Nearly every other form of electricity generation is associated with causing more premature deaths than does nuclear, and there are currently nations that have been safely relying on nuclear energy for decades.

In 2018, 71.7 percent of the electricity produced in France, 55 percent in Slovakia, 53 percent in Ukraine, 50.6 percent in Hungary, and 40 percent in Sweden came from nuclear power plants.[187] Further, nuclear facilities generated more than one-quarter of the electricity in Armenia, Finland, the Czech Republic, Bulgaria, Slovenia, Switzerland, and Belgium.[188]

No offense to the wonderful people of Slovakia and Hungary, but does anyone really believe that these countries are better equipped to safely manage nuclear energy than the United States, the most powerful, scientifically advanced, and wealthiest nation on the planet?

Nuclear energy also offers a greater potential for technological breakthroughs and innovation. Advocates of wind and solar energy often tout recent increases in efficiency and claim that more improvements are just around the corner. However, the rate of these increases has decelerated. A 2019 report from the Manhattan Institute analyzed the cost reductions and energy output of wind and solar energy over the past few decades. The Manhattan

Institute researchers found that wind and solar energy improvements are slowing substantially. The report concludes, "The era of 10-fold gains is over."[189] But with nuclear power, there is still lots of room for improvement.

Due to public fears and miles of regulatory red tape, the advancement of nuclear technology has been relatively stagnant over the past fifty years, but there are now in the works a number of new developments that could revolutionize the future of energy. Rolls-Royce is attempting to develop small modular reactors (SMRs). These mini reactors would require a fraction of the land needed for other forms of renewable energy, would generate a consistent flow of baseload energy, would dramatically reduce the costs associated with nuclear power, and could be easily scaled to meet specific energy needs.[190]

"SMRs are the next evolutionary step of nuclear power: compact, affordable, quick to construct, emission-less, and even transportable," wrote Ariel Cohen, a program director and senior fellow at the Atlantic Council, in a 2020 article for *Forbes*.[191]

Advancements in nuclear fusion are also underway. In 2020, assembly on the largest fusion program, the ITER Project, began in southern France. The ITER Project has the potential of providing essentially unlimited clean energy by replicating the reactions that power stars like the sun. Several nations, including the United States, are contributing to this potentially game-changing project.[192]

If nuclear power is safer, more likely to experience revolutionary technological improvements, and more cost-efficient, reliable, and environmentally friendly than wind and solar, why the heck do so many people in financial institutions, international corporations, and government—including President Biden and Vice President Kamala Harris—want to spend trillions of dollars building millions of wind turbines and billions of solar panels instead of nuclear power plants?

A BIG "GREEN" GRAB FOR POWER

It is hard to imagine a more ideal justification for a long-term take-over of the global economy than the claim that climate change poses an existential threat to humanity. And in the face of certain doom, it's easy to argue that the only way to solve this crisis is to vest gargantuan amounts of power in the hands of the ruling class. That way, they can save us all by managing the economy away from a climate catastrophe that's always just ten years down the road. Nice and tidy.

Nuclear power might reduce carbon dioxide emissions, which people like Biden say they care about, but it does nothing to help elites gain control over society. So naturally, most of them don't want anything to do with it.

The very existence of the Great Reset movement proves how important climate change has become to global elites. Sure, far-reaching, deadly pandemics are useful, and yes, the coronavirus has created that "golden opportunity" many have been waiting for to justify a "reset" of capitalism. But in the end, nothing can match the opportunity presented by the claim that there is a looming, nearly unstoppable threat to all life on earth, posed by global warming—an argument Great Reset supporters have made repeatedly since the movement began.

Gita Gopinath, the chief economist at the International Monetary Fund and a staunch supporter of the Great Reset, said at a June 2020 World Economic Forum meeting that shifting economies to green priorities should be a part of every nation's economic strategy under the Reset.

> But how do we get to a more planet-friendly way of doing economic activity? What's needed is to ramp up production of alternative forms of energy. And second, to have infrastructure that's much more climate-friendly. In both these measures, the public sector can play a very big role.

Once you have those in place—alternatives to energy and greener, physical infrastructure—then you can obviously put on top of that carbon pricing, too, so companies and firms internalize the impact of their activities on the climate.[193]

Alluding to climate change, Sharan Burrow, the general secretary of the International Trade Union Confederation, told WEF, "We want an end to the profit-at-all-costs mentality, because if we don't build an economic future within a sustainable framework in which we are respectful of our planetary boundaries, and the need to change our energy and technology systems, then we will not have a living planet for human beings."[194]

Jennifer Morgan, the executive director of Greenpeace International, said that the Great Reset needs to "put the health of people and the planet first."[195]

"That's what's happening on COVID-19," Morgan added, "but it has not yet happened on climate change in many cases, because the fossil fuel interests and the large industrial farming interests want to keep things the way they are. And what we're learning from this pandemic is it is possible to switch it."[196]

Also at the June World Economic Forum meeting, U.N. secretary-general António Guterres said, "We must build equal, inclusive, sustainable societies, that are more resilient in the face of pandemics and climate change."[197]

In April 2020, James Shaw, the climate minister for New Zealand and another supporter of the Great Reset, wrote in an article for the *Guardian* that the COVID-19 pandemic "is a time for governments, regions, and cities around the world to mobilise and deploy resources to tackle the climate crisis at the same time as rebuilding their economies, all whilst creating high value green jobs."[198]

Shaw said readers must imagine "a future that is more equitable, more prosperous, and more innovative—and all within planetary limits," adding later that governments must now "make bold decisions for the collective good."[199]

Prince Charles, one of the leading voices behind the Great Reset, said at the June 2020 WEF event, "The threat of climate change has been more gradual—but its devastating reality for many people and their livelihoods around the world, and its ever greater potential to disrupt, surpasses even that of COVID-19.[200]

"If we look at the planet as if it were a patient," Prince Charles added, "we can see that our activities have been damaging her immune system, and she has been struggling to function and thrive due to the strain we have put on her vital organs."[201]

Klaus Schwab, the head of the World Economic Forum, has identified climate change as the "next global disaster" and has said that if the world does not soon adopt the Great Reset, global warming will have "even more dramatic consequences for humankind" than COVID-19.

"We have to decarbonize the economy in the short window still remaining and bring our thinking and behavior once more into harmony with nature," Schwab said.[202]

Yeah, nothing says "harmony with nature" quite like strip-mining the world for the rare earth minerals needed to construct billions of solar panels and storage batteries, grinding up millions of acres of land to build "green" energy facilities, and mass-murdering millions of birds with huge wind turbines, right, Klaus?

JUSTIFYING THE "MACHINE"

In January 2019, Greta Thunberg spoke at the World Economic Forum in Davos. Her message was terrifying and revealing. "I don't want you to be hopeful," she said, "I want you to panic. I want you to feel the fear I feel every day. And then I want you to act."[203]

Notice that her message was not focused on determining the best path forward based on logic and reason; it was focused simply on taking action based on emotion and fear. This fear infects virtually every aspect of the modern climate change narrative and is frequently used to justify extreme actions, including those that would destroy the global economy and require massive government takeovers.

When Thunberg demanded that government leaders tear down the global economy at the United Nations in late 2019, she had no idea that lurking around the corner was a pandemic that would, within just a few months, radically alter the world's political, economic, and social landscape. COVID-19 made what had previously seemed possible only to wildly idealistic teenagers like Thunberg into a policy platform for many of the planet's most powerful and influential figures.

It is easy for relatively wealthy Swedish teens to demand that hundreds of thousands of people around the world lose their jobs. It's no big deal for them to call for economies to collapse in the name of stopping climate change. But it's not as simple for people who have to play the role of economic executioner—even for those who have long hoped for the same sorts of changes Thunberg demanded.

What so many elites around the world initially did not have the stomach to do, the pandemic did for them. By providing the ruling class with a reason that voters could tolerate for killing the global economy (the possibility of millions of people dying at the hands of a novel virus), COVID-19 offered leaders in business, government, and activism a "golden opportunity" to change, well, everything, and to make potentially trillions of dollars while doing it. (More on that in chapter 5.)

I care deeply about the environment and the importance of protecting the planet and its natural resources. I believe humanity has a sacred responsibility to be good stewards of the earth God has provided to all of us. And unlike many Hollywood elites, who like to tweet about how much they care about the planet between sips of champagne on a private jet traveling halfway around the world, I have put my money (and snow shovel) where my mouth is. I have spent a small fortune trying to power my home using renewable energy sources, because I truly do want to help protect the planet. But the truth is, as much as I would love for wind and solar power to be the answer to the world's energy problems, the evidence overwhelmingly shows it isn't. Yet the ruling class continues to insist we all have to use it. Why?

As history has repeatedly shown, sometimes there's just too much power to be seized and too much money to be made to worry about what is in the best interests of Main Street America.

4

MODERN MONETARY THEORY: FUEL FOR A GLOBAL ECONOMIC TAKEOVER

And I sincerely believe with you, that banking establishments are more dangerous than standing armies; and that the principle of spending money to be paid by posterity, under the name of funding, is but swindling futurity on a large scale.

—Thomas Jefferson, in a letter to John Taylor, May 28, 1816[204]

I N 1910, U.S. SENATOR NELSON ALDRICH OF RHODE ISLAND, the chairman of the National Monetary Committee, instructed several of America's highest-profile bankers to covertly meet at night in a train station in New Jersey. Among those who attended were Henry P. Davison, senior partner at JP Morgan and Company; Paul Warburg, founder of the investment firm Kuhn, Loeb, and Co.; Frank A. Vanderlip, vice president of the National City Bank of New York (now called Citibank); and Charles D. Norton, president of Morgan's First National Bank of New York.[205]

These wealthy, extremely well-connected men selected by Aldrich, one of the most powerful senators of his day, were told that they must hide their identities, use only first names with each other, and dress as if they were going on a duck-hunting expedition. (You know, because late-night duck-hunting train rides are not suspicious at all.) The bankers were then informed that they would be heading to a lavish resort in Georgia—on Jekyll Island—where they would join other important businessmen and policymakers to formulate a plan to reshape America's banking system.[206]

Once they arrived at Jekyll Island, hidden under a fog of secrecy, these members of America's economic elite began crafting legislation that would eventually become the Federal Reserve Act of 1913, the law that created the Federal Reserve Banks. The central banking structure of the United States, a system that has controlled U.S. monetary policy for more than one hundred years, was created by a real-life, honest-to-goodness conspiracy.

The meeting at Jekyll Island was not the first time powerful bankers and government officials attempted to create a central bank. Two other prominent efforts were made to establish a central bank in the United States prior to the passage of the Federal Reserve Act, but both were short-lived. What made the third attempt successful, and what can we learn from this important moment in history?[207]

After the panic of 1907, the economy of the United States was, to say the least, rattled. Unemployment was high and the banking system was on the verge of collapse. The panic was the latest in a series of recessions that shook U.S. financial markets, prompting politicians and bankers to come up with a big-government solution to deal with past and future economic upheavals, one that would provide even greater influence to ruling-class elites.[208] Sound familiar?

By 1910, increased interest in solving the perceived banking "crisis" developed among many of the most authoritative people on Wall Street. In November 1910, the Academy of Political Science at Columbia University, the New York Chamber of Commerce, and the Merchant's Association of New York hosted a conference to formulate potential answers to the questions that had been plaguing bankers for decades. Economists, policy analysts, and many high-level representatives from the nation's largest banks took part in the meeting, and according to attendees, it was at this conference—one almost no one in America knows about today—that the real groundwork was laid for the nation's new central bank.[209]

At the end of the conference, attendees were told to spread the word and convince the American people of the need for the radical overhaul outlined there. Christopher Stuart Patterson, dean of the University of Pennsylvania and member of the Indianapolis Monetary Commission, told those who attended the meeting, "That is just what you must do in this case, you must uphold the hands of Senator Aldrich. You have got to see that the bill which he formulates...obtains the support of every part of this country."[210]

Shortly after the conference, Senator Aldrich orchestrated the meeting at Jekyll Island to develop specific legislative language for developing a new central bank, and the rest is history.

The secret meetings that occurred in 1910 were not organized by globalist European elites, but they do have special relevance to the Great Reset and the topic of this chapter, modern monetary theory. Had the Federal Reserve never been created, the twenty-first century fascism of the Great Reset would be virtually impossible to achieve, because without central banks churning out trillions of new dollars, how could government elites pay for all of their shiny new socialist programs?

Perhaps even more important, the events of 1910 teach us that a relatively small group of elites can and do make gargantuan, history-changing alterations to global economic markets, and they can do so without most people really understanding the repercussions of their actions or even knowing that they have occurred.

I am certainly not suggesting that important decisions are made at every, or even most, academic conferences. But once in a while, a conference of powerful people takes place and the world suddenly changes, a fact worth remembering as the Great Reset movement plans its next great conference of influencers in 2022.

THE BIG QUESTION

Millions of Americans face many problems—poor education, joblessness, homelessness, and a lack of affordable health care, just to name a few. There is no shortage of things that *could* be better. And ruling-class elites have no shortage of supposed solutions to these problems—free college, universal basic income, government housing, and government-run health care. You name it, and politicians from both political parties want to provide it, and often for "free."

The confounding question inevitably arises, however: "How are you going to pay for it?" This is the question that probably used to keep elites in Washington up at night, stalking their dreams like Freddy Krueger. One minute, they are fantasizing about a world powered by billions of solar panels, and then, out of nowhere, someone sporting a bladed glove asks about "paying for things," waking politicians, lobbyists, and solar power business executives from their Great Reset slumber.

In the past, policy proposals would be rejected frequently because they were considered too expensive. To fund their pet projects, lawmakers routinely would have to search for what congressional insiders call "pay-fors," which often come in the shape of new taxes or increases to existing tax rates. Political candidates would cobble together schemes for how they could theoretically fund all the programs they promised to pass if elected.

This boogeyman struck the deep-blue state of Vermont in 2014. Soon after passing a state-level universal health care plan, then-governor Peter Shumlin was distraught to find his team had failed to craft a realistic plan to pay for the ambitious project. It turned out that any state plan to fund the government-run health care system would have required massive tax increases that would have put the state at "risk of economic shock."[211] Shumlin was eventually forced to abandon the planned universal health care program, a move he called "the greatest disappointment of my political life so far."[212]

Shumlin's single-payer-health-care debacle shows just how powerful the "how are you going to pay for it?" question has been in U.S. politics, even recently. This single-payer program failed in Bernie Sanders's home state of Vermont, perhaps the most liberal state in America, even though there was plenty of political demand for government-run health care and a governor who campaigned and won his election by promising to enact a plan just like it. Yet Green Mountain Care still went belly-up because no one could figure out how to pay for it.

Even on a national level, massive price tags have rendered countless proposals dead on arrival in recent years. One of the most notable examples is Alexandria Ocasio-Cortez's Green New Deal. This monster of a plan included a wish list for many on the left, including 100 percent renewable energy, universal health care, a federal jobs guarantee, and college debt cancellation. But like Shumlin's single-payer health care dreams, the Green New Deal was murdered by sticker shock. Even many Democrats ended up rejecting the proposal because of its high expenses. The Green New Deal nonbinding resolution failed to earn a single vote in the U.S. Senate, and it was never approved by the Democrat-led House of Representatives.

The American Action Forum (AAF) ran the numbers on the Green New Deal. When all was said and done, AAF determined that Ocasio-Cortez's plan could cost upward of $94 trillion over just ten years.[213] That is equivalent to cutting every single American a check to the tune of $280,000. I'll take what's behind door number two, Monty.

Again, think about the power of asking, "How are you going to pay for it?" The Green New Deal did not die in the Democrat-controlled House because of its more unpopular provisions. It also was not because of the economic harm that would result from enacting the plan in states like Pennsylvania and Colorado, nor the environmental destruction that comes along with relying completely on energy sources like wind and solar, which we unpacked in the previous chapter. No, it was the $94 trillion number that dominated the headlines. The plan was so expensive, Nancy Pelosi even stopped supporting it. Now, *that* is really saying something.

Why is the "pay for it" question so politically important? The answer is probably obvious to most of the people reading this book; it is because money and resources are scarce. We have a limited supply of wealth, labor, and time, which makes it valuable. This is a basic truth that is pervasive in economics and is even part of its definition. As Investopedia puts it, "Economics is the study of how people allocate scarce resources for production, distribution, and consumption, both individually and collectively."[214]

Scarcity is the cornerstone upon which everything else in economics is built. Fundamental principles like supply and demand, price signals, and opportunity costs are all anchored to this one core concept. Dealing with scarcity has always been a gigantic problem for elites in the Democratic and Republican Parties looking to use government to build massive new programs. How can they possibly overcome this economic obstacle?

Well, they could raise taxes on the middle and upper classes, but that works only to an extent. Eventually, people feel "taxed enough already," don their tricorne hats, and throw politicians out of power.

Of course, policymakers could "tax the rich," but that eventually fails, too, as wealthy people find ways to stash their cash overseas and/or move businesses out of high-tax regions.

Sometimes governments simply resort to force—they cannot figure out a good way of taxing people, so they just steal property, nationalize industries, and even throw people in prison. Although that option is always on the table, the advent of the twenty-four-hour cable news cycle really makes full-blown persecution more difficult than it used to be. (Don't you miss the good ol' days, when dictators could mass-murder people without news crews getting in the way?)

To advance programs that centralize power in the hands of the ruling class while winning over Main Street Americans, elites needed something much stronger than tax increases but not as overtly authoritarian as gulags, and they found their answer in the allure of modern monetary theory (MMT).

MMT has already been adopted by governments all over the world—although you will not find leaders spending much time talking about it—and it is currently an important part of the strategy that supporters of the Great Reset are using to help usher in their transformation of the global economy.

MODERN MONETARY THEORY

My first real taste of modern monetary theory came in a March 2019 town hall event on education policy in Brooklyn, New York. Alexandria Ocasio-Cortez (AOC) took the stage to espouse the merits of increasing educational opportunities for more people in the city. A constituent in the crowd then began to raise his or her voice. It is hard to make out what the heckler was saying, but you can bet it's a version of the big question discussed in the previous section. AOC's shouting response was revealing: "My concern is that this right here, where we're fighting each other, is exactly what happens under a scarcity mindset."[215]

In the minds of AOC and a growing number of other politicians in Washington, D.C., humans have essentially reached a post-scarcity world. We can have anything we want and more if we just exert our political wills hard enough. In their worldview, the "how are you going to pay for it?" question is outdated; it belongs in the dustbin of history, alongside the horse and buggy. Instead of paying for things, policymakers should dig up traditional economic cornerstones and cast them aside in favor of nearly unlimited government spending.

Some might be tempted to write off AOC's views on government spending and scarcity as incredibly uncommon and thus not worth serious consideration or concern. However, there is an entire movement of academics who champion this new way of looking at scarcity as it relates to monetary policy—the modern monetary theory movement. Although its membership remains relatively small, it has had, because of the important implications of its beliefs, a tremendous and far-reaching impact on public policy over the past few years.

Currently, the face of modern monetary theory is Stephanie Kelton, a professor of public policy and economics at Stony Brook University. Kelton is about as well connected as an economist can be. In 2015, she served as the chief economist of the Democratic Party's staff on the U.S. Senate Budget Committee. Kelton was also the senior economic adviser to Bernie Sanders's 2016 and 2020 presidential campaigns, and a member of Joe Biden and Bernie Sanders's 2020 "Unity Task Force," which was given the responsibility of reforming the platforms of the Biden campaign and the Democratic Party.[216] Additionally, Kelton is the author of the popular new MMT book *The Deficit Myth: Modern Monetary Theory and the Birth of the People's Economy.*[217] (More on Kelton's book later.)

Other notable MMT economists include L. Randall Wray, a professor of economics at Bard College, and Pavlina Tcherneva, a program director and associate professor of economics at Bard College and a research associate at the Levy Economics Institute.

If you read my previous book, *Arguing with Socialists*, some of this might sound familiar to you. But stick with me, because there is plenty of new information in this chapter to keep this refresher course entertaining, enlightening, and important.

Modern monetary theory might sound complicated, but it is actually very simple. According to MMT theorists, everyone should stop worrying so much about the national debt and deficits, because the U.S. government can print and spend as much money as it wants to in order to achieve the goals set by the federal government's bureaucratic masterminds and political elite. That's pretty much it.

When most people first hear about modern monetary theory, they usually say something like, "That's a bunch of malarkey." Actually, almost no one under the age of one hundred says "malarkey" (sorry, Joe Biden), but you get the idea. As with so many other concepts I am going to discuss throughout this book, try to avoid dismissing MMT as a crackpot theory that no *reasonable* person would ever try to implement. MMT is appealing to many because of its potential to dramatically increase the power of government and fatten the pockets of the corporate class, not because it is supported by history or because of its academic merits. (Also, as I am sure you already know, politicians and bureaucrats are often anything but reasonable.)

HOW MMT "WORKS"

It is hard to ignore election season. There is a steady stream of political ads on every television and radio station, candidate lawn signs that pop up and never seem to be taken down on time, and heated shouting matches at family gatherings. "No, you're the racist, Uncle Ned!"

Ahh, isn't politics fun?

In addition to all the screaming and terrible campaign ads, election season is also a time when Americans are reminded about how the U.S. national debt and annual deficits have grown out of control. Even Barack Obama positioned himself at first as a fiscal hawk when campaigning in 2008. During one stop in Fargo, North Dakota, then-candidate Obama complained that the spending practices of President George W. Bush's administration, which had added $4 trillion to the national debt over Bush's two terms in office, were so out of hand that they had become "unpatriotic." I guess that makes the multitrillion-dollar deficits of 2020 look like an act of economic terrorism.[218]

As strange as it might sound, supporters of modern monetary theory have criticized Obama for pointing out George W. Bush's spending problems and have even suggested that one of Obama's biggest mistakes as president was not spending enough money. Yes, you read that correctly—according to MMT, Barack Obama, the man who presided over the largest addition to the national debt in history (prior to the COVID-19 pandemic), should have spent trillions *more* following the 2008 financial crash, and he shouldn't have lost a wink of sleep over it.

Under modern monetary theory, because the United States is a currency issuer, there is no danger that the country will ever become insolvent. The federal government has a monopoly on dollar production (money printing), so it cannot run out of money.

Thus, MMT advocates say if we need more cash, all the government must do is turn on the printing presses—or more accurately, move numbers around on an electronic spreadsheet.

In a 2019 interview with CNBC, Kelton explained this idea more completely, highlighting the distinction between a money user and a money issuer.

MMT starts with a really simple observation and that is that the U.S. dollar is a simple public monopoly. In other words, the United States currency comes from the United States government. It can't come from anywhere else. And therefore, it can never run out of money. It cannot face a solvency problem, bills coming due that it can't afford to pay. It never has to worry about finding the money in order to be able to spend. It doesn't need to go and raise taxes or borrow money before it is able to spend.

So what that means is that the federal government is nothing like a household. In order for households or private businesses to be able to spend, they've got to come up with the money, right? And the federal government doesn't have to behave like a household. In fact, it becomes really destructive for the economy if the government tries to behave like a household. You and I are using the U.S. dollar. States and municipalities—the state of Kansas or Detroit—they're also using the U.S. dollar. Private businesses are using the dollar. The federal government of the United States is issuing our currency, and so we have a very different relationship to the currency. That means that in order to spend, the government doesn't have to do what a household or a private business has to do: find the money. The government can simply spend the money into the economy and when it does, the rest of us end up receiving that spending as part of our income.[219]

According to Kelton, the federal government "doesn't have to behave like a household," as we have all been told for years by countless politicians, including Obama. They have all gotten it wrong. Under Kelton's theory, the Federal Reserve should effectively give the government a hall pass to spend as much money as it wants. Doesn't that sound great? Free ponies for everyone! Scratch that, make it two ponies. I am feeling generous.

You are probably wondering, "But what about the national debt?" The U.S. debt has already surpassed $28 trillion—and at this rate it could be a quadrillion by the time this book goes to the printer.[220] Won't that have some serious long-term consequences for the economy?

Fret not, Kelton says. The national debt is just a number. "Let's remember what the national debt is," Kelton said in an interview with CNBC. "The national debt is nothing more than a historical record of all the dollars that the government spent into the economy and didn't tax back that are currently being held in the form of safe U.S. Treasurys."[221]

Under MMT, debt and deficits are nothing to fear. They are encouraged. Kelton explained:

> Normally, I think people tend to hear deficit and think it's something that we should strive to eliminate, that we shouldn't be running budget deficits, that they're evidence of fiscal irresponsibility. And the truth is the deficit can be too big. Evidence of a deficit that's too big would be inflation. But the deficit can also be too small. It can be too small to support demand in the economy and evidence of a deficit that is too small is unemployment. So, deficits can be too big, but they can also be too small. And the right level of the deficit is the one that gets you a balanced overall economy. The one that allows you to achieve high levels of employment and low inflation.[222]

As Kelton noted, modern monetary theory supporters believe deficit spending should be used to reach full employment, but that's not where deficit spending should end. MMTers say it should also be used to achieve every other goal elites have for society. In a 2019 article for *Barron's*, writer Matthew Klein compared MMT to a "peacetime version of wartime economic management," and he suggested MMTers believe "governments can do whatever is necessary to satisfy the 'public purpose' as long as they maintain their authority over the populace."[223]

Just imagine all the things the government could do if it were not limited by that looming big question. Should we "cancel" all student loan debt, no matter how rich the borrower is? Why not? Debt and deficits don't matter. Should we pass a $94 trillion Green New Deal? Why not? Debt and deficits don't matter. Should we continue to nation-build around the world? Why not? Debt and deficits don't matter.

Modern monetary theory is the *perfect* tool for politicians who make grandiose promises without any plan to pay for them—which is just about every politician these days.

If you are just now hearing about this wild theory, you are likely thinking one or both of the following:

1. If the government can just print money, why would it need to tax anyone?
2. Wouldn't all this massive money printing result in inflation?

Good questions, hypothetical reader. Let's address them one at a time.

TAXATION UNDER MMT

Under a standard economic model—which is to say, reality—governments and politicians are generally constrained by limited tax revenue. (I say "generally" because yearly deficits and growing national debt are proof the government is rarely able to live within its means.) To initiate a new spending program, politicians are required to figure out the answer to the big question we have been discussing throughout this chapter: "How are you going to pay for it?"

This requirement forces politicians to walk through the political minefield of revenue-generation schemes. Maybe we can raise taxes on businesses? Boom! The higher-unemployment mine goes off. How about we raise taxes on sugary drinks? Bang! The constituent-anger mine explodes. Perhaps government could issue an extra thirty-cent tax on every gallon of gasoline? Kapow! The yellow-vest-protest mine bursts.

This trek through the political "how will you pay for it?" minefield is never fun for politicians, who are typically interested in doing whatever it takes to keep voters happy so they can win more elections in the future, the sole reason most politicians wake up in the morning.

But under MMT, taxes serve a very different purpose. Instead of being used to raise revenues to pay for government spending programs, they function as tools that help government manage the economy more closely and as weapons to punish those businesses and groups that government does not like, for whatever reason.

This is all made very clear in Kelton's book *The Deficit Myth*. In chapter 1, Kelton outlines four ways in which taxation can be used under a modern monetary theory system.[224]

I. USE OUR CURRENCY…OR ELSE!

According to Kelton, the first reason government should continue using taxes under modern monetary theory is that "taxes enable governments to provision themselves without the use of explicit force." Or put another way, they require people to use dollars instead of some other kind of currency.[225]

In Kelton's world, people must be *pushed* into using her freshly printed, government-issued Monopoly money, not merely *persuaded* to do so. Alternative currencies, such as cryptocurrencies, cannot be tolerated as a payment for taxes owed. Government and big banks can create all the money they want, but if nobody uses or demands those pieces of paper decorated with Founding Fathers and government buildings, then that paper becomes useless and elites lose their power to control monetary policy. This is an unacceptable scenario from the perspective of those who support modern monetary theory.

In the past, the idea that there could ever be an America in which there is widespread use of an alternative currency seemed too far-fetched for most people to consider, but technological advancements have made new currencies possible in a way that generations before us never dreamed of. Cryptocurrencies like Bitcoin, Ethereum, and Chainlink are part of decentralized networks and not commissioned by any government, yet they have become increasingly popular over the past decade as millions of people have started to question the long-term stability of the dollar.

The values of these digital currencies are based solely on the popularity of the currency and the blockchain technology on which each is based.[226] Bitcoin, for example, cannot "print" more units of its currency, making it attractive for many people concerned about government's addiction to debt and deficits.

Of course, America is hardly on the verge of adopting Bitcoin as its primary currency. The point is, the use of cryptocurrencies has expanded in recent years, especially with the rise of ecommerce, and it is only likely to continue expanding in the years to come.[227]

For Stephanie Kelton and other MMTers, cryptocurrencies represent a threat to the power of government and bankers. Taxation is a surefire way to guarantee that the dollar remains in use. What better way to force someone to use the dollar than to charge that person a tax that is payable only with government-printed currency?

2. INFLATION CONTROL

The most common knee-jerk reaction to MMT is the fear that it will cause unsustainable amounts of harmful inflation. Reasonable people are concerned that if government, with the backing of financial institutions, gets in the habit of running the printing presses whenever it wants money—which is pretty much all the time— then we will all soon end up with Zimbabwe levels of inflation.

Admittedly, modern monetary theorists do spend a lot of time thinking and worrying about inflation. It is probably the thing the academic wing of the MMT movement is most concerned with. How, then, do they propose avoiding inflation while simultaneously printing trillions of new dollars?

Kelton explains in her book that according to MMT, inflation is the warning sign of overspending, not deficits. Remember, in modern monetary theory, deficits are almost always a good thing. Deficit spending ensures that the economy is running at full steam, properly using its available resources, and leaving no potential workers on the sidelines. If there is a single willing worker sitting idly by without a job opportunity, modern monetary theory supporters would argue that the government is not spending enough money, regardless of how much cash it is already printing.

This does not mean government officials could wake up tomorrow and print $50 trillion, though. It is possible to spend too much cash in modern monetary theory. It occurs when private sector entities and government both vie for limited resources and too much money is chasing too few goods and services in one or several parts of an economy.

If inflation occurs, how should government deal with this problem? Reduce government spending? Of course not. Instead Kelton suggests raising taxes to "force us to cut back a little to make room for additional government spending."

Kelton further argues, "If the government wants to boost spending on health care and education, it may need to remove some spending power from the rest of us to prevent its own more generous outlays from pushing up prices."[228]

Stop for a moment and think about what this highly influential economist is suggesting. Under modern monetary theory, the government might need to battle inflation by destroying the wealth of the people, including the middle and working classes, in order to make room for more government spending. I guess that whole free lunch thing really is a myth after all.

There is a lot more I could say about the specter of inflation and the policy prescriptions modern monetary theorists have proposed to avoid it, but we will get to that shortly. For now, let's get back to our list.

3. WEALTH REDISTRIBUTION

As I have already shown at length, modern monetary theory gives the government a blank check to pay for all the social programs it wants, from "free" college tuition to government-guaranteed jobs programs and 100 percent renewable energy. However, even if those programs were to work exactly as intended (and, in my opinion, they never do), social programs cannot on their own address wealth inequality.

But where government social programs fall short, modern monetary theorists say, taxes can fill in the gaps. Kelton wrote, "MMT sees taxes as an important means to help redress decades of ...rising inequality."[229] According to Kelton and others, taxes can help reduce wealth inequality by confiscating wealth from those deemed too rich, theoretically balancing the scales.

Some MMT academics take an even more radical view of the use of taxation. Professor L. Randall Wray wrote the following response in reaction to questions about how taxes relate to modern monetary theory.

> For far too long left-leaning Democrats have had a close symbiotic relationship with the rich. They've needed the "good" rich folk, like George Soros, Bill Gates, Warren Buffet, Bob Rubin, to fund their think tanks and political campaigns. The centrist Clinton wing, has repaid the generosity of Wall Street's neoliberals with deregulation that allowed the CEOs to shovel money to themselves, vastly increasing inequality and their own power. And they in turn rewarded Hillary— who by her own account accepted whatever money they would throw in her direction.
>
> Today's progressives won't fall into that trap. "How ya gonna pay for it?" Through a budget authorization. Uncle Sam can afford it without the help of the rich.
>
> And, by the way, they're going to tax you anyway, because you've got too much—too much income, too much wealth, too much power. What will we do with the tax revenue? Burn it. Uncle Sam doesn't need your money.
>
> In reality, taxes just lead to debits to bank accounts. We'll just knock 3 or 5 zeros off the accounts of the rich. Of course, double entry bookkeeping means we also need to knock zeros off the debts held by the rich—so we'll wipe zeros off the student loan debts, the mortgage debts, the auto loan debts, and the credit card debts of American households. Yes, debt cancellation too.[230]

After many years of watching academics and corrupt politicians closely, I am rarely shocked, but I've got to admit, when I first read this quote by L. Randall Wray, I was floored. It's worth looking at the most important part again: "They're going to tax you anyway," Wray said, "because you've got too much—too much income, too much wealth, too much power. What will we do with the tax revenue? Burn it. Uncle Sam doesn't need your money."

Well, Wray could not possibly be any clearer about how MMT economists plan to use taxes: to punish those individuals and families who already have "too much" wealth, whatever that means. And what will they do with all the cash? Drench it with gasoline and light it on fire—sort of like the Joker in *The Dark Knight*, just with less face paint and fewer henchmen dressed as clowns. Under MMT, the government does not need tax revenue. All it needs is power over its own currency.

Pavlina Tcherneva, a professor of economics at Bard College and research associate at the Levy Economics Institute, has repeated many of the same arguments put forward by Wray and Kelton, referring to those foolish liberals concerned about generating tax revenue as "tax-the-rich-to-pay-for-progress lefties." And she has argued that relying on taxing the rich is "an imaginary umbilical cord that holds [the] progressive agenda hostage to [the] oppressors."

"To me," Tcherneva wrote, "this is the definition of a self-induced paralysis."[231]

4. CONTROL OF SOCIETY

Imagine you are on your way home from work, and you are driving a little faster than usual because, well, you've had one too many Diet Cokes and foolishly left the office without using the restroom. Of course, today is your unlucky day. A local police officer catches you driving 37 mph in a 30 mph zone, and before you know it, you are back on your way home with a new passenger in the seat beside you—a $120 speeding ticket.

Fines like these exist as deterrents to unwanted or unsafe behaviors. Society, through its elected representatives, has determined that speed limits are needed for protecting other drivers on the road, and police officers have been tasked with ensuring that people follow the law. Speed limits might be annoying or unnecessarily strict at times, but most Americans agree that they do serve an important purpose.

Of course, every driver also knows that in addition to acting as a deterrent, speeding tickets function as a vital revenue generator for local law enforcement. So from government's perspective, everyone is a winner when a driver receives a speeding ticket: the community is a little safer, and the government coffers are more secure.

Over time, politicians stumbling through the political minefield of revenue-generation schemes have realized that speeding tickets are not the only way to raise revenues while eliminating "bad" behaviors. Today fines are issued for all sorts of "sins," especially to punish those less sympathetic groups, like cigarette smokers. Why not squeeze a few bucks out of them by levying a new tobacco tax? They should not be smoking anyway, right?[232]

In many cases, governments have gone overboard, imposing a slew of excessive fines and "sin taxes" to help raise revenue for the town, city, state, or federal government—all under the guise of promoting public health, safety, or some other allegedly noble cause.

However, in a world dominated by modern monetary theory, there is no reason for governments to pass laws for the purpose of raising tax revenue. The federal government can simply print all the money it needs and then distribute it to state and local officials. So does that mean Kelton and other MMT supporters believe their system would lead to a reduction in fines and sin taxes? Of course not.

As Kelton notes, under modern monetary theory, "governments can use taxes to encourage or discourage certain behaviors, to improve public health, battle climate change, or deter risky speculation in financial markets."[233] So rather than disincentivizing government from imposing controls on society, a system utilizing modern monetary theory would empower policymakers to use the tax code to manipulate people, even if they no longer have a financially motivated reason to do so.

RISK OF INFLATION

Now that we have a solid understanding of how taxes fit into modern monetary theory, let's turn to the big elephant in the room: How do modern monetary theorists plan to stop inflation?

Traditionally, when policymakers float the idea of expanding the Federal Reserve's balance sheet or running the printing presses to fund a new government program, those of us concerned about the national debt brace for the devaluation of our currency, commonly called *inflation*. In extreme cases, we are reminded of the recent rampant inflation in Venezuela in 2018 or stories from 1920s Germany, where money became so worthless under the disastrous policies of the Weimar Republic that families wallpapered their homes with cash.

In 2008 in Zimbabwe, hyperinflation caused by irresponsible money printing practices became so bad, inflation levels topped out at 89.7 sextillion percent, forcing the government, which could barely function under these conditions, to issue bills with increasingly higher denominations.[234] In 2009, Zimbabwe released a $100 trillion bill—the largest denomination ever printed.[235] But hey, even though the hyperinflation in Zimbabwe made it difficult for families to put food on the table, at least everyone could become a trillionaire.

Do not worry, America. MMTers swear that Zimbabwe's hyper-inflation hell will not happen in the United States. To defend their position, they usually cite several key arguments.

First, the U.S. dollar is a world reserve currency, which means countries across the globe use and accept the dollar when conducting trade, adding an extra level of stability that most other currencies do not enjoy.[236] (This one is important, so we will come back to it soon to discuss further.)

Second, modern monetary theorists like L. Randall Wray argue that most of the worst examples of hyperinflation were brought on by "very specific circumstances," such as civil war or huge external debts denominated in a foreign currency.[237] The U.S. dollar's status as a world reserve currency defends against both of these threats, but especially the latter.

Third, modern monetary theorists say there is no reason to worry about hyperinflation because Americans have access to an unstoppable weapon of monetary security—the Congressional Budget Office (CBO). And no, I am not joking. Kelton said in 2019,

> So the best defense against inflation is a good offense, and what MMT does is to try to be … kind of hypersensitive to the risks of inflation. I don't see any other macro school of thought pay as careful attention as we do to the inflation risk question. And so what we would say is: Look, if you are Congress and if you are considering a new spending bill, instead of thinking about the ways in which that new spending will add to the deficit or add to the debt, you should be thinking about the ways in which that new spending has the risk of accelerating inflation. And then avoid doing that.
>
> So instead of going to the Congressional Budget Office and saying, "Would you take a look at this piece of legislation and give us feedback? We'd like to know what this bill will do to the

debt and the deficit over time," Instead, go to the Congressional Budget Office or other government agencies and say, "We're considering passing this trillion-dollar investment in infrastructure. This is our bill would you look at it? And we plan to do this spending over the course of the next five years. Tell us if that would create problems in the real economy. Evaluate the inflation risk and come back to us and give us some feedback."[238]

Let's stop here for a second before my head explodes. Kelton's preposterous answer to the inflation question is to have the fate of the world's largest economy rely on the predictions of the Congressional Budget Office? Are you kidding me? The CBO is the same dysfunctional agency that has been issuing a steady stream of false projections for decades. Its 2012 projection for Obamacare enrollment was off by a whopping 150 percent.[239] For a monetary system that needs to be "hypersensitive to the risks of inflation," putting all your eggs in the CBO's broken basket seems like a catastrophically bad idea.

Oh, and it does not end there either. Kelton also says that inflation can be prevented under MMT by vesting government with enough authority that it could micromanage the economy and thus control inflation.

"And so when you think about how to fight inflation," Kelton said, "I think the first question is to understand what the source of the inflationary pressure is and then to move forward with a policy tool that you think is going to help you get at that inflation. If you've got inflation resulting from energy price increases it's probably not going to do much to have the Fed raise interest rates or even to have Congress raise taxes. You've got to do something else that's going to work."[240]

This "solution" is the one that provides the *real* secret herbs and spices that make MMT such an important part of the plan to create twenty-first century fascism. Let's use Kelton's example of the energy market to illustrate this point.

In Kelton's modern monetary theory fantasy, policymakers begin using freshly printed money to chase their goal of 100 percent renewable energy. Money begins to flow into politically connected companies that start producing big, beautiful, new solar panels and wind turbines. Energy prices then start to increase. This is deemed "inflation," but the public has no reason to be concerned, because political elites (who are often barely functional human beings to begin with) are given the green light to craft "policy tools" and use the tax code to fight against rising prices. What could possibly go wrong?

Well, for starters, why should we believe that the same people who created this brand-new inflation-causing energy system would be smart enough to fix it? Why didn't they just design the system to avoid inflation in the first place? And if government officials are so good at problem-solving and planning, why haven't they figured out a way to get Amtrak to turn a profit or the Postal Service to stop hemorrhaging billions of dollars per year?

Further, does anyone really think politicians are going to cut off funding to well-connected renewable energy companies amid a transition to a world free of fossil fuels? Surely, politicians would not put concerns about inflation before the "existential threat" of global warming, right?

In the end, Kelton's system would depend on a scapegoat to blame when everything goes horribly wrong. In this case, it would almost certainly be fossil fuel companies, who have in recent decades fallen out of favor with the ruling elites. It would not be hard to convince those in charge to give oil and gas companies the axe to help bring prices down after government's money printing effort drives them up.

You can play out these types of scenarios in virtually every sector of the economy. Ultimately, the trillions of new dollars created by government would result in inflation, either in the economy as a whole or in specific sectors, forcing bureaucrats to selectively identify the "sources of inflationary pressure" and then craft policy tools to deal with those problems. It is a perfect plan for those trying to control society, but as for the rest of us—well, we will be left out in the cold, especially if the entire country is required to run on wind and solar.

At present, elites at the Federal Reserve have essentially one major monetary lever in their toolbox, the baseline interest rate. During periods of economic malaise, the Fed "turns the dial" and lowers interest rates in an attempt to boost markets by infusing them with cash from lower-interest loans. When inflation creeps in, the Fed "turns the dial" in the other direction, raising interest rates to curb rising prices.

Modern monetary theory throws out the dial and replaces it with a gigantic control panel full of levers, knobs, and switches that allow bureaucrats to manage the economy and society as they see fit. Sounds like something people calling for a Great Reset of the global economy would like. Huh.

Those calling for a Great Reset like the idea of modern monetary theory so much, they invited the face of MMT, Stephanie Kelton, to speak on behalf of the economic theory during a November 2020 World Economic Forum virtual event promoting the movement.[241]

During her segment, Kelton told the panel they need not worry about debt and deficits, and she then explained how MMT could be used to justify massive spending programs designed to transform society.

"[Governments] can establish where it is they want to go and they can provide the kind of large-scale and patient finance that can remain in place for the duration of the time that we are going to be making transformative investments in our economy moving forward," Kelton promised the Great Reset overlords, who, I can just imagine, couldn't have been happier to hear about the magic of modern monetary theory.

END OF THE DOLLAR

While MMTers attempt to paint their proposed monetary system as merely a more efficient way of managing the economy, it is in reality an incredibly risky experiment. And what happens if the experiment goes awry?

As I mentioned earlier, modern monetary theorists try to soothe critics' concerns about hyperinflation by saying that even if government bureaucrats and policymakers do not manage things perfectly in the future, the U.S. dollar's status as the world's reserve currency would protect Americans from a hyperinflation nightmare.

There is no question that the dollar's world reserve currency status would help *at first*, but who is to say that the dollar would remain the global reserve currency in a universe in which the United States chose to embrace modern monetary theory? As recently as July 2020, Goldman Sachs warned that the dollar is increasingly at risk of losing its world reserve status. Strategists for Goldman specifically cited the Federal Reserve's swelling balance sheet and growing debt levels as the primary reasons for their worries.[242]

If the United States were to aggressively travel further down the money printing road, as Stephanie Kelton and others have suggested, it is entirely possible—and probably inevitable—that other economic powerhouses like China would demand that international commerce occur using alternative currencies like the euro or the Chinese yuan.

Many global institutions and government leaders in Europe and Asia have already started floating the idea of shifting the reserve currency to the International Monetary Fund's Special Drawing Rights (SDR). SDR is essentially composed of a basket of currencies and designed to act as a stable medium of exchange for international trade.[243] (A quick sidenote: the International Monetary Fund is one of the biggest supporters of the Great Reset, but I am sure that's just a coincidence.)

If the government and the Federal Reserve continue to pursue an MMT system, the U.S. dollar will become increasingly vulnerable to losing its world reserve currency status. This would likely cause the same hyperinflation that Kelton and others insist would never occur under their model, because countries would have no place to spend their greenbacks except in the United States, leading to an unprecedented flood of dollars returning to U.S. shores. This would drive up prices in key industries like real estate and likely send America into an economic depression that could exceed coronavirus lockdown levels, as hard as that is for many to imagine.

This scenario would be a truly horrifying economic nightmare, the likes of which the country has never seen before. It should give pause to everyone who has embraced or even flirted seriously with modern monetary theory and its reckless principles.

Oh, and things could be even worse than the situation I just described. A Special Drawing Rights model relying on a printed currency could end up being our best-case scenario. Some influential economists and world leaders associated with the World Economic Forum are trying to dethrone the dollar by replacing it with a global *digital* currency.

Consider WEF board member Mark Carney, an economist and banker with an unquestionably impressive resume. Carney previously served as the governor of the Bank of Canada as well as governor of the Bank of England.[244] Carney spends his days convincing other elites that the U.S. dollar is too influential in global markets and should be replaced with a digital currency.[245]

In his role as the governor of the Bank of England, Carney began to lay the groundwork to give digital currencies greater standing with the bank and throughout the world.[246] And at the 2019 Economic Policy Symposium at Jackson Hole, Wyoming—an annual conference attended by many of the world's central bankers[247]—Carney touted the benefits of a new digital currency replacing the dollar as the world's reserve currency.

"[A digital currency] could dampen the domineering influence of the U.S. dollar on global trade," Carney said. "The dollar's influence on global financial conditions could similarly decline if a financial architecture developed around a new [digital currency] and it displaced the dollar's dominance in credit markets."[248]

Carney is not alone. One of the biggest advocates for expanding the power of government-controlled digital currencies is the Chinese Communist Party. China is currently in the lead when it comes to creating the first digital currency backed by a large central bank.

The digital yuan would allow the Chinese Communist Party to maintain unprecedented control over its country's finances. Chinese officials have already said they plan to use the digital yuan to better manage the economy and track and eliminate "illegal" transactions—which, in China, could be something as simple as going to a website the Communist Party does not like.

And if China is doing it, you just know the rest of the world's governing elites are paying attention, especially at the World Economic Forum, where influential Chinese citizens serve as board members.

Given Carney and China's connections to the World Economic Forum, it should not surprise you to hear that WEF is already preparing to give their "expert opinion" on how to regulate government-controlled digital currencies, which many at WEF believe to be inevitable.

In January 2020, the WEF announced the creation of the very first "global consortium focused on designing a framework for governance of digital currencies." Speaking about the consortium in early 2020, WEF founder and executive chairman Klaus Schwab said, "We hope that hosting this consortium will catalyse the conversations necessary to inform a robust framework of governance for global digital currencies."[249]

Even the Federal Reserve in the United States is now trying to get in on the "fun." On February 28, 2021, Fed chairman Jerome Powell said exploring the creation of a central bank digital currency is a "high priority project for us."[250]

Referring to the possibility of a digital currency, Powell added, "This is going to be an important year. This is going to be the year in which we engage with the public pretty actively."[251]

And remember that idea of an International Monetary Fund SDR system for the world reserve currency that I mentioned earlier in the chapter? It turns out that its supporters are also considering pushing for a digital SDR currency. Back in 2019, during a Bank of England forum, Christine Lagarde, who was then the director of the IMF and who currently serves as president of the European Central Bank, discussed the idea of developing a digital version of SDR. This concept, dubbed "IMFCoin," could easily become the world's new reserve currency, a scenario Lagarde said is *not* "a far-fetched hypothetical."[252]

The amount of power and control over the world that would come with the full embrace of an MMT system, especially if mixed with a digital currency, is almost too much to fathom. Not only would government and central banks be able to create as much money as they wanted to, they could, depending on how the new monetary framework operates, create and distribute cash with a push of a button—literally.

"There's another round of angry riots in Paris over high energy costs? Let's just put some newly minted digital cash in their digital wallets and politely tell them to go home. Oh, we tried that and they aren't listening? Let's just empty their wallets then of all their cash and see if that gets their attention."

It is also worth considering how digital currencies could be used to control economic behavior. If all currency were to become digitized and physical mediums of exchange were phased out, then banks, financial institutions, and governments would be able to track and control nearly every transaction in the world. Although there is no way of knowing exactly how they might try to use this unprecedented power, it is not hard to imagine how it could expand the authority of elites and impact regular folks on a daily basis.

We have all heard about local governments' attempts to tax—and in some cases ban—certain unhealthy foods, everything from foods containing trans fats to sugary drinks. In a world with a centralized digital currency, what's to stop the ruling class from putting a limit on the number of Cokes you buy each week? Or the number of burgers you eat? Or the number of alcoholic beverages you consume or cigars you smoke? What's to stop elites from preventing you from buying alcohol, cigarettes, or Twinkies entirely? They *are* bad for you, you know.

And what about limits on energy consumption? Perhaps you have done more than your "fair share" of traveling this year and are deemed not important enough for a travel exemption. We cannot have you polluting the planet on yet another "unnecessary" family vacation.

I am confident the Second Amendment will survive the Great Reset—at least on paper. It is incredibly difficult to change the Constitution, and there are just too many states that will never agree to ratify an amendment that overturns the Second Amendment for gun rights to be stripped away in Congress. But a Great Reset world that runs on a government-controlled global digital currency could make gun and ammunition sales virtually impossible. Powerful bankers and international institutions cannot make it illegal to ban guns in America, but they could stop people from buying or selling guns using their global currency, effectively killing most of the gun and ammunition industries.

And if you think for a moment that Americans might be able to escape this sort of control because transactions occurring within our country might still continue to be made using U.S. dollars, remember that the Federal Reserve is also strongly considering adopting its own digital currency. So whether it's elites in Europe and China making the rules or elites at the Fed, the point is, you won't be the one in control of your economic decision making—at least, that's how things seem to be shaping up.

I could go on for days citing other potential problems that could arise from a centralized, government-controlled digital currency, but I think you get the point. If international elites were to have authority over the world's digital currency, they would have the power to control most of the global economic activity and, by extension, human behavior. As the old saying goes, "He who has the gold makes the rules." Or more accurate but not quite as catchy, "He who has the otherwise worthless digital currency everyone has been required to accept as the only valid medium of exchange makes the rules."

Now, at this point you might be wondering, "If modern monetary theory is an important component to the Great Reset, why are some elites at the World Economic Forum trying to undercut the dollar's position as the world's reserve currency?" Why can't the ruling class just continue relying on the dollar, perhaps a digital dollar like the one Powell has alluded to?

Unfortunately, all we can do is speculate, but there are plenty of good justifications that ruling-class elites might have for wanting to move on from the dollar. For starters, one of the biggest impediments to the globalist agenda over the past several decades has been the unwillingness of the United States to go along with internationalism. There have been many moments throughout modern history when globalists thought they had the world right where they wanted it, but then those darn Americans got in the way and did something unexpected, like elect Donald Trump as president.

There is a seemingly endless amount of material I could point to showing that global elites view America's role in the world as one of the biggest, if not *the* biggest, impediments to ushering in Great Reset–like alterations to the international economy, but some of the best evidence comes by way of George Soros, one of the most influential voices in the globalist movement.

Since the 1980s, Soros and his Open Society Foundations, one of the wealthiest philanthropic organizations on the planet, have spent more than $14 billion on a variety of causes in more than one hundred countries.[253] Leaked documents from Soros's Open Society Foundations show it is "clearly devoted to the eradication of national sovereignty" and using crises to advance its political and social goals.[254]

The elimination of national sovereignty is Soros's guiding principle, one that has helped to shape most of his political and philanthropic work.

In an article for the *Guardian* by Daniel Bessner, a professor at the University of Washington and contributing editor for the popular socialist magazine *Jacobin*, Bessner correctly notes that in Soros's mind, "the two major threats" to an "open society" are capitalistic "hyperglobalisation and market fundamentalism."[255] He explains,

> Soros argued that the history of the post-cold war world, as well as his personal experiences as one of international finance's most successful traders, demonstrated that unregulated global capitalism undermined open society in three distinct ways. First, because capital could move anywhere to avoid taxation, western

nations were deprived of the finances they needed to provide citizens with public goods. Second, because international lenders were not subject to much regulation, they often engaged in "unsound lending practices" that threatened financial stability. Finally, because these realities increased domestic and international inequality, Soros feared they would encourage people to commit unspecified "acts of desperation" that could damage the global system's viability.[256]

For Soros, the only way to address these and other related perceived problems is to establish a new "global system of political decision-making."[257] (Wow, that sounds an awful lot like the Great Reset. Just another coincidence, I am sure.) However, Soros has continuously identified one gigantic roadblock standing in the way of his dream of advancing the cause of internationalism: America.

Bessner explains that "as early as 1998, Soros acknowledged that the US was the primary opponent of global institutions; by this point in time, Americans had refused to join the International Court of Justice; had declined to sign the Ottawa treaty on banning landmines; and had unilaterally imposed economic sanctions when and where they saw fit."[258]

Soros spelled out this belief clearly in his 2007 book *The Age of Fallibility*—which, by the way, is agonizingly boring.

The main obstacle to a stable and just world order is the United States. This is a harsh—indeed, for me, painful—thing to say, but unfortunately I am convinced it is true. The United States continues to set the agenda for the world in spite of its loss of influence since 9/11, and the Bush administration is setting the wrong agenda. The Bush agenda is nationalistic: it emphasizes the use of force and ignores global problems whose solution requires international cooperation.[259]

Soros's views are pervasive in international circles of influence, so is it really surprising that many globalists are keen on pushing the dollar out of its position of prominence? Would they really want to trust control of the lifeblood of their Great Reset system—a currency operating under MMT principles—to a country with a strong independent streak like the United States? I doubt it. From their perspective, it would be much better if the international ruling class had its own currency, preferably one that was easy for elites to manage. And what could possibly be easier to control than a digital currency?

MMT "SUCCESS" STORIES

Modern monetary theorists are often confronted by skeptics concerned about elites gambling with America's future on a largely unproven economic theory. When that happens, Kelton and other supporters of MMT usually respond by arguing that many of their ideas have been tried before—and with great success—in the mysterious, ancient land of Japan. The following argument by Kelton is just one example out of many showing how modern monetary theorists usually present this important claim.

So it's impossible really to put a number, nobody can. How much debt is too much debt? If you look at Japan today you see a country where the debt-to-GDP ratio is something like 240 percent. Well above, orders of magnitude above, where the U.S. is today or even where the U.S. is forecast to be in the future. And so, the question is how is Japan able to sustain a debt of that size? Wouldn't it have an inflation problem? Wouldn't it lead to rising interest rates? Wouldn't this be destructive in some way? And the answer to all of those questions, as Japan has demonstrated now for years is simply: No. Japan's debt is close to 240 percent of GDP—almost a quadrillion, that's a very big number, yen. Long-term interest rates are very close to zero, there's no inflation problem. And so despite the size of the debt there are no negative consequences as a result and I think Japan teaches us a really important lesson.[260]

Before addressing Kelton's argument, take a moment to marvel at her assertion. A 240 percent debt-to-GDP ratio is completely acceptable? If translated to America, that would amount to a national debt of more than $51 *trillion*. You know what that means, right? Ponies for everyone! Uncle Sam is picking up the tab.

Now, I admit that Kelton is correct in asserting that Japan has yet to suffer through high levels of inflation, even though it has amassed staggering levels of debt. However, as with everything else in life, there is no such thing as a free lunch. Japan is far from the MMT utopia that Kelton would have you believe.

Although Japan's government has spent trillions on "construction-related public investment" over the past three decades—precisely the type of spending that MMTers propose—economic growth has almost totally stagnated, and Japan's problems began long before the coronavirus pandemic hit.[261] From 1995 to 2018, Japan's GDP *decreased* by more than 8 percent. Over the same period, the United States experienced a 168 percent growth in GDP.[262]

Further, in Japan, the percentage of the GDP composed of government spending has also steadily increased over the past two decades, showing that substantially more economic power has been vested in the hands of the Japanese government over that period.

With all this in mind, should Americans really consider Japan an MMT success story? Is an anemic economy, massive amounts of debt, and an increased size of government something most Americans pine for? I am no mind reader, but I think it is a safe bet that when faced with these facts, most people in the United States would want nothing to do with modern monetary theory.

MMT IN AMERICA

When I first heard about the concept of modern monetary theory, I, probably like you, thought it was nothing more than yet another delusional fantasy concocted by ivory-tower elites that had as much chance of becoming reality as I have of winning a gold medal in figure skating at the next Olympics. (Just to be clear, I am not exactly a graceful ice-skater.)

But if 2020 taught us anything, it is that the groundwork for a large-scale shift to modern monetary theory has already been laid. Thanks to the COVID-19 pandemic, the United States appears to be on the MMT train at this very moment, even though most Americans still have never heard of the concept.

In the aftermath of the Great Recession of 2008, politicians began constructing a plan to "stimulate" the economy. Competing plans outlined ways to get people back to work and stabilize markets. After much negotiating between reckless politicians in the Republican and Democratic Parties, President Obama signed into law the American Recovery and Reinvestment Act of 2009, a plan with an $830 billion price tag.[263]

At that time, many conservatives chastised Obama for being fiscally reckless, while liberals celebrated Obama for taking "bold" action to save the country. However, in 2019 and 2020, MMTers like Kelton called Obama "basically a conservative when it came to fiscal policy,"[264] and congressional Republicans and their Republican president passed legislation that in a single year added more money to the national debt than nearly every other president in history did during their full terms in office.

This proves that modern monetary theory has already moved from being a fringe concept supported by a small band of mostly unknown academics to a mainstream practice embraced by politicians, both in the GOP and in the Democratic Party. Additionally, some of MMT's biggest names have risen to the highest rungs of power in America. As I mentioned earlier in the chapter, Kelton served as the chief economist of the Democratic Party's staff on the U.S. Senate Budget Committee and as a key economic adviser to Bernie Sanders during his 2016 and 2020 presidential campaigns. Kelton also served on Joe Biden's 2020 "Unity Task Force," where she heavily influenced Biden's platform and first-year policies.[265]

Just one decade ago, MMT academics like Kelton were being laughed out of the room. Today they are advising presidents and congressional budget committees. And the popularity of modern monetary theory is likely to grow within the academic community in the years to come, especially in the wake of George Soros's sudden and strange infatuation with a small liberal arts college in Upstate New York.

At a January 2020 speech before the—you guessed it—World Economic Forum, Soros announced that he was launching "a new kind of global educational network" to "advance the values of the open society," including Soros's commitment to internationalism.[266] Soros pledged $1 billion to the new association, which he named the Open Society University Network.[267] Interestingly, the two colleges leading the network are Central European University, a graduate college in Vienna founded by Soros, and Bard College, a small liberal arts school in the United States that enrolls about 2,200 undergraduate students.

Soros also named in 2020 the president of Bard College, Leon Botstein, as the Open Society University Network's first chancellor, a position Botstein has filled while continuing to serve as Bard's president.[268] Even more remarkably, less than seven months after Soros announced the creation of the Open Society University Network, his Open Society Foundations agreed to give Bard $100 million. Boy, George Soros sure loves Bard College.

If Bard sounds familiar to you, it is probably because earlier in this chapter, I mentioned it when discussing L. Randall Wray and Pavlina Tcherneva, two of the world's leading modern monetary theory economists, both of whom work as influential professors at Bard College. Bard is also home to the Levy Economics Institute, the epicenter of modern monetary theory scholarship. Not only does the Levy Economics Institute feature the work of Wray, Tcherneva, and other MMT academics *and* organize the International Conferences on Modern Monetary Theory, but it also counts as one of its researchers the queen of modern monetary theory, Stephanie Kelton.[269]

Now, I suppose it is possible that it is just a coincidence that George Soros chose to make Bard College, the mecca of the modern monetary theory movement, the leading institution in Soros's new $1 billion global educational network. I suppose it is also possible that there is some special reason not related to modern monetary theory that Soros has decided to give the college $100 million and to name its president the chancellor of his international network. But in my experience, when it comes to Mr. Soros, there is no such thing as a coincidence.

I cannot prove it beyond a reasonable doubt, of course, but I am willing to bet that the reason Soros is building his new educational network around Bard College is because of the small school's devotion to modern monetary theory and because Soros knows that if modern monetary theory were to be fully embraced by leading U.S. institutions, it would inevitably push the entire world toward a more centralized governing structure, one that would give powerful elites control over nearly every economic decision, either directly or indirectly. This is the goal that Soros has been working toward for decades, and with a modern monetary theory system fully in place, he—as well as supporters of the Great Reset—knows it could finally become a reality.

FUELING THE MACHINE

Like elites' plan to create the Federal Reserve system more than one hundred years ago, embracing MMT will probably start with a meeting of the country's most powerful government officials, bankers, and businesspeople, who will travel from every corner of the globe to devise a plan to reset the world economic system.[270] And when they do, I am sure they will erroneously assure the American people that creating trillions of new dollars out of thin air and disregarding the national debt would open the door to a new era of economic growth. Thanks to this book, you'll know why you shouldn't trust them. (And thanks to this book, if you see Mitch McConnell, Nancy Pelosi, and Stephanie Kelton dressed as duck hunters and boarding a train, you will know exactly what is going on.)

The Great Reset is a machine manufactured to usher in a new, highly sophisticated, technologically advanced, twenty-first century brand of international fascism, one with a corporatist twist. But powerful machines like the Great Reset cannot operate without fuel. That is what modern monetary theory provides, by offering seemingly endless amounts of money that could be used to pay for just about anything government, corporations, and financial institutions can dream up.

COVID-19 created the conditions for the machine's existence. Without an urgent global crisis that could normalize modern monetary theory and burn down well-established economic and societal norms, the world would never have allowed the Great Reset to emerge as a viable option. People like Greta Thunberg could have screamed, shouted, and shamed all day long, but it never would have resulted in the "progress" she wanted, because everyone else in society had way too much to lose.

But as important as COVID-19 has been for the Great Reset, it is climate change that provides the key long-term justification for a far-reaching, sustained transformation of society. Without a decades-long "existential crisis" for governments and business leaders to rally around, the coronavirus pandemic would be nothing more than a fleeting public policy challenge—a large one, no doubt, but temporary and thus not useful for the sort of grand structural changes dreamed up by the Great Reset's leaders.

It is climate change policies, fueled by modern monetary theory, that ultimately provide the foundation upon which can be built the "new world order" that Greenpeace's Jennifer Morgan alluded to in her Great Reset presentation before the World Economic Forum in mid-2020.[271] But what exactly does that "new world" look like? That is the topic of the next chapter, "The Great Reset: Building a Twenty-First Century Fascism Machine."

5

THE GREAT RESET: BUILDING A TWENTY-FIRST CENTURY FASCISM MACHINE

First of all, we have to have the definition of "Reset" correctly. "Reset," we can't think of it in terms of sort of pushing a button and going back to the way things were .... The normal was a crisis. The normal was itself not working.

—John Kerry, speaking at a World Economic Forum event titled "Redesigning Social Contracts in Crisis," June 24, 2020[272]

AN INTERNATIONAL CONSPIRACY BETWEEN POWERFUL bankers, business leaders, and government officials; secret meetings in the Swiss Alps; and calls for a "new world order"—the Great Reset is one henchman-with-an-eyepatch away from being a great plot for the next James Bond movie. (Which, by the way, means that when Hollywood inevitably makes a blockbuster Great Reset film, the role of Glenn Beck will be played by Daniel Craig. Makes perfect sense to me, but not so much to my wife.)

In previous chapters, I have shown how the Great Reset would be fueled (modern monetary theory), how the conditions have come about that make the Reset possible (the coronavirus pandemic), and what the justification is for the destruction of the current world economic system (claims of an "existential" climate change crisis). But to this point, I have deliberately avoided explaining the specific policy changes that Great Reset supporters have in mind when they talk about their plans for the future, and there is a good reason for that: parts of the Great Reset are complicated—very complicated.

Unlike conservative political figures like Ted Cruz and Rand Paul, or left-leaning politicians like Bernie Sanders and Alexandria Ocasio-Cortez, who typically have no problem telling the American people exactly where they stand on the issues, those who favor the Great Reset often shroud their plans using coded language, largely unknown economic theories, and incredibly complex charts and diagrams that make whatever the heck that guy in *A Beautiful Mind* was sketching look like a children's maze on the back of a Denny's kid's menu.

Making matters worse, the Great Reset's biggest backers have deliberately chosen to use terminology that *sounds* appealing to many supporters of free markets—like "capitalism," "investments," and "stakeholders"—while meaning something very different from what many of us think of when we hear these ideas discussed in the United States.

Of course, at times the Great Reset movement could not be clearer. When advocates of the Reset say, "To achieve a better outcome, the world must act jointly and swiftly to revamp all aspects of our societies and economies, from education to social contracts and working conditions," they mean it.[273] Likewise, when they say, "We need a 'Great Reset' of capitalism," they mean that too.[274] And when they say, "We are completely rethinking the tools of economic policy," they are not lying.[275]

But as shocking as these and many other Great Reset-related statements are, they do not come even remotely close to painting the truly horrifying transformation of the world that the Great Reset movement has in mind when it talks about building its new global society. And although you will not hear Great Resetters openly calling for authoritarianism, the Great Reset is clearly a new kind of soft authoritarianism that is not too far off from the merging of markets, corporatism, authoritarianism, collectivism, and modern technology that has been embraced by the Communist Party of China in recent decades.

Its confusing terminology and vague language are what make the Great Reset so dangerous—and frankly, brilliant. Openly calling for a takeover of the global economy by the ruling class would immediately alienate 90 percent of the general population, but by tying in the Green New Deal, a government jobs guarantee, and a host of other large social welfare programs, they have managed to win over some progressives and socialists who care deeply about those issues. And by painting the movement as a pro-business, pro-capitalism plan to improve the economy, they have managed to win over some establishment political figures on the right.

But at its core, the Great Reset is not truly pro-socialism, and it's not pro-capitalism either—it's just a rebranding of the same old tired ideas that elites have pushed a million times before: "Give us more power, and we promise we'll take care of you and fix the world's ills. Let us manage more of the economy, and we promise you'll all be wealthier for it. Give us the authority to punish the 'bad guys' in society, and we'll save the planet from annihilation."

I admit that the Great Reset is a little cleverer (is that even a word, Mr. Editor?) than some of the schemes that the ruling class have trotted out before, but in the end, no matter what label the elitist snake oil salesman slaps on the front of the bottle, it is still poison he's trying to sell you. Or as former Texas governor Ann Richards once said, "You can put lipstick on a hog and call it Monique, but it is still a pig."[276] And make no mistake about it, the Great Reset *is* a pig—a big, fat, trough-licking pig.

The trick to stopping the Great Reset, then, is knowing how to recognize the poison and then how to keep our friends, family, and neighbors from guzzling it down. So what exactly is the Great Reset, and how do global elites plan to impose it on the entire world?

THE ROAD TO SERFDOM

The first thing you need to know about the Great Reset is that, at least at the time of this writing, there is no official Great Reset manual, framework, or agreement that all Great Reset advocates have signed up for. It is possible such a platform will be released when the World Economic Forum holds its next annual meeting, but currently you cannot go to one single place and see everything that the Reset entails.

The Great Reset has often been presented one component at a time, as though you are given a puzzle with all the pieces and the theme but without a picture of what it would look like completed. The obscurity of the final picture is, I believe, deliberate. It is much harder for people who would otherwise be deeply concerned about the Great Reset to spend too much time worrying about it, because it takes a lot of effort just to figure out what the Reset really is.

Luckily for you, my research team and I have spent months putting all the Great Reset pieces together so you do not have to.

The best place to find information about the Great Reset is on the website of the World Economic Forum (WEF). As I have noted throughout this book, the World Economic Forum is one of the leaders of the Great Reset movement. It hosts a large archive of articles, interviews, podcasts, and videos about the Reset—much of which features academics, business and government leaders, and activists from around the world, including America.

In an article published on June 3, 2020, on WEF's website, World Economic Forum founder and executive chairman Klaus Schwab discusses, in broad but relatively clear terms, some of the main goals of the Great Reset.

"There are many reasons to pursue a Great Reset," Schwab wrote, "but the most urgent is COVID-19. Having already led to hundreds of thousands of deaths, the pandemic represents one of the worst public-health crises in recent history. And, with casualties still mounting in many parts of the world, it is far from over."[277]

Schwab then cites climate change, income inequality, and other "crises" as key justifications for a "'Great Reset' of capitalism" and then he explains, "Left unaddressed, these crises…will deepen and leave the world even less sustainable, less equal, and more fragile. Incremental measures and ad hoc fixes will not suffice to prevent this scenario. We must build entirely new foundations for our economic and social systems."[278]

Schwab says there are "three main components" to the Great Reset "agenda." One is mostly uncontroversial: "to harness the innovations of the Fourth Industrial Revolution to support the public good, especially by addressing health and social challenges. During the COVID-19 crisis, companies, universities, and others have joined forces to develop diagnostics, therapeutics, and possible vaccines; establish testing centers; create mechanisms for tracing infections; and deliver telemedicine. Imagine what could be possible if similar concerted efforts were made in every sector."[279]

There are few people in the Western world who believe that technological advancements won't play a key role in future economic development, and some of the innovations Schwab cites, such as telemedicine, are something I have been talking about for many years. Unfortunately, here in America it took a pandemic to convince many in government to loosen regulations and make key reforms so that telemedicine and similar services made possible by recent technological achievements are available to everyone. I guess talking to your doctor through applications like Skype was just too much innovation for bureaucrats to handle. Don't you just love government?

The other two components Schwab outlines is where the real fun begins. According to Schwab,

> The first [component of the Great Reset] would steer the market toward fairer outcomes. To this end, governments should improve coordination (for example, in tax, regulatory, and fiscal policy), upgrade trade arrangements, and create the conditions for a "stakeholder economy." At a time of diminishing tax bases and soaring public debt, governments have a powerful incentive to pursue such action.
>
> Moreover, governments should implement long-overdue reforms that promote more equitable outcomes. Depending on the country, these may include changes to wealth taxes, the withdrawal of fossil-fuel subsidies, and new rules governing intellectual property, trade, and competition.[280]

Okay, now you might be thinking, "Glenn, this sounds like your standard progressive tax-and-spend platform, but you promised me so much more. Where's this big 'reset' of society you've been talking so much about?"

Hang with me, because we are going to get there soon. For now, I just want you to remember that Schwab has said that the Great Reset would "steer the market toward fairer outcomes," "create the conditions for a 'stakeholder economy,'" and "implement long-overdue reforms that promote more equitable outcomes." All of these ideas are going to get fleshed out in a lot more detail later in this chapter, but you can already see that Schwab's ideas require dramatically altering the global economy and empowering *someone*—we'll find out who that someone is soon—with the authority to redistribute wealth and power. It is also important to remember that Schwab, who is really just one of many important Great Reset advocates, is especially interested in something called a "stakeholder economy," a concept that is vital for understanding the full weight of the Great Reset.

Later in the same article, Schwab explains that another major component of the Great Reset agenda is to "ensure that investments advance shared goals, such as equality and sustainability." He continues:

> Here, the large-scale spending programs that many governments are implementing represent a major opportunity for progress. The European Commission, for one, has unveiled plans for a €750 billion ($826 billion) recovery fund. The US, China, and Japan also have ambitious economic-stimulus plans.
>
> Rather than using these funds, as well as investments from private entities and pension funds, to fill cracks in the old system, we should use them to create a new one that is more resilient, equitable, and sustainable in the long run. This means, for example, building "green" urban infrastructure and creating

incentives for industries to improve their track record on environmental, social, and governance (ESG) metrics. [281]

The new system Schwab is referring to is a total reworking of the way people think about businesses and how to evaluate them. Rather than focus on profits, private property rights, supply, and demand from consumers—the cornerstones of free market economies—Schwab wants to develop a system based largely on "environmental, social, and governance (ESG) metrics," which, as we'll explore later, is another, much more complex way of suggesting that companies should be rewarded for working toward achieving social justice goals, like fighting climate change, addressing racial inequity, and removing Aunt Jemima from syrup bottles.

This does not mean, however, that the Great Reset is a socialist system. It is easy to fall into that trap—I did many times in the year leading up to this book's release. The Great Reset is fundamentally about shifting wealth and power into the hands of elites, as you'll see later in the chapter. All this "social justice" stuff that Schwab and other Resetters like to talk about is just a smoke-and-mirror show. In the end, the Great Reset machine could be used to pursue *any* goals the ruling class deems important.

As I warned you about earlier, in Schwab's article he is deliberately being very vague, but there are already several reasons to be alarmed.

First, Schwab wants to reset capitalism and create a new system.

Second, that new system would be focused on equality of outcomes—not equality under the law—a goal rejected by all market-based economies. And although Schwab does not say it in the passage quoted here, we will discover elsewhere that the "equality" Schwab wants isn't just among people *within* a nation but *between* nations as well. The Great Reset is, without a doubt, an internationalist movement.

Third, Schwab wants national governments and central banks to spend massive amounts of money—money they do not have—to make his proposed changes. Schwab says elsewhere in the article that this will "require stronger and more effective governments."[282]

EXPANDING SOCIAL PROGRAMS

In a variety of articles, speeches, presentations, interviews, and videos, Great Reset supporters make it abundantly clear that their plan for building a more "equitable" society requires large, government-funded socialist or progressive programs, which would be paid for by increasing taxes on the wealthy and businesses, as well as through the printing of money by central banks like the Federal Reserve in the United States.

Gita Gopinath, the chief economist at the International Monetary Fund, said during an interview with WEF promoting the Great Reset, "I believe it's very important for countries to recognize there are essential services that need to be provided in terms of healthcare, education, good governance and a social safety that cannot be compromised on."[283]

Sharan Burrow, the general secretary of the International Trade Union Confederation (ITUC), also supports the Great Reset. During a similar interview, Burrow said, "I can see how we could use this opportunity to design a better world, but we need both national and multilateral institutions to make it work."[284]

Later Burrow added, "We must ensure this design is inclusive of universal social protection. The world could fund it right now—and yet 70% of the world's population has no social protection. It must be respectful of public services rather than simply trying to profit from them."[285]

Here Burrow is not clear by what she means by "universal social protection," which is not a term you often hear in the United

States. However, on the website of the International Trade Union Confederation, which claims to represent two hundred million workers in 163 countries, the organization spells out in detail what Burrow was referring to. In a June 2020 campaign brief titled "A Global Social Protection Fund Is Possible," the ITUC writes, "The Covid-19 pandemic has brutally exposed the fault lines of the global divide between those that have universal social protection, including health and income support, and those that don't."[286]

ITUC later explains,

> Social protection is essential for human security and social justice. It is a foundation for peaceful societies committed to building shared prosperity. It creates the basis for economic development and builds resilience against personal, national or global shocks.
>
> A social protection floor includes basic income security including cash transfers where necessary; pensions for the elderly; disability benefits; unemployment benefits and support; maternity protection; and child benefits amongst other nationally identified needs.
>
> In addition and equally important, universal access to essential social services—including health, education, water, sanitation and housing—is vital.[287]

Providing the entire world's population with a litany of government-funded social programs? I would love to see the price tag on that one. No doubt it would make the $94 trillion Green New Deal in America look like an off-brand can of tomatoes on the discount shelf at Dollar General.

The stated purpose of the Great Reset's proposed expansion of government "social protection" is to promote left-wing goals. Kristalina Georgieva, the managing director of the International

Monetary Fund, said in a June 2020 address about the Great Reset that any economic recovery must focus on "fairer growth."[288]

"We know that—if left to its own devices—this pandemic is going to deepen inequality," Georgieva said. "That has happened in prior pandemics.[289]

"We can avoid this if we concentrate on investing in people—in the social fabric of our societies, in access to opportunities, in education for all, and in the expansion of social programs so we take care of the most vulnerable people," Georgieva added. "Then we can have a world that is better for everyone."[290]

In the same talk, Georgieva then explained that the creation of the government-run health care system in the United Kingdom following World War II serves as an important "example from the past" of how governments can use crises to enact progressive reforms.

"I want to conclude with an example from the past," she said. "William Beveridge, in the midst of the Second World War, put forward his famous report in 1942 in which he projected how U.K. should address what he called the 'five giant evils.' That famous 'Beveridge Report' led to a better country after the war—including the creation of the National Health Service that is saving so many lives today in the U.K."[291]

Of course, Georgieva left out how the National Health Service has for decades been poorly managed, underfunded, and associated with rationing and long wait times. According to the *New York Times*—a publication that often promotes left-wing causes like single-payer health care —"Denying lifesaving care to conserve public resources is nothing new for Britain's National Health Service.[292]

"In expensive treatments for cancer and other diseases, the health service officially limits what it will spend to postpone a death: 30,000 pounds, or about $37,000, for each year of full 'quality' life provided to a patient," the *Times* reported.[293] (In case you were ever wondering how much you mean to the government, the United Kingdom's bureaucrats went through the trouble of assigning a specific value to your life. How thoughtful of them.)

In addition to calls for expanding "universal social protection" through government-run or government-managed health care and education programs, individual Great Resetters and others aligned with the World Economic Forum have also demanded a variety of large government programs that may or may not be part of a final Great Reset platform that could be released in 2022.

Guy Standing, a professor in development studies at the University of London and nominee for the Most Literal Name Ever award, authored an article in April 2020 for the World Economic Forum titled "Coronavirus Has Shown Us Why We Urgently Need to Make a Basic Income a Reality." In the article, Standing argues that "in this pandemic, the economy will not survive without [a] quasi-universal" basic income program.[294]

Standing is not alone in demanding new basic income programs. In April 2020, Kanni Wignaraja, assistant secretary-general of the United Nations, and Balazs Horvath, chief economist for the Asia-Pacific group at the U.N. Development Programme, argued that the COVID-19 pandemic has made it apparent that it is now "time to add a new element to the policy packages that governments are introducing, one we know but have abandoned: Universal Basic Income (UBI). It is needed as part of the package that will help us to get out of this yawning pit."[295]

It is impossible to say what additional multitrillion-dollar government social programs will be dreamed up at the World Economic Forum's various Great Reset meetings in the years to come. But based on the other parts of the Great Reset platform, I think it's a safe bet, to say the least, that they would expand the power and influence of government bureaucrats and the ruling class.

Before we move on, I want to once again stress the importance of resisting the urge to view the Great Reset as a socialist or even progressive framework. There are socialist and progressive elements to the plan, as I have just pointed out, but we have also already encountered what should be a big red flag: throughout this book, I've noted repeatedly that corporations, bankers, and some of the world's wealthiest people have proudly stood behind the Great Reset. Does anyone really believe that these Wall Street cutthroats and billionaire entrepreneurs have suddenly become card-carrying members of the Democratic Socialists of America? Of course they haven't.

The real reason there are so many corporate and financial industry interests lining up to promote the Great Reset is because of money and power—the true driving force behind the Reset. We are going to get into that topic in a lot more detail later in the chapter, but it is important to keep this point in mind as we navigate our way through this complex issue. The progressive and socialist elements to the Reset are merely there to win support from some groups on the left while simultaneously expanding the power of elites. The ruling class has *not*, no matter what they say, had a real come-to-Bernie moment—which probably explains why you typically won't find Sanders at Davos cocktail parties.

A GLOBAL GREEN NEW DEAL

As I explained at length in chapter 3, the most important long-term justification used by supporters of the Great Reset is that it is necessary for saving humanity from the "existential crisis" posed by climate change.

In that chapter, I noted that Schwab has argued, "We only have one planet and we know that climate change could be the next global disaster with even more dramatic consequences for humankind.

We have to decarbonize the economy in the short window still remaining and bring our thinking and behavior once more into harmony with nature."[296]

How exactly do Klaus and friends aim to bring Americans "into harmony with nature"? By imposing an expansive, never-before-attempted, global Green New Deal that would wipe out the use of most fossil fuels and replace conventional energy with wind, solar, and other earth-destroying "green" energy sources.

Martina Larkin, a member of the Executive Committee at the World Economic Forum, wrote in May 2020 that the "Green Deal must be at the heart of the COVID-19 recovery" in Europe.[297] According to Larkin:

> A new forecast by climate experts at the Global Carbon Project predicts that carbon dioxide emissions could fall by the largest amount since the Second World War due to the impact of COVID-19 on economic activity. This means carbon output could fall by more than 5% year-on-year, which is the first dip since a 1.4% reduction following the 2008 financial crisis.
>
> However, as economic activity resumes and countries and companies develop recovery strategies, we need to fast-track the structural changes towards a fossil-free economy. The European Green Deal could be the opportunity to leap-frog in this ambition....
>
> Achieving this transformative agenda and making Europe a leader in the global climate transition requires a massive mobilization of public and private investments. The Commission estimates that reaching the net-zero 2050 target requires at least €1 trillion of public and private investment over the next decade.[298]

However, as Larkin knows well, most European nations, just like the United States, do not have any cash available for all the "public and private investment" needed to build billions of solar panels. They are running huge deficits. So how do they plan to pay for the Green New Deal? By printing money, of course, in line with the principles of Stephanie Kelton and other modern monetary theorists. There simply is no feasible way to pay for plans this ambitious without a monetary framework that would allow for absurdly high levels of government deficit spending.

Larkin and Schwab are not the only Great Reset supporters who have called for massive "green" infrastructure plans as part of a COVID-19 recovery. Just about everyone I could find who supports the Great Reset also backs some version of the Green New Deal, both in Europe and elsewhere, and many began attempting to link the pandemic to "green" infrastructure proposals in the earliest days of the coronavirus crisis.

In March 2020, the World Economic Forum published an article titled "Could COVID-19 Give Rise to a Greener Global Future?" The article was written by two academics and the copresident of the Club of Rome, a powerful nonprofit organization most famous for its 1972 book *The Limits to Growth*, which predicted that modern civilization may not survive the twenty-first century because of resource depletion.[299] According to the authors of the March article, the only way to save the planet is to use the COVID-19 pandemic to rebuild the global economy using policies such as the Green New Deal.

They wrote,

The coronavirus pandemic is a wake-up call to stop exceeding the planet's limits. After all, deforestation, biodiversity loss, and climate change all make pandemics more likely....Governments that succeed in containing epidemics all tacitly follow the same mantra: "Follow the science and prepare for the future." But we can do much better. Rather than simply reacting to disasters, we can use the science to design economies that will mitigate the threats of climate change, biodiversity loss, and pandemics. We must start investing in what matters, by laying the foundation for a green, circular economy that is anchored in nature-based solutions and geared toward the public good.[300]

They then called on lawmakers to redirect public funding linked to fossil fuels "toward green infrastructure, reforestation, and investments in a more circular, shared, regenerative, low-carbon economy."[301]

At the June 2020 World Economic Forum virtual meeting, António Guterres, the secretary-general of the United Nations, said the Great Reset should be used to build economies that are more "sustainable," a term often used by Great Resetters as a stand-in for "green" energy. Guterres also called for economies to become more "resilient in the face of…climate change and the many other global changes we face."[302]

What Larkin, Guterres, and Schwab don't mention, however, is that financial institutions, investors, and corporations would amass untold trillions of dollars if the Green New Deal were to become a reality and spread globally. More on that a little later.

GLOBAL "COOPERATION"

If you are wondering how all of this can be achieved on a grand scale without increasing the power of global governing bodies like the United Nations, then you are not alone. Although Great Resetters never say that they want to abandon all notions of national sovereignty in favor of world government, they do make it clear that greatly empowering international organizations like the United Nations will be necessary under a Great Reset model.

Schwab admits that the "level of cooperation and ambition this [the Great Reset] implies is unprecedented," but, he says, "it is not some impossible dream."[303] It simply will require "global cooperation" on a gigantic scale.

"This global pandemic has also demonstrated again how interconnected we are," Schwab said. "We have to restore a functioning system of smart global cooperation structured to address the challenges of the next 50 years. The Great Reset will require us to integrate all stakeholders of global society into a community of common interest, purpose and action."[304]

I hate to sound like a "conspiracy theorist" again, but a "global … community of common interest, purpose and action" sounds an awful lot like Schwab is suggesting we put international governing bodies in charge of the world economy, doesn't it?

Feike Sijbesma is a member of the board of trustees at the World Economic Forum and the cochair of the Global Center on Adaptation (GCA). He is a little clearer about the Great Reset's intention to usher in a glorious new era of enhancing global government—or at the very least, a high degree of global "cooperation" that would "change" societies around the world.

According to Sijbesma,

[The Great Reset] requires improving global multilateral cooperation and aligning both the recovery of our economies and priorities of societies. For the Great Reset to succeed, we have to change the way we do business and manage health, nature, the environment, and societal issues at the same time.

Despite the unprecedented impact and global spread, there was little cooperation between countries. In many aspects, it was everyone for themselves when buying ventilators, face masks, tests, and more. As healthcare for governments is a domestic issue, countries did not explore multilateral joint approaches and solutions. Let's hope this was not the litmus test for other cross-border crises like climate change. Only via collaboration between countries, can we address such issues.[305]

THE "STAKEHOLDER ECONOMY"

It is easy to look at the long list of left-wing government programs appearing earlier in the chapter and think that this is all that Resetters have in mind when they talk about pushing the reset button on the global economy, but the truth is, as crazy as it might sound, the trillions of dollars in new spending, total destruction of the world's existing energy industry, and creation of countless social programs like universal basic income and government-managed health care are not the most important parts of the Reset or even part of the foundation of the plan.

At the beginning of this chapter, I cited Klaus Schwab's broad outline for the Great Reset, and at the time, I told you that his call to "steer the market toward fairer outcomes" by, in part, creating "the conditions for a 'stakeholder economy'" was something you should take note of, because it plays a pivotal role in grasping just how big the Great Reset transformation would be.[306] Now that you have a better understanding of some of the more overtly social-istic elements of the Great Reset, let's turn our attention to what Schwab and many others in the Great Reset movement mean by building a "stakeholder economy."

At first, the idea of a stakeholder economy, also commonly referred to as stakeholder capitalism, sounds pretty darn innocuous, even boring. After all, the whole idea of government and business officials caring about "stakeholders"—a term that normally means "one who is involved in or affected by a course of action"[307]—does not sound very radical. But if you start to dig deeper into the Great Reset pit, you will quickly see that "stakeholder capitalism" represents a dramatic departure from our common understanding of market-based economics.

Stakeholder capitalism is an economic system in which companies are effectively required to put social justice causes and/or the goals of elites—which, of course, vary wildly depending on the parties involved—before profits, supply and demand, the desires of consumers, and other market forces that normally direct capitalist systems, which, don't forget, have created the most prosperous, healthy, safe societies humankind has ever known. Our more traditional understanding of capitalism is often called "shareholder capitalism" by Great Resetters, because they say it prioritizes the interests of the shareholders—another word for owners—of corporations over the interests of the wider community.

After calling for "a change in capitalism," Feike Sijbesma explained in an article for the World Economic Forum that under the Great Reset, "the [economic] focus should shift from short-term and profit-only to longer-term, incorporating value creation for people and the planet, moving from shareholder value to stakeholder interests."[308]

Schwab, who has long advocated for stakeholder capitalism, said in January 2020, "Business has now to fully embrace stakeholder capitalism, which means not only maximizing profits, but use their capabilities and resources in cooperation with governments and civil society to address the key issues of this decade. They have to actively contribute to a more cohesive and sustainable world."[309]

Sijbesma further explained that the principles that must be embraced by companies in a stakeholder capitalist system focus on a "longer-term economic strategy" that is "anchored in addressing the Sustainable Development Goals (SDGs)" produced by the United Nations.[310]

When Great Resetters talk about shifting to a stakeholder model, they typically mean one centered on U.N. SDGs, so it is important to understand what the Sustainable Development Goals involve and why Great Reset promoters are so interested in them.

The Sustainable Development Goals were created at a meeting of the United Nations in September 2015. The SDGs, which serve as a successor to the United Nations's Agenda 21 sustainable development plan—yes, *that* Agenda 21—represent commitments made by U.N. nations to "end poverty and hunger everywhere; to combat inequalities within and among countries; to build peaceful, just and inclusive societies; to protect human rights and promote gender equality and the empowerment of women and girls; and to ensure the lasting protection of the planet and its natural resources"—and all by 2030.[311] If you ever hear anyone talk about "Agenda 2030," it's almost certainly in reference to the United Nations's Sustainable Development Goals.

According to the United Nations, this "collective journey" is "accepted by all countries and is applicable to all, taking into account different national realities, capacities and levels of development and respecting national policies and priorities."[312]

In their commitment to the Sustainable Development Goals, member nations said they imagined "a world free of poverty, hunger, disease and want, where all life can thrive." They also said,

> We envisage a world free of fear and violence. A world with universal literacy. A world with equitable and universal access to quality education at all levels, to health care and social protection, where physical, mental and social well-being are assured. . . . A world where human habitats are safe, resilient and sustainable and where there is universal access to affordable, reliable and sustainable energy. . . . A world of universal respect for human

rights and human dignity, the rule of law, justice, equality and non-discrimination; of respect for race, ethnicity and cultural diversity; and of equal opportunity permitting the full realization of human potential and contributing to shared prosperity.[313]

They further committed to a world in which every country enjoys sustained, inclusive and sustainable economic growth and decent work for all. A world in which consumption and production patterns and use of all natural resources—from air to land, from rivers, lakes and aquifers to oceans and seas—are sustainable. One in which democracy, good governance and the rule of law as well as an enabling environment at national and international levels, are essential for sustainable development, including sustained and inclusive economic growth, social development, environmental protection and the eradication of poverty and hunger. One in which development and the application of technology are climate-sensitive, respect biodiversity and are resilient. One in which humanity lives in harmony with nature and in which wildlife and other living species are protected.[314]

I get their desire to aim high, but creating "a world free of...want"? You know, I *want* a unicorn and clouds made of cotton candy. Is the United Nations promising these things too? Fat dads like me love cotton candy clouds and demand to know.

I realize all of this sounds like your standard pie-in-the-sky globalism from the United Nations, and that is because that is exactly what the Sustainable Development Goals are. But this does not mean they are meaningless. They certainly have a lot of value to supporters of the Great Reset, who want to use these goals as a springboard to control economic activity while making their corporate friends filthy rich. But how exactly would that work?

Schwab and other Great Reset supporters want to transform the current global economy into one in which every company focuses more on advancing SDGs, or whatever else the ruling class deems important, than on profits. In December 2019, Schwab and the World Economic Forum released its *Davos Manifesto 2020*, which outlines some of the core values of a new stakeholder economy.[315]

In a stakeholder economy, the manifesto notes, "the purpose of a company is to engage all its stakeholders in shared and sustained value creation. In creating such value, a company serves not only its shareholders, but all its stakeholders—employees, customers, suppliers, local communities and society at large."[316]

Or put in much clearer terms, in a stakeholder capitalist system, companies should first serve the collective according to the demands of the ruling class in government, not their customers and owners. Stakeholder capitalism is just another way of saying "collectivist capitalism," which really is not capitalism at all.

To many Americans, perhaps even some reading this book, this concept might not sound all that worrisome. You might be thinking, "Okay, so under the Great Reset, companies would have to factor in other considerations in addition to profits. So what?"

Before dismissing my concerns, stop and think for a minute about the implications of this idea. A "profit-driven" model for business ensures that companies put the consumer first. Under this system, individuals dictate the products and services that are produced, by voting with their dollars. Companies that want to survive listen to the demands of their customers and even try to anticipate them. But in a stakeholder system, individuals are replaced by an elite group of Bond villain wannabes in the ruling class. *They* dictate which products and services are produced and who ought to be hired to provide them to customers—not you, the individual.

UNDERSTANDING ESG

How can the Great Reset overlords know which companies are properly pursuing the "right" goals? To help push businesses in the direction the elites in society deem best, the World Economic Forum, business leaders, financial institutions, activists, and government officials from around the world have developed environmental, social, and governance (ESG) metrics that can help companies, investors, governments, and the public know who the "good" businesses are and which scoundrel companies are interested only in turning a profit, developing new products, and hiring more employees. I mean, there is nothing worse than a company looking to hire more employees and earn a profit in a marketplace, right?

Although there are several versions of these ESG metrics available today, the metrics promoted by the World Economic Forum and the International Business Council, a group created by WEF in 2001, are perhaps positioned best to become the international standard in the coming years.

The final draft of the WEF metrics, titled *Measuring Stakeholder Capitalism: Toward Common Metrics and Consistent Reporting of Sustainable Value Creation*, was released in September 2020 and prepared in collaboration with experts from Bank of America and the "Big Four" accounting firms: Deloitte, KPMG, PricewaterhouseCoopers, and Ernst & Young, all of which are worth *tens of billions of dollars* and widely considered to be the most influential and powerful firms in the world—you know, real down-to-earth people who know what life is like for the average, everyday worker.[317]

The World Economic Forum's ESG standards include twenty-one "core metrics" and thirty-four "expanded metrics." Together they allow auditors to develop a comprehensive ESG score that can be used to determine whether a company is in line with the demands of the ruling class.[318]

The standards are divided into four "pillars": Principles of Governance, Planet, People, and Prosperity. Although some of the core metrics that compose each pillar are reasonable and even advisable—like closely tracking "incidents of corruption confirmed during the current year but related to previous years"—many others are clearly designed to advance social justice causes favored mostly by those on the left.[319]

In the Principles of Governance pillar, WEF suggests that companies be scored based on the "membership of under-represented social groups" serving in a company's governing body, as well as those leaders' "competencies relating to economic, environmental and social topics."

In the Planet pillar, companies are evaluated based on their greenhouse gas emissions, their compliance with the Paris Climate Accords, their "land use and ecological sensitivity," and their "water consumption and withdrawal in water-stressed areas," among other environmental standards.

The People pillar is full of woke ideology, including an ESG measure for the "percentage of employees per employee category, by age group, gender and other indicators of diversity (e.g. ethnicity)," as well as pro–labor union measures such as the "percentage of active workforce covered under collective bargaining agreements."[320]

Let's stop for a second and think about what the World Economic Forum's ESG model would look like in the real world. Under WEF's standards, a company with relatively larger profits, high employee and customer satisfaction, and high-quality products and services—a company that would universally be considered well managed under a free market system—could be rated lower than a company in the same industry that is less efficient and has fewer profits and worse products and services but has the right ratio of Asian-to-Black workers, low carbon dioxide emissions in their supply chain, and the "ideal" number of transgender members on the board of directors.

Now, let's get one thing out of the way right from the start: private businesses should have the right to engage in any number of silly, stupid, wasteful, noble, kind, compassionate, or ridiculous causes or to hold themselves to standards that I think are foolish or counterproductive. As far as I am concerned, if businesses want to create an ESG system that rewards corporations that give raises only to workers who like the color green or that pay salaries ending in odd numbers or that are owned by people named Glenn, then I'm fine with that. Investors, employees, and consumers should have the right to decide who they want to do business with, and if people want to spend their time and money doing business with only the wokest of woke companies, then that should be their right.

But for the most part, that system has always existed in every market economy. Nothing has stopped consumers from buying from only those companies that choose to embrace their ideals, and nothing has stopped investors from investing in them.

So what do Klaus Schwab and the other Great Reset elites have in mind when they say they want to advance the ESG model, tear down the existing "shareholder capitalism" system, and replace it with an economy focused on stakeholders?

The answer is almost certainly twofold: the transformation could be brought on by either government mandates or the use of monetary incentives made possible by newly printed cash from central banks. Under the first option, governments around the world could start building stricter regulatory schemes that directly or indirectly force businesses to focus on improving ESG scores, rather than profits, in order to continue operating in certain nations or regions or to continue being a publicly traded corporation. Some governments have already started putting into place regulations that force companies to "act responsibly" and in line with the concerns of elites.

As World Economic Forum project specialist Elisabeth Andvig noted in a May 2020 WEF article calling for a Great Reset,

> Legal and societal pressures on businesses operating around the world are rapidly evolving. There is a call for efforts to better align the activities of corporations with society's drive to build a more inclusive, equitable and sustainable economy. . . . The implementation of the Sustainable Development Goals (SDGs) and Agenda 2030 will depend on positive contributions from the private sector, through responsible business conduct and responsible investments. . . . Doing the right thing is about more than just complying with the law. However, legal obligations are increasingly requiring companies to act responsibly.[321]

In some cases, American investors and businesses themselves are begging for regulatory agencies to use their powers to impose social justice and environmental causes. In July 2020, a group of more than three dozen large investors, activists, nonprofits, pension funds, and former politicians—which together manage nearly $1 trillion in assets—sent a letter to the Federal Reserve (America's central bank), the Securities and Exchange Commission, and other regulatory bodies asking them to impose rules that would supposedly help stop climate change.

According to the *New York Times*, the letter read, in part, "The climate crisis poses a systemic threat to financial markets and the real economy, with significant disruptive consequences on asset valuations and our nation's economic stability."[322]

The *Times* further reported, "That financial threat, combined with the physical risks posed by climate change, may create 'disastrous impacts the likes of which we haven't seen before,' the letter says. It urges the Fed, the Securities and Exchange Commission and other agencies to 'explicitly integrate climate change across your mandates.'"[323]

These investors are asking the U.S. government to do everything in its power to *force* other companies to adopt their woke causes, bringing to mind the old statist slogan "Ideas so good, they are mandatory."

Similarly, according to the World Economic Forum, Ma Jun, the chairman of the China Green Finance Committee and an avid supporter of the Great Reset, has called for the Reset to include "tighter reporting and regulation for companies," to ensure they are working harder to advance environmental goals.[324]

Regulatory agencies in the United States are listening. In March 2021, Perkins Coie, a highly influential international law firm, reported,

> Over the past few weeks, the U.S. Securities and Exchange Commission has taken several actions that put climate change front and center, reflecting the importance to many investors of climate change related disclosures.
>
> In early February, the SEC announced the addition of Satyam Khanna as a senior policy advisor charged with coordinating and overseeing efforts related to climate and other environmental, social, and governance (ESG) issues. Mr. Khanna is the first-ever senior policy advisor for ESG issues at the SEC. Since then, the SEC has announced a rapid series of additional initiatives....
>
> President Biden's nominee to be the next SEC chair, Gary Gensler, said during his confirmation hearing that investors want more information about climate risks and that disclosure requirements should be grounded in what reasonable investors find material. If confirmed, Mr. Gensler indicated to the Senate

Committee on Banking, Housing, and Urban Affairs, he would likely pursue rulemaking around climate risk disclosures and perhaps other ESG topics.[325]

Additionally, in August 2021, *Bloomberg* writer Bill Dudley outlined some of the radical developments underway at the U.S. Federal Reserve, led by Chair Jay Powell, who is eagerly working to build a regulatory framework that can be used to push banks and the companies they do business with to adopt climate and energy policies favored by the Left.

> Powell and the Fed's Board of Governors created two new entities—the Financial Stability Climate Committee, to focus on the broader financial system, and the Supervision Climate Committee, to focus on individual institutions. This matters, because it means top officials are committed to regularly evaluating and responding to the threat [of climate change]. They're already working to ensure that banks embed climate change in their business decisions—analyzing exposures, identifying concentrations of risk and considering how to manage them over time.[326]

The recent developments at the SEC and Federal Reserve are vital because they will serve as the foundation for future Great Reset economic transformations in the United States, by providing lawmakers in Washington with tools needed to push companies toward full ESG adoption. And they are already acting as a warning to American businesses that future regulatory changes are just around the corner.

But as troubling as things are in America, the situation is much worse in Europe, where many political figures have been working for years to make ESG standards mandatory for all large businesses and many small businesses. As my coauthor, Justin Haskins, reported in June 2021, "In March, the Parliament of the European Union passed a resolution that seeks to require nearly all of the EU's largest companies—and many smaller businesses, too—to adopt and prioritize ESG metrics. And especially important for U.S. businesses and consumers, the resolution would further require that EU companies only work with those who share the European Union's environmental, social and governance standards."[327]

In a report about the European ESG resolution, international law firm Shearman & Sterling noted, "If adopted, all EU Member States will be required to implement the Directive into their national laws. This will result in substantive due diligence requirements being imposed on companies, whether based in the EU or selling their products and services into the EU, across their entire value chain, with potential sanctions for non-compliance."[328]

Understanding what European Union officials mean by "value chain" is extremely important. In their resolution, "value chain" is defined as "all activities, operations, business relationships and investment chains of an undertaking and includes entities with which the undertaking has a direct or indirect business relationship, upstream and downstream, and which either: (a) supply products, parts of products or services that contribute to the undertaking's own products or services, or (b) receive products or services from the undertaking."[329]

That means if the E.U. resolution were to become law—and as of the time of this writing, that is looking more and more likely—all U.S. businesses having any "direct or indirect" relationship with an E.U. business, "upstream and downstream," would be forced to operate under some or all of Europe's proposed ESG system.[330]

Now, it's not true that all Great Resetters are calling for the use of regulations to impose ESG standards on private companies, at least not in every situation. In some cases, they talk about adopting ESG voluntarily. In 2019, Schwab encouraged businesses to adopt stakeholder capitalist principles voluntarily, so that they can "move beyond their legal obligations and uphold their duty to society."[331]

This is where the second method for creating a stakeholder economic system comes into play. Rather than use regulations to impose environmental, social, and governance standards on companies, some Great Resetters want to use massive government and central bank spending programs to push companies toward adopting ESG standards, a move that looks eerily similar to proposals backed by people like modern monetary theorist Stephanie Kelton, who has long suggested that the best way to "progress" society is to not only expand the power of government but also print trillions of dollars and tie social justice strings to the money.

Pursuing modern monetary theory principles like those supported by Kelton would make it unnecessary to completely dismantle private property ownership. Government and central banks would become the biggest and most important "consumers" in the marketplace, which, of course, would not and could not function as a true market because of the outsized power and influence of government and central bank spending programs.

"ALIGNING INCENTIVES"

Say, for example, government funding makes up 20 percent of a business's income, directly or indirectly. On many issues, that business is going to be far more interested in keeping the government happy than focused on pleasing individual consumers, and this perversion would only get worse as the government raises its level of involvement. Eventually, individual consumers would become nothing more than an afterthought.

As I mentioned at the start of this chapter, this strategy was clearly stated in Klaus Schwab's article outlining his "main components" of the Great Reset, published in June 2020.

> The second component of a Great Reset agenda would ensure that investments advance shared goals, such as equality and sustainability....Rather than using these funds, as well as investments from private entities and pension funds, to fill cracks in the old system, we should use them to create a new one that is more resilient, equitable, and sustainable in the long run. This means, for example, building "green" urban infrastructure and creating incentives for industries to improve their track record on environmental, social, and governance (ESG) metrics.[332]

Another, much less misleading word for the "incentives" Klaus speaks about here is "coercion." And if enough money is tied to ESG metrics, that coercion could effectively become necessary to businesses in order for them to survive, especially if it is coupled with all the new taxes and regulations Schwab and other Great Resetters also support.

Additionally, it is important to note that Great Resetters do not always use the words "environmental, social, and governance metrics" when they are referring to building their new stakeholder economy but instead use terms like "sustainable investment" and "realigning incentives" to convey the same radical idea.

Writing for WEF and Project Syndicate in July 2020, Tolullah Oni, a physician and researcher at the University of Cambridge, said, "Although several global philanthropic initiatives have sought to improve urban health and resilience, undoubtedly with positive results, today's flawed systems need more fundamental disruption. Simply put, the world needs a new Marshall Plan for planetary health—akin to a New Deal for a post-pandemic recovery."[333]

According to Oni, this new "Marshall Plan" would "serve as a global guide, aligning incentives and shifting default behaviors toward the shared goal of sustainable healthy urban development. It will require the agreement and participation of national and local governments, private developers, investors, and multilateral organizations, which will take time."[334]

"Aligning incentives and shifting default behaviors" is another way of saying "bribing businesses to do what we think is in the best interests of the collective," in line with ESG goals.

This is exactly what Great Reset supporter Sharan Burrow, the general secretary of the International Trade Union Confederation, had in mind when she said during an interview about the Great Reset, "We need to design policies to align with investment in people and the environment. But above all, the longer-term perspective is about rebalancing economies."[335]

Burrow elaborated further in the interview, saying, "We want an end to the profit-at-all-costs mentality, because if we don't build an economic future within a sustainable framework in which we are respectful of our planetary boundaries, and the need to change our energy and technology systems, then we will not have a living planet for human beings."[336]

This is the same sort of thinking used by the French government in 2020 when crafting COVID-19 relief packages for airlines suffering under government lockdowns. As reported by the *Guardian* in April 2020, "Some governments are seeking to attach strings to rescue plans. France's minister for ecological transition, Elisabeth Borne, insisted Air France was not getting 'a blank cheque.' The government has set 'ecological commitments,' she said, including a 50% reduction in carbon emissions on domestic flights by 2024, as well as investing in more fuel-efficient planes."[337]

Many financial institutions have already laid the groundwork for punishing companies that will not go along with the Great Reset's mandates. In February 2021, Bank of America, citing its "long-standing support for the Paris Climate Agreement," issued a press release announcing that it had "outlined initial steps to achieve its goal of net zero greenhouse gas (GHG) emissions in its financing activities, operations and supply chain before 2050."[338]

The press release further noted, "Bank of America continues to actively engage with its clients to help accelerate their own transitions to net zero, and it plans to establish interim science based emissions targets for high-emitting portfolios, including energy and power. In addition, Bank of America released its broader 2030 operational and supply chain goals as part of a holistic commitment to environmental sustainability."

Notice that Bank of America's "goal of net zero greenhouse gas (GHG) emissions" applies not only to the company's "operations and supply chain," which means that everyone who does business with Bank of America would have to go along with its goals in order to keep BoA as a customer, but also to the bank's "financing activities," which is another way of saying, "If you don't go 'green,' we're not going to give your business a loan."

In the same press release, Bank of America also touted the close relationship its CEO, Brian Moynihan, has with the World Economic Forum and his involvement with the development of WEF's ESG metrics. And then it included this creepy quote from Bank of America vice chairman Anne Finucane, who, according to the press release, "leads the company's environmental, social and governance, sustainable finance, capital deployment, and public policy efforts": "It is critical that we leverage all parts of our business—beyond our direct operations—in order to accelerate the transition to a net zero global economy. We recognize that this will be no easy task, but we believe our commitment will help spur the growth of zero carbon energy and power solutions, sustainable transportation and agriculture, and other sector transformations, while generating more climate resilient and equitable opportunities for our future."

Boy, that sounds awfully similar to the sort of thing one might hear while attending a Great Reset meeting in Davos. Again, pay special attention to what Bank of America is saying here. Its plan is to "leverage all parts of our business—beyond our direct operations—in order to accelerate the transition to a net zero global economy." In other words, the plan is to push the world toward elites' goal of a global economy that has net zero carbon dioxide emissions, whether the world wants it or not, by using the full weight and power of one of the wealthiest, most influential banks on earth.

Bank of America is hardly the only private financial institution pushing ESG standards and green energy mandates. In March 2021, Jane Fraser—the CEO of Citi, a bank worth more than $200 billion—published an article on the company's website titled "Citi's Commitment to Net Zero by 2050."

In the article, Fraser declared, "The climate crisis is among the top critical challenges facing our global society and economy today and there is an urgent need for collective action. We believe that global financial institutions like Citi have the opportunity—and the responsibility—to play a leading role in helping drive the transition to a net zero global economy and make good on the promise of the Paris Agreement."[339]

How exactly does Fraser envision Citi "helping drive the transition to a net zero global economy"?

After bragging about the various actions Citi has taken to reduce its own carbon footprint and to facilitate financing for "low-carbon solutions," Fraser wrote, "Our ESG agenda can't just be a separate layer that sits above what we do day-to-day. Our commitments to closing the gender pay gap, to advancing racial equity, and to pioneering the green agenda have demonstrated that this is good for business and not at odds with it. And we will continue to be part of the solution to these challenges and enable others to do so as well.[340]

"Net zero means rethinking our business and helping our clients rethink theirs," Fraser added. "For banks, what some don't realize is that net zero includes not just our own operations but also our core business impacts," including the bank's financing activities.

YEARS IN THE MAKING

It is not a coincidence that the announcement from Citi's CEO about the bank's commitment to shift toward a model that will eventually limit financing opportunities to businesses that fit into its ESG framework came within a month of Bank of America issuing a nearly identical promise. Thanks to a swift shove from government, the world's financial institutions have been moving in this direction for many years.

As Iain Murray, the vice president for strategy and a senior fellow at the Competitive Enterprise Institute, reported back in 2014 for the Blaze,

> Firearm sellers, pawn shops, payday lenders, and even porn stars around the nation have recently found their bank accounts canceled despite years of good relationships with their banks.
>
> When pressed, the banks say that it is because of heightened regulatory supervision of "high risk" industries. This has been traced back to a shadowy Obama administration program launched in 2013 called "Operation Choke Point." ... Operation Choke Point is a Department of Justice-led initiative aimed at "choking off" the financial oxygen of potential financial fraudsters who use Third Party Payment Processors (TPPPs) to process payments. It does this based on a 2011 guidance document from the Federal Deposit Insurance Corporation (FDIC)

on how banks should manage their relationships with TPPPs that deal with industries that might present "reputational risk" to the bank. Until recently, that guidance contained a list of about 30 "high risk" industries, including ammunition, drug paraphernalia, pornography, home-based charities, and many others.[341]

Once the public found out about Operation Choke Point, the backlash caused the leadership at the Federal Deposit Insurance Corporation to withdraw its list of "high-risk" industries. But as Murray noted, Operation Choke Point continued, "though in a slightly different guise." He explained,

> The underlying guidance about "reputational risk" remains unchanged. All the government has done is remove examples of what might constitute such risk from its websites. As a result, banks now have to judge for themselves what constitutes the sort of reputational risk that could trigger a federal subpoena.
>
> Meanwhile, Justice Department attorneys are using their own judgment about reputational risk to serve as a basis for whom to investigate. If today's focus is on payday lenders, who is to say, for example, that pornography will not be the next industry to come under the spotlight? ... What about a coal company, when so many are now convinced that coal pollutes the planet and the nation should move toward "renewable" energy?[342]

Although Operation Choke Point was eventually disbanded by the Trump administration in 2017,[343] a clear signal had been sent to banks and other financial institutions: don't do business with industries disfavored by many in the federal government.

Around the same time that 195 countries signed the Paris Climate Agreement in 2015, thereby committing to dramatically reduce their carbon dioxide emissions, banks and financial institutions around

the world—with Operation Choke Point and other, similar policies in mind—began to shift their focus heavily toward concerns
over climate change and how they could better position their businesses in a post-Paris Agreement world.

It started with the development of the Partnership for Carbon
Accounting Financials (PCAF) in 2015. PCAF members—which
include "commercial banks, development banks, asset owners/
managers, insurance companies, etc."—collaborate "to develop and
implement greenhouse gas (GHG) accounting in their organizations," as well as to help spur discussions on "climate change and the
role of the financial institution to facilitate the transition towards a
low-carbon society."[344]

PCAF-compliant financial institutions numbered more than
one hundred as of March 2021 and included many of the largest
institutions in America, such as Bank of America, Citi, Morgan
Stanley, and TD Bank.

Following the signing of the Paris Agreement, banks and financial institutions worked together to further develop and expand
rules, regulations, and guidelines to transform their industry,
culminating in the formation in 2019 of the U.N. Principles for
Responsible Banking (PRB), "the first-ever global sustainability
framework for the banking industry."[345]

PRB signatories "commit to align their business strategy and practice with the Sustainable Development Goals and the goals of the
Paris Climate Agreement"—or put more simply, signatories agree to
stop financing any business that refuses to adopt elites' climate change
mandates. As of September 2020, more than 190 banks had agreed
to the Principles for Responsible Banking, and these signatories "look
after the business of more than 1.6 billion customers worldwide and
represent around 40% of global banking assets."[346]

However, fear of government mandates is not the only thing
banks and financial institutions have had in mind when building

their Great Reset ESG frameworks. Perhaps most important of all is the promise of cold, hard cash.

THE PAYOFF

It is important to understand that the most corrupt—and terrifying—elements of the Great Reset also help explain why so many business leaders and financial institutions have agreed to promote this movement. Many have gone beyond mere promotion and even helped develop some of its primary components. This includes presidents and CEOs from Microsoft, Bank of America, Mastercard, BP, and other highly influential businesses and investment firms.[347]

The crony corporatists running these multibillion-dollar companies have seen the writing on the wall: governments around the world are increasingly pushing for "green" mandates and sustainable development, as well as restrictions on speech—whether businesses and their customers like it or not. Plus, central banks are literally printing trillions of dollars that governments are directing toward the causes they favor, including many focused on social justice. If you were running a business, especially a large multinational corporation, it would be stupid not to do everything in your power to get your hands on some of that "free" cash, right?

It is also worth noting that many investors and businesses are not waiting around for what they believe to be the inevitable rise of ESG standards and increased government action. Investors and large corporations do not merely plan twelve months into the future; they plan *twelve years* into the future. Instead of utilizing a potentially catastrophic wait-and-see approach, they are adopting policies now with the hope that it will put them in the good graces of the money printing overlords in central banks and governments across the planet, including the United States.

Nowhere has this been made clearer than in the presentations and articles posted to the website of the Principles for Responsible Investment (PRI) group, one of the world's most influential advocates for adopting ESG standards. In 2005, the United Nations brought together a group of twenty influential investors from twelve countries, as well as seventy experts from the investment industry, to develop the Principles for Responsible Investment.[348]

According to PRI, "The six Principles for Responsible Investment are a voluntary and aspirational set of investment principles that offer a menu of possible actions for incorporating ESG issues into investment practice. The Principles were developed by investors, for investors. In implementing them, signatories contribute to developing a more sustainable global financial system."[349]

When PRI officially launched in 2006, there were a total of one hundred signatories. Today there are more than three thousand, and together they control more than $100 trillion in assets. (Yes, you read that correctly—*$100 trillion.*)[350]

Although PRI is officially independent, it continues to work very closely with the United Nations and other Great Reset allies, and even though it's a purely voluntary association, it openly acknowledges that it fully expects governments to *demand* in the near future many of the so-called sustainable principles that it supports. Even more important, PRI's investors are convinced that governments and central banks will soon start shoveling even more cash into the coffers of all those businesses that agree to sign on to the Great Reset agenda.

You do not need to be a genius to see that the Principles for Responsible Investment group is more concerned with finding ways to profit off cronyism and government mandates than with fighting climate change or battling income inequality.

In a section of PRI's website titled "What Is the Inevitable Policy Response?" PRI states that "it is inevitable that governments will be forced to act more decisively than they have so far" on the issue of climate change.[351]

"The question for investors now is not if governments will act," PRI claims, "but when they will do so, what policies they will use and where the impact will be felt. The IPR [Inevitable Policy Response] project forecasts a response by 2025 that will be forceful, abrupt, and disorderly because of the delay."[352]

PRI then goes on to encourage its investors to focus on putting money into companies, projects, and other investments that are closely aligned with "green" energy. Why? Is it because PRI is full of people desperate to win the love and affection of Bernie Sanders and Alexandria Ocasio-Cortez? No. It is because green energy projects are where the government-printed, modern monetary theory money will be under Joe Biden and many other government administrations around the world over the next several years.

THE "BIG THREE"

It is tempting to think that government is the primary driver of corporations' move toward ESG and other woke causes, and it has undoubtedly played a significant role. However, perhaps the biggest reason so many corporations have agreed to adopt Great Reset principles in recent years is because of the voting power and influence of large Wall Street investment management companies, not the authority of government agencies.

In the previous section, I explained that investors are promoting ESG in part because they believe government regulations and spending programs are moving in that direction, and they don't want to be left behind when the Great Reset is fully in place. Corporations looking to attract new investors and raise their stock prices are reworking their business models to please these investors. But that's only part of the story. In many cases, corporations are effectively being *forced* to change by powerful investment groups. How can investment management firms coerce companies to enact radical new corporate policies, including ESG scoring systems? By owning so much stock that they can alter corporate policies through shareholder resolutions or even replace corporate board members who refuse to go along with the Great Reset.

The consolidation of stock ownership in the hands of a small group of investment management companies is a relatively new and exceedingly dangerous development. The three largest stock index fund managers—BlackRock, Vanguard, and State Street Global Advisors—have quadrupled their average combined stake in S&P 500 companies over the past two decades.[353]

According to research by Lucian Bebchuk, a professor at Harvard Law School, and Scott Hirst, an associate professor at the Boston University School of Law, the average ownership stake of the "Big Three" investment firms was 5.2 percent in 1998. In 2017, it was 20.5 percent. Even more important, the Big Three "collectively cast an average of about 25% of the votes at S&P 500 companies."[354] That means when the Big Three firms demand that corporate America jumps, most CEOs can respond only with, "How high?"

This consolidation of voting power is likely to get worse in the coming years. Bebchuk and Hirst believe "that the Big Three could well cast as much as 40% of the votes in S&P 500 companies within two decades."[355] If that were to occur, three Wall Street firms, working in conjunction with a relatively small group of other share-holders, could effectively control nearly all of corporate America.

Although the influence of the Big Three has yet to reach the 40 percent mark, many corporations today are effectively controlled by a combination of the ten investment groups and financial insti-tutions with the most assets under management. Collectively, the total assets controlled by the "Big Ten" investment groups—a list that includes goliaths like JPMorgan Chase, Fidelity, and Goldman

Sachs—are worth more than $34 trillion.[356] To put that into perspective, Americans spent $12.5 trillion on goods and services in 2020, and the total U.S. GDP in 2020 was less than $21 trillion.[357]

Many of the largest asset managers are deeply involved in the ESG movement, and some have openly supported the Great Reset. For example, Laurence Fink, the CEO of BlackRock, is on the board of directors at the World Economic Forum and is a vocal proponent of the Reset.[358]

State Street Global Advisors—the folks who installed the *Fearless Girl* statue across from Wall Street's bull statue as a publicity stunt in 2017—launched a widespread campaign in 2017 to force companies to have more women on their board of directors. The move was part of the company's strong commitment to ESG standards. In 2018, the publication *Institutional Investor* reported State Street expanded the policy and said it "will vote against the entire slate of board members on the nominating committee of any company not meeting its gender diversity criteria."[359]

According to the *Institutional Investor*, as of 2018, "State Street says that more than 300 companies have added a female board director in response to its demands, and that another 28 have pledged to do so."[360]

Additionally, it is important to note that every one of the ten largest asset managers has signed the Principles for Responsible Investment.[361]

As is often the case, if you want to truly understand why big corporations or large government agencies act the way they do, *follow the money*.

SHIFTING STANDARDS

Even if you happen to believe that banks and investment management groups should be shoving other businesses toward green energy and other environmental causes, it's important to remember the fluid nature of ESG standards. As I discussed earlier, many of the metrics in ESG systems revolve around environmental causes, but this does not mean that is where they end.

ESG elites have begun to add metrics that punish businesses who work with some weapons manufacturers. How long before firearm manufacturers and sellers lose access to business loans or other services because banks are worried about their precious ESG scores falling by a point or two? How long before fast-food giants and soda manufacturers are deemed "too dangerous" for the public health? Once the full ESG system imagined by Great Resetters is firmly in place, no business or industry will be able to survive the ire of the ruling-class elites who run it. Even individual politicians could be targeted.

In 2021, Americans witnessed some of the earliest attempts by banks to use their power to punish specific political figures in the United States. According to a report by Bloomberg.com, officials at Deutsche Bank and New York-based Signature Bank said in January 2021 they will no longer do business with Donald Trump, despite both banks' long-standing relationships with the Trump family and its businesses. According to the banks, the decision was based on political matters, not financial concerns.[362]

Even more stunning, Bloomberg.com further reported that Signature Bank announced it "will not do business in the future with any members of Congress who voted to disregard the electoral college," referring to members of the U.S. House and Senate who questioned the validity of the 2020 presidential races in several states after evidence emerged pointing to the possibility of voter fraud.[363]

Other industries and large corporations have also engaged in the targeting of individuals. Shortly after the January 6, 2021, riots at the U.S. Capitol, book publisher Simon & Schuster announced the cancellation of Senator Josh Hawley's book *The Tyranny of Big*

Tech. In Simon & Schuster's announcement, they vaguely alluded to Hawley's demands for investigations into potential voter fraud occurring during the 2020 presidential election as the primary reason for the cancellation. Simon & Schuster also suggested that by demanding election investigations, Hawley helped to encourage the riots—a ludicrous assertion.[364]

Even more troubling, courts will likely do very little to stop ESG's infringement of individual liberties, because ESG standards don't necessarily need to be controlled by government directly. So whenever international elites wanted to manipulate society, silence political opponents, or engage in otherwise horrifying, tyrannical behavior, all they would have to do under an ESG system would be to add another metric or two to the global ESG framework, and they could effectively nullify free speech (an issue I discuss more extensively later on), the right to keep and bear arms, or a number of other constitutionally protected rights. And this all could be accomplished without the consent of the American people.

YOUR VERY OWN ESG SCORE

Some might be tempted to think, "Yeah, well, I'm not a politician, gun rights group, or oil company, so I've got nothing to worry about." But that's a *huge* mistake. If banks and other financial institutions can target well-funded special interest groups, President Trump, and sitting members of Congress, some of the most powerful and influential people in the world, what makes you believe they would think twice about debanking, silencing, or punishing *you*, regardless of your political views, if you belong to a political group, club, organization, association, religion, or business considered to be standing in the way of elites' goals?

The framework for providing ESG scores to Main Street Americans—not just big companies—has already been built. You might have investment accounts that have received ESG scores without your even knowing about it.

In March 2021, a friend of mine who works for a think tank and is well acquainted with the Great Reset—let's call him Chris—reached out to my staff after he discovered that his account with Merrill Lynch, one of the world's largest investment services companies (and a subsidiary of Bank of America), had been given an ESG score. The score had been formulated by examining the ESG scores of the various companies Chris had invested in.

Now, Chris is just a regular guy with a 401(k) retirement account. He's young and doesn't have an investment portfolio overflowing with cash. He's a regular, hardworking guy—probably very similar to a lot of people reading this book now. He never asked for his investments to be given an ESG score, and he wasn't happy—to say the least—to find that his ESG score was an abysmal 4.7 out of 10. (What a degenerate!) But Merrill Lynch gave him an ESG score anyway, and because they are such nice people over there, they also offered guidance on how Chris could improve his account's ESG score in the future.

Are you getting nervous yet? You should be.

In full disclosure, my research team has been contacted by a very large financial institution that wasn't happy with the warnings about ESG scores that I have issued on my radio and television shows. The bank, which I will not name here because the conversation was off the record, controls *hundreds of billions of dollars in assets*. Now, the financial institution's main complaint was *not* that my reporting on ESG scores has been factually inaccurate but rather that my fears about ESG scores are overblown. In conversations with my staff, bank officials insisted that they were not forcing individual investors to do anything based on an account's ESG score. And that is true—for now.

But the most terrifying part of the Great Reset's ESG system is not what they are doing today (although there's plenty there to worry about, to be sure); it's what could be done with these ESG scores and other, similar metrics in the future. The framework to manipulate and control the economy is being built now. Much of it has been in place for years, and we did not even know it.

A huge number of the world's largest, wealthiest corporations have already bought into the ESG system. They have employees who spend most of their days conducting internal audits related specifically to ESG scoring. CEOs from all over the world are regularly working with groups like the World Economic Forum to refine and expand ESG scores.

The SEC, as we've already shown, is now getting involved in ESG reporting and beginning the process of issuing ESG-related regulations. S&P Global, the organization that produces the S&P 500 and Dow Jones Industrial Average stock indexes, now even has an S&P 500 ESG stock index.[365]

Investment companies like Merrill Lynch have started providing individual investors, even people with relatively small accounts, with ESG scores based on the stocks and index funds they have invested in.

Bank of America, Citi, and other large banks have said that they are going to use their considerable wealth and power "to accelerate the transition to a net zero global economy," in part by requiring their "financing activities, operations and supply chain" to go "green."[366]

President Trump, special interest groups, and members of Congress have been banned from doing business with some banks and retailers because of their political views.

Politicians and pundits, some of whom have millions of followers, have been banned or censored on social media platforms—a problem we will discuss at length in the next section—for speaking out about the possibility of election fraud or for questioning the justification given by elites for stopping people from attending church services in the midst of a pandemic, while also encouraging protesters to take to the streets by the tens of thousands to demand social justice.

China has already developed and started to roll out a social credit system that includes "a set of databases and initiatives that monitor and assess the trustworthiness of individuals, companies and government entities." According to the *South China Morning Post*, "Each entry"—meaning a human being—"is given a social credit score, with reward for those who have a high rating and punishments for those with low scores."[367]

Businesses in China are also subjected to a credit scoring system. "Business entities, including foreign businesses in China, are subject to a corporate credit system, tracking information such as tax payments, bank loan repayments and employment disputes," the *Morning Post* also reported.

And who are the key people in charge of running China's social credit system? Government bureaucrats and banks.

According to the *Morning Post*, "The databases are managed by China's economic planner, the National Development and Reform Commission (NDRC), the People's Bank of China (PBOC) and the country's court system."[368]

Does any of this sound familiar to you? It's almost as though Klaus Schwab took his ESG playbook directly from China—or that China took Schwab's ideas, which have been around for more than fifty years, and put them into action long before anyone in America had ever heard of environmental, social, and governance metrics.

In our modern world—which is full of authoritarian power grabs, a growing divide between ruling-class elites and everyone else, endless money printing, "golden opportunity" pandemics, a dishonest media, and the emergence of an authoritarian China as a global superpower—you would have to be certifiably insane if you weren't at least a little concerned about the possibility of every regular Joe and Jane in America receiving a score measuring how closely their investment decisions align with those of the ruling class.

BIG TECH TYRANTS

Much of the Great Reset is focused on economic changes, but it would be a mistake to think that Resetters are not interested in making expansive alterations to other parts of society as well. As WEF head Klaus Schwab wrote in June 2020, "To achieve a better outcome, the world must act jointly and swiftly to revamp *all aspects of our societies* and economies, from education to social contracts and working conditions."[369]

But what exactly do Schwab and other Resetters have in mind when they make these far-reaching statements? At the very least, it includes left-wing ideas about enhancing "social justice," as countless articles published on the World Economic Forum's website illustrate.

In October 2020, David Sangokoya, the head of the WEF's Civil Society Communities and Social Justice Initiatives, authored an article titled "Social Justice, Inclusion and Sustainable Development Need a 'Great Reset.' Here Are 3 Key Steps We Can Take."[370]

In the article, Sangokoya summarizes the findings of a September 2020 WEF meeting of "more than 3,800 leaders from government, business and civil society" called the Sustainable Development Impact Summit. According to Sangokoya, "Sessions [held at the summit] on social justice were of significant interest to business leaders navigating the ramifications of the pandemic and how to define their stakeholder responsibilities to social justice and sustainability."[371]

Sangokoya then describes the "three key takeaways" from the summit "on driving a Great Reset in social justice, inclusion and sustainable development impact," including this one: "Widespread environmental crises and global Black Lives Matter protests have sparked palpable restlessness for change. There is a need to accelerate both sustainability and social justice agendas—from both employees and consumers."[372]

Of course, over the past few years, we've learned that one of the ways corporations can "accelerate" social justice agendas is to stifle the free speech of anyone who stands in the way of the Great Reset—or any other cause embraced by elites, for that matter. That's why the Great Reset agenda includes the WEF's Global Alliance for Responsible Media. (They never seem to run out of new Orwellian names for their little authoritarian clubs, do they?)

The purpose of the Global Alliance for Responsible Media is to partner corporations and advertisers with publishers and platforms to "do more to address harmful and misleading media environments; and to develop and deliver against a concrete set of actions, processes and protocols for protecting brands."[373]

According to WEF, among the perceived "problems" publishers and platforms need to do more to address are "bullying," "hate speech," and "disinformation," all of which are words regularly used by elites to unfairly smear, well, just about anyone who does not agree with their vision for the world.

Some European countries have already started requiring social media companies to restrict free speech. In May 2020, CNN reported, "The French parliament passed a controversial hate speech law . . . that would fine social media companies if they fail to remove certain illegal content within 24 hours—and in some cases, as little as one hour."[374]

CNN further reported, "The new regulation calls for the tech platforms to remove hateful comments—based on race, religion, sexual orientation, gender or disability, as well as sexual harass-ment—within 24 hours after they are flagged by users."[375]

Companies that fail to comply with the twenty-four-hour rule would be fined as much as $1.36 million per violation, but there would be "no fines if platforms prematurely remove content that is later deemed acceptable."[376]

The law was based on similar legislation already in place in Germany, the Network Enforcement Act, which mandates that social media companies "remove hate speech and fake news within 24 hours of it being flagged, or face penalties of up to roughly $60 million," according to CNN. "They also must publish reports every six months detailing the number of complaints of illegal content they have received."[377]

Courts struck down much of the French law in June 2020 for violating the country's constitution,[378] but that has not stopped some affiliated with the World Economic Forum from continuing to promote similar mandates.

WEF continues to display on its website a March 2018 article titled "How Technology Can Be Used to Combat Online Hate Speech," authored by La Trobe University lecturer Andre Oboler. In the article, Oboler suggested that "government should follow the lead of Germany in imposing financial penalties on major social media companies if they fail to reduce the volume of abusive content on their platforms."[379]

Oboler further said that "we must develop ways of correctly identifying and measuring the amount of abusive content being posted and removed to ensure that companies are complying."

Although it is unlikely such a law would survive a challenge in the U.S. Supreme Court, it is vital to remember that a model like the one proposed by supporters of the Great Reset would work around the free speech protections guaranteed by the First Amendment, because it would not *mandate* that companies do anything to stop free speech; it would just heavily coerce them into eliminating speech, until they effectively have no choice but to act in line with the demands of the ruling class.

It is not hard to imagine how Great Reset ideas about limiting speech, especially when coupled with the other Great Reset initiatives previously discussed, could result in an unprecedented and dangerous assault on speech in the United States. This is especially true for conservatives and other free speech advocates, who are already experiencing the earliest stages of the Left's digital purge of freethinkers, conservative voices, and even some political figures.

In the wake of the riots at the U.S. Capitol building in January 2021, which occurred following a rally promoted by President Trump, a long list of social media companies banned Trump from using their services, including Facebook, Instagram, Snapchat, and Twitter.[380] But social media platforms did not stop at President Trump himself. An unprecedented wave of social media bans soon followed that spread well beyond Trump.

As the *Federalist*'s Joy Pullmann noted in a January 2021 column, "The purge wasn't at all limited to Trump himself. It's also pursuing his supporters. YouTube banned all videos discussing voter fraud. Reddit shut down its Donald Trump subreddit. On Jan. 8, Facebook shut down the Walkaway campaign that shared the stories of people who left the Democratic Party to vote for Trump, and banned every one of the group's owners from using Facebook."[381]

Facebook also permanently banned clothing retailer PatrioticMe from advertising any of its products on its platform, apparently for violating some unknown Facebook "community standard." To give you a sense of some of the *dangerous* products offered by PatrioticMe, read the following description of the site by one reporter covering the ban: "The apparel sold by PatrioticMe has, well, an obvious patriotic flair. These are shirts adorned with red, white, and blue or an outline of the United States. Hoodies with the American flag.

Hats you could proudly wear to your Fourth of July cookout and every other day too, just because you love America."[382]

According to the same reporter, "A portion of every sale [made on PatrioticMe] is donated to the Tunnel to Towers Foundation, a charity founded to honor the sacrifice of New York City firefighter Stephen Siller, who gave his life to save others as a first responder on Sept. 11, 2001. Tunnel to Towers provides mortgage-free smart homes to veterans or first responders with catastrophic injuries suffered in the line of duty or to gold star families with surviving spouses and young children."[383]

Wow, what a bunch of monsters. I sure am glad Facebook is cracking down on the sale of all those violence-inducing "hoodies with the American flag" that are helping veterans and first responders gain access to mortgage-free homes.

Then there was AR15.com, "the biggest gun forum in the world." AR15.com committed the unspeakable crime of letting law-abiding Americans talk online about firearms and gun ownership—a constitutionally protected, God-given right, by the way. Hosting company GoDaddy suddenly terminated access to the website in January 2021 for allegedly violating GoDaddy's terms of service, without initially providing any detailed explanation for the decision or the ability to appeal.[384] But as bad as these attacks on speech were, they pale in comparison to the shocking treatment of Parler, an online social media platform similar to Twitter.

In 2018, after years of social media companies deplatforming, mistreating, and unfairly targeting conservatives, including many of the people who work for my media company, Blaze Media, John Matze and Jared Thomson launched a new platform, Parler.[385] Unlike establishment social media platforms such as Facebook and Twitter, Parler promised to protect users' privacy and promote free speech by allowing voices from all walks of life to share their political, religious, or ideological views without fear of being punished by Big Tech or its flawed algorithms. Rather than rely on unaccountable speech police at companies like Google and Facebook, Parler empowered users with a wealth of tools to customize their experience on the platform.

Contrary to what you will read in dishonest mainstream media outlets, Parler was not a "conservative" social media platform. Anyone could join, and many people who were not conservative did.

Parler's rise to prominence was nothing short of amazing. After initially numbering only thousands of users, Parler's user list skyrocketed into the *millions* within just two years of its launch. In July 2020, Parler reported 2.8 million users, and by early November 2020, the app reported 8 million users. In the week following the 2020 election alone, "Parler gained more than 3.5 million users, putting it at the top of Apple's App Store list of free apps."[386]

By the end of November, the number of users on Parler hit 10 million, and at the conclusion of 2020, the app's user base was on track to hit 20 million in 2021. Countless media outlets, politicians, and radio hosts had joined in 2020—myself included. On Apple's iOS app store, the application used by every single iPhone user in the world to download new applications for their phone, Parler had recorded a whopping 8.1 million new installs in 2020, making it the tenth most downloaded social media application in the store over the course of the year.[387]

Parler was well on its way to becoming a real competitor to establishment social media giants at the start of 2021, with some analysts anticipating that the value of the company could soon be $1 billion or more. But all of that soon changed. The *New York Times* recorded the incredible chain of events in a January 13 news report—see, I told you I read the *New York Times*—which noted, "By Saturday morning, Apple listed Parler as the No. 1 free app for its iPhones. But, by Saturday night, Parler was suddenly fighting for its life."[388]

The *Times* further reported, "First, Apple and Google removed the app from their app stores because they said it had not sufficiently policed its users' posts, allowing too many that encouraged violence and crime. Then, late Saturday, Amazon told Parler it would boot the company from its web-hosting service on Sunday night because of repeated violations of Amazon's rules."[389]

"Amazon's move meant that Parler's entire platform would soon go offline unless it was able to find a new hosting service on Sunday," the *Times* added.

The Sunday deadline came and went, and as expected, Amazon shut Parler down. Parler initially anticipated that it could quickly shift its operations to an Amazon competitor, but one web hosting service after another refused Parler's business, and it was not long before other third-party vendors and businesses also banned Parler from using their services.

Within just one week of the moves by Apple, Google, and Amazon—three of the wealthiest, most powerful companies on the planet, all of which are run by people hostile to conservatism—Parler's CEO announced that one of the only services the platform still had up and running was its company email account.

The justification used by Big Tech to attack the country's most popular social media outlet guaranteeing free political speech is that Parler had not done enough to remove posts considered dangerous by Amazon, Apple, and Google. The legacy media was quick to come to the aid of these tech tyrants, insisting—often without providing any evidence—that Parler had become a bastion of hate and extremism.

Contrary to the unfair characterizations of Parler appearing in many biased media outlets, Parler did not and does not now allow users to post literally anything they want. Parler's terms of service prohibit all sorts of material considered harmful to the platform's community. In a July 2020 article for the left-leaning online publication *The Conversation*, academic Audrey Courty reviewed Parler's terms of service and community standards and found that "a closer look at its user agreement suggests it moderates content the same way as any platform, maybe even more."[390]

Courty also noted,

> Parler's community guidelines prohibit a range of content including spam, terrorism, unsolicited ads, defamation, blackmail, bribery and criminal behaviour.
>
> Although there are no explicit rules against hate speech, there are policies against "fighting words" and "threats of harm." This includes "a threat of or advocating for violation against an individual or group."
>
> There are rules against content that is obscene, sexual or "lacks serious literary, artistic, political and scientific value." For example, visuals of genitalia, female nipples, or faecal matter are barred from Parler.[391]

Courty's analysis is generally in line with other reports by media about Parler that were published throughout 2020. Numerous media outlets went out of their way to talk about how even though Parler's marketing campaign presented the platform as a free speech haven, Parler also frequently moderated content considered extremely offensive or violent. Some critics of Parler even suggested the platform was hypocritical for doing so.

Newsweek published an article titled "Parler, the Ted Cruz-Approved 'Free Speech' App, Is Already Banning Users."[392] Fortune.com posted an article in July 2020 titled, "Conservative Social Media Darling Parler Discovers That Free Speech Is Messy."[393] The *Washington Post* published a piece called "The Conservative Alternative to Twitter Wants to Be a Place for Free Speech for All. It Turns Out, Rules Still Apply."[394]

It was not until Parler's popularity soared to even greater heights that the platform suddenly became, in the eyes of the media, an ultraviolent website that *must* be closed down because, according to the press, only radical extremists use it.

In addition to being misleading and/or factually incorrect, many of the criticisms leveled against Parler in 2021 were wildly hypocritical. It is true that there were (and probably still are) some vile, disgusting, and violent posts on Parler. And I do believe Parler should have done more to remove such content, and to do it more quickly. Parler officials themselves admitted that they had a backlog of thousands of complaints at the time Amazon took the site down.

However, it is also true that Facebook, Twitter, and Google regularly hosted equally vile, disgusting, and violent rhetoric. And no one knows that better than I do—well, no one except for Donald Trump. My family and I have been subject to tens of thousands of threats, personal attacks, and foul insults over the years through social media platforms. And that's just counting the mean stuff my producer Stu has written about me.

I have not seen a shred of evidence to suggest that Facebook and Twitter have permanently banned all the users who posted this material about me, my staff, and my family, much of which, I'm sure, violates their community standards. (And I know for a fact that Stu is still allowed to post his nonsensical rantings all over the internet.)

Facebook, Google, and Twitter have also routinely been used by violent groups to stage riots and events meant to cause destruction and impose fear—including groups associated with the January 2021 Capitol Hill riot. Further, there is no denying that social media platforms like Twitter and Facebook have in some cases gone out of their way to *protect* accounts controlled by truly dangerous political or social leaders.

Take, for example, the Twitter account of Ayatollah Ali Khamenei, the supreme dictator—eh, I mean "supreme leader"—of Iran, a country that has for decades violated human rights, supported terrorism, destabilized the Middle East, and even waged a stealth war against the United States. While accounts and tweets from conservatives were being banned by Twitter's thought police in 2020 and 2021, Khamenei's account and its many violent tweets remained intact, including one from 2018 that reads, "Our stance against Israel is the same stance we have always taken. #Israel is a malignant cancerous tumor in the West Asian region that has to be removed and eradicated: it is possible and it will happen."[395]

How many of Twitter's standards do you think Khamenei violated with that whopper? Or perhaps calling for the genocide of a historically abused religious and ethnic group does not mean much to Twitter? I suppose it is true Khamenei could be worse in the eyes of the social media speech police—at least he didn't vote for Donald Trump, right?

Further, Twitter continues to allow radicals like Louis Farrakhan and Chinese propagandists to regularly spew false information to their huge social media followings. And Twitter and other social media giants have also refused to warn readers when pundits spread demonstrably false information and conspiracy theories about "Russian collusion," including claims that were widely debunked years ago.

They have also chosen not to silence politicians who have openly called for people to harass government officials in the Trump administration and conservative public figures, nor have they banned users who openly sympathized with the rioters who burned and looted cities throughout the summer of 2020.

In 2018, Congresswoman Maxine Waters told her supporters, "If you see anybody from that Cabinet [in the Trump administration] in a restaurant, in a department store, at a gasoline station, you get out and you create a crowd and you push back on them, and you tell them they're not welcome anymore, anywhere."[396]

That sure sounds like Representative Waters is inciting criminal activity, doesn't it? Yet Twitter continues to allow Maxine to engage with her 1.6 million followers on its platform on a daily basis.

CNN host Chris Cuomo—the brother of Andrew Cuomo, everyone's least favorite *Sopranos* character and one of the worst governors in American history—said in the midst of a period of widespread rioting and looting in the summer of 2020, "And please, show me where it says protesters are supposed to be polite and peaceful. Because I can show you that outraged citizens are what made the country what she is and led to any major milestone. To be honest, this is not a tranquil time."[397]

Yet Chris Cuomo is still able to communicate with his 2.1 million Twitter followers every single day.

In waging its war on Parler, Big Tech could not have been clearer: If you are a free speech–friendly platform that tries to limit violent speech but struggles, like all social media companies, to root out every single vile post, you deserve to be destroyed. But if you are a media outlet or platform that allows or promotes dangerous, reckless, or misleading information but generally still favors and promotes causes that ruling-class elites and their allies like, then you deserve special legal protections that allow Big Tech investors to earn billions of dollars and amass unprecedented amounts of power.

Welcome to the start of the Great Reset, ladies and gentlemen.

Some Americans on the left and even some libertarians on the right argue that Americans should not be concerned about digital crackdowns on speech. We are frequently told, "Private companies can do whatever they want to control speech on their platforms. It's the free market." But the truth is, there is nothing "free" about Big Tech's actions, and there won't be anything "free market" about a Great Reset ESG system that awards woke companies for stifling speech. Companies will merely be acting to stay on the good side of government and big financial institutions, as many do now, because that is where the money will be in a world dominated by ESG scores and modern monetary theorists like Stephanie Kelton.

When confronted with arguments alleging that anyone who stands against Big Tech tyrants is working against free market capitalism, it is important to remember that corporations— whether they be massive online retailers or social media giants like Facebook—are themselves the products of government. Not only are corporations subject to countless regulations governing their behavior, but they are also made possible only by special laws that do not exist in a marketplace free of government interference.

Big corporations do not pay the same tax rates as individuals, operate under many of the same rules as individuals, or face the same legal liabilities as individuals. And that is especially true of numerous large technology companies, which in countless cases are able to exist only because federal law allows them to avoid lawsuits when users post illegal or defamatory content on their platforms.

There used to be a time when even many elites understood that corporations should not have unlimited power. Consider the following quote from the opinion issued in 1946 by the Supreme Court in *Marsh v. Alabama*, a case in which the court determined that a private corporation could not prohibit a Jehovah's Witness from distributing religious materials in a company-owned town, because the ban was in violation of the First Amendment.

"Ownership does not always mean absolute dominion," wrote Hugo Black, a justice appointed by one of the twentieth century's most progressive presidents, Franklin Roosevelt. "The more an owner, for his advantage, opens up his property for use by the public in general, the more do his rights become circumscribed by the statutory and constitutional rights of those who use it. Thus, the owners of privately held bridges, ferries, turnpikes and railroads may not operate them as freely as a farmer does his farm."[398]

Make no mistake about it, large corporations ought to be given a great deal of authority over their products, services, and property, but it should never be forgotten that corporations are not divine institutions fully endowed with inalienable rights but rather the creations of government that exist to offer to the public—*everyone* in the public—goods and services. There is no reason why they should have the power to silence political or religious speech, and Americans who are demanding that corporations be required to promote individual rights as a condition of having access to special legal protections ought not to feel even slightly ashamed for doing so.

IT CAN'T HAPPEN HERE—WAIT, CAN IT?

When I talk to others about the Great Reset, I am often met at first with a healthy dose of skepticism. Not only is all that "stakeholder capitalist" language misleading and confusing, but many people also have difficulty accepting that something like the Reset really could happen in America. This is, after all, the home of the largest, most powerful financial markets on the planet, the world's most profitable companies, and the biggest and best economic engine humankind has ever seen. "Yeah, Glenn, we get it. Those Europeans love big government systems and elitism, and they have cozied up to fascism before. But America is not Europe. What are you so worried about?"

Well, in addition to snakes—I *really* hate snakes—I am worried that many of the leaders of the biggest institutions in the world, from the United Nations and the International Monetary Fund to multibillion-dollar corporations on Wall Street, have started adopting many of the Great Reset's principles and promoting its expansion. And many of the people involved are American and have already started to promote the Reset in the United States.

According to a report by KPMG, *thousands* of companies, located in more than fifty countries, already have ESG systems in place, including 82 percent of large companies in the United States.[399] Further, American financial institutions have already built massive ESG databases to track and even predict companies' ESG scores.

Moody's database has more than 140 million company ESG scores, covering 220 countries, and it now sells a tool to help banks, corporations, and other institutions *predict* the ESG scores of small- and medium-sized companies around the world, including countless companies that have never once submitted ESG data or reports.[400] That means if you do not turn an ESG report in to Moody's, it might invent one for you, whether you like it or not.

Most important, although it has not received nearly enough media attention—shocking, I know—many politicians, activists, and bureaucrats in Washington, D.C., support the Great Reset's policies and are deeply committed to making them a reality, even if they do not typically use the "Great Reset" slogan on the campaign trail or in the halls of Congress. And first among them is none other than President Joe Biden.

The Biden administration and its allies are not merely calling for Great Reset policies; they have already started to put in place the policy and regulatory framework necessary to make the Reset a reality. And they have done so at a speed that, at the end of the Trump administration, almost no one thought was possible.

How exactly are the Biden administration and other elites planning on altering American society in line with Great Reset principles? That is the subject of my next chapter.

6

JOE BIDEN AND THE GREAT RESET OF AMERICA

Why should Russians have all the fun of remaking a world?
—Stuart Chase, an Adviser to President Franklin
Roosevelt, in his book *A New Deal*, 1932

THE FIRST FIFTY YEARS OF THE TWENTIETH CENTURY WERE filled with nearly unimaginable horror and despair. Twenty million people died in World War I, the "war to end all wars," and another 21 million were wounded. As many as 100 million people perished during the 1918–1919 influenza outbreak.[401] Seventy-five million people were killed during World War II, including the millions of European Jews who were murdered during the Nazis' Holocaust.

During the Dust Bowl and Great Depression, 15 million Americans were unemployed, and the United States faced unprecedented chaos in its financial industry. Nearly half of all U.S. banks failed.[402] Segregation gripped the Southern United States, severely limiting the opportunities and rights of African Americans. The *Titanic*—the world's first "unsinkable ship"—sank.

However, despite these grave tragedies, the United States endured—and in many respects, significantly progressed—offering periods of immense, positive economic and societal changes. The horse-driven carriage was replaced by the motor vehicle. Widespread access to electricity transformed America's economy and dramatically improved living standards. The Wright brothers showed the world that humans could take flight. More than 15 million people emigrated to America's shores from 1900 to 1915, helping to push the U.S. economy far beyond its global competitors and greatly expanding the country's urban centers.[403]

For better or worse, the period from 1900 to the end of World War II is best defined by one word: *disruption*. And as has always been the case in human history, whenever there is disruption, there is great opportunity for radical change. Or as they are fond of saying in America's favorite television documentary series, *Game of Thrones*, "Chaos is a ladder."

The rise of progressivism in the United States in the early twentieth century would not have been possible without the era's tremendous disruption. Progressives knew this, and they took advantage. In the early days of the Progressive movement, leaders developed a playbook for remaking society by shifting power into the hands of elites, who would use centralized bureaucratic agencies, international organizations, and large businesses and financial institutions to enact their far-reaching reforms. Although progressive elites' plan has gone through a variety of phases, it has remained mostly unchanged over the past one hundred years. The faces and some methods have evolved, to be sure, but the foundational goals and strategies are nearly identical to those established at the start of the Progressive Era.

One of the clearest articulations for progressives' plan for a new society was revealed in the 1940s by Stuart Chase, perhaps the most influential American economist of his time and a member of President Franklin Delano Roosevelt's famous "brain trust."[404] Chase is most famous in progressive and socialist circles today for developing the "New Deal" political slogan later adopted by FDR.[405]

In the early 1940s, the Twentieth Century Fund, an influential organization devoted to promoting progressive causes, commissioned Chase to write a series of small books called *When the War Ends*.[406] The purpose of the book series was to advocate for the advancement of a new society following the conclusion of World War II.

In the first book of the series, titled *The Road We Are Traveling*, published in 1942, Chase claims there is no hope of returning to a "system of free enterprise" at the conclusion of the war. Why? Because, according to Chase, "the basic conditions which made it a good and workable system for a century and more, have so changed that it has now become unworkable over great areas."[407]

In its place, Chase believed, the global economy had already started the process of transforming into something entirely new, a "managerial revolution" that is "displacing the system of free enterprise, all over the world." Because this "revolution" had not yet been named, Chase called it simply "X."

Chase's vision for a novel economic model was not merely part of a proposed alteration of society; it was viewed by Chase and others as *essential* and even *inevitable*. In Chase's mind, the world was moving toward system X, whether Americans liked it or not, and although he acknowledged that some folks might be worried by such a change, Chase, like most elitist progressives of the period, believed everyone would be better off under a "managerial" state.

"Win, lose or draw," Chase wrote, "we can never return to the world of 1928, or even of 1939. This may alarm many Americans but it does not alarm me. The old world was not so perfect that a better one cannot be found."[408]

In *The Road We Are Traveling*, Chase outlined the framework of that "better" world, much of which had already become the guiding principles of the Roosevelt administration prior to the start of World War II.[409] In a subsection of his book, titled "Free Enterprise into 'X,'" Chase listed eighteen characteristics of X:

+ A strong, centralized government.
+ An executive arm growing at the expense of the legislative and judicial arms. In some countries, power is consolidated in a dictator, issuing decrees.
+ The control of banking, credit and security exchanges by the government.
+ The underwriting of employment by the government, either through armaments or public works.
+ The underwriting of social security by the government— old-age pensions, mothers' pensions, unemployment insurance, and the like.
+ The underwriting of food, housing and medical care by the government. The United States is already experimenting with providing these essentials. Other nations are far along the road.
+ The use of the deficit spending technique to finance these underwritings. The annually balanced budget has lost its old-time sanctity.
+ The abandonment of gold in favor of managed currencies.

+ The control of foreign trade by the government, with increasing emphasis on bilateral agreements and barter deals.

+ The control of natural resources, with increasing emphasis on self-sufficiency.

+ The control of energy sources—hydroelectric power, coal, petroleum, natural gas.

+ The control of transportation—railway, highway, airway, waterway.

+ The control of agricultural production.

+ The control of labor organizations, often to the point of prohibiting strikes.

+ The enlistment of young men and women in youth corps devoted to health, discipline, community service and ideologies consistent with those of the authorities. The CCC camps have just inaugurated military drill.

+ Heavy taxation, with especial emphasis on the estates and incomes of the rich.

+ Not much "taking over" of property or industries in the old socialistic sense. The formula appears to be control without ownership. It is interesting to recall that the same formula is used by the management of great corporations in depriving stockholders of power.

+ The state control of communications and propaganda.[410]

Chase is very clear that not every single part of X ought to be pursued in the manner in which it had been imposed outside of the United States. For example, it appears Chase was not an advocate of dictatorships, despite having acknowledged that some forms of system X included totalitarian rule. However, for Chase, system X was the future. "It is a question not of kind but of degree," he wrote.[411]

Throughout the 1930s and 1940s, American progressive elites set out to implement their own version of system X, and to a large extent they were successful.

By the end of the Franklin Roosevelt administration, more federal social programs had been created than at any other time in U.S. history. Instead of relying primarily on a belief in the power of the free markets and individual choice, millions of Americans became dependent on the federal government's Civilian Conservation Corps (CCC), Farm Security Administration (FSA), Resettlement Administration (RA), National Youth Administration (NYA), and countless other alphabet soup government bureaucracies.

Progressives also used the era's disruption to transform government and financial institutions. State legislatures lost their ability to elect U.S. senators. The size of the House of Representatives was permanently capped at 435, all but ensuring the creation and maintenance of a legislative oligarchy in Washington, D.C. Federal bureaucracies seized more and more power from state and local governments. The Federal Reserve System was created, and federal officials began the process of ending the gold standard, paving the way for massive future government debt.

Progressives' vision for establishing a vast federal bureaucracy of "experts" to manage society was well on its way to becoming fully realized from 1900 to 1940, and then again during President Lyndon Johnson's "Great Society" reforms in the 1960s. Fortunately, pushback from political opponents, several key losses in the Supreme Court, the conclusion of World War II, and most important, the rise of totalitarian communism in China and Russia thwarted progressives' plan to impose X—not entirely but enough to stop them from reaching their ultimate goal.

By the end of the Reagan administration in 1989, communism had largely been defeated, and the political and social winds had shifted back in favor of conservatism and limited government.

Ronald Reagan's brilliant public relations strategy for defeating the Soviets—which focused on the fundamental differences between free, capitalistic societies and the brutal socialistic models used by regimes in places like the Soviet Union and Cuba—inspired a new generation to recognize and appreciate America's exceptional past and foundational goals.

For the most part, conservative values dominated the post–Soviet era, until, that is, President Barack Obama rose to power—which, as at the start of the Progressive Era, was largely the result of an ineffective Republican president and a government-created crisis, the financial system's collapse in 2008.

Like the end of FDR's reign, the final year of the Obama era was full of optimism for progressives. After decades of failing to recapture the momentum enjoyed during the days of FDR's New Deal and Lyndon Johnson's Great Society, President Obama managed to get the country moving back toward the vision of reshaping American society imagined by President Wilson, FDR, and influential intellectuals of the Progressive Era, like Stuart Chase.

In 2016, Hillary Clinton was well positioned to finish what Obama started, but then something happened, something remarkable—and I mean "remarkable" in nearly every sense of the word. Donald Trump, a reality television star and real estate mogul, was elected president of the United States, a feat he managed to accomplish by running on an "America First" platform that denounced most of the essential parts of system X. And whether you love him or loathe him, if you're fair-minded, you have to admit that there's a good chance that had the COVID-19 pandemic never occurred, Donald Trump would still be president today.

As I discussed at length in chapter 2, it was COVID-19 that provided global elites with another "golden opportunity" to reset the world's economy and finish the job started by European and American elites in the Progressive Era.[412] Today's Great Reset movement is attempting to write the final chapter of a story that began more than a century ago, not in 2020, as so many believe.

The Great Reset is nothing but a more perfected version of system X. Like Chase's framework, the Great Reset depends on a powerful, centralized government led by large executive branch government bureaucracies. Similarly, the Reset depends on the control of banking, credit, and security exchanges. It also involves huge social programs like those dreamed up by Chase. The Green New Deal and European Green Deal were even named after Chase and FDR's "New Deal" reforms.

The Great Reset also requires the use of "managed currencies." Without such a system, modern monetary theory, the fuel of the Great Reset machine, would be impossible.

Further, the Reset depends on "control of agricultural production," "transportation," and "energy sources,"[413] right in line with Chase's description of system X.

"Heavy taxation" is another shared component of system X and the Great Reset, as is system X's government "control without ownership"—the primary purpose of environmental, social, and governance metrics.

With all this in mind, it is clear that system X *is* the Great Reset, and the Great Reset *is* system X.

Understanding that the Great Reset is part of a much larger narrative is vital for many reasons, but perhaps the most important is that it reveals just how close we are to seeing our national sovereignty, right to self-determination, and protections for individual liberty slip away. Within the larger historical context, the movement for individual liberty is hanging on by a thread. We have been fighting this battle for more than a century, and we are now seemingly one breath away from catastrophe.

For those of you who still think that President Biden and America's other leaders in the Democratic and Republican Parties are working for you and that they would never let Great Reset elites transform the United States so they have even greater power over Main Street America, the remainder of this chapter is going to be a rough wake-up call.

President Biden might present himself as a Scranton-born, Corn Pop-fighting, lunch pail-carrying champion of blue-collar America, but he and numerous members of his administration, as well as many of Biden's closest political allies outside of the White House, are as devoted to the globalist, corporatist principles of the Great Reset as anyone working at the World Economic Forum has ever been. And numerous members of Congress and key social and political leaders are right there with him. Their mission is to finish the implementation of system X under the Great Reset banner, and they will not stop until they succeed where so many others before them have fallen short.

Countless members of the press have argued that this is all just a wild conspiracy theory cooked up by the "far right" to scare you. Why should you believe Glenn Beck when the New York Times is portraying the Great Reset in a completely different light? Well, here's something you won't hear the New York Times say, especially when it comes to the Great Reset: Do not take my word for it. Do your own homework, and you will see that the Great Reset is all too real and that it is an overt power grab by the ruling class, one that might be impossible to fully reverse once it is in place.

The remainder of this chapter will present you with incontro-vertible evidence, most of which comes from politically unbiased or left-leaning sources, that proves beyond any doubt that Joe Biden and other influential U.S. political leaders are working feverishly to impose the Great Reset. These evidences are *not* the only proof out there, but they are a good place to start. If you keep an open mind, use the original sources I provide throughout this chapter, and allow yourself to view the data objectively, I am confident you will see why I am so convinced that the Reset is on the verge of becoming a reality in America.

THE EVIDENCE, EXHIBIT A:
AL GORE AND ELITES' CLIMATE CHANGE "SOLUTIONS"

As I noted in chapter 1, Al Gore—the self-proclaimed savior of the world—called for the Great Reset in a June 2020 interview with NBC's *TODAY* television show, during which he tied huge "green" infrastructure plans to the coronavirus recovery.

"So, I think this is a time for a 'Great Reset,'" Gore said, after arguing in favor of electric cars and renewable energy sources like wind and solar. "We've got to fix a lot of these problems that have been allowed to fester for way too long. And the climate crisis is an opportunity to create tens of millions of new jobs, clean up the air, and reduce the death rate from pandemics, by the way, because the air pollution from burning fossil fuels heightens the death rates from coronavirus."[414]

Gore, a close political ally of Joe Biden, has not only supported the Reset on television, he is also a member of the World Economic Forum's board of trustees.[415]

Gore's well-funded Climate Reality Project has also worked closely with the WEF's Global Shapers youth activist organization over the past several years. The Climate Reality Project has trained more than 1,300 Global Shapers on best practices for engaging in climate and environmental activism.[416]

Gore's involvement with the Global Shapers is extremely important, since the WEF announced in June 2020 that these youth activists will play a vital role at future Great Reset meetings.[417] According to the WEF, there are now Global Shaper groups in four hundred cities, and it is not hard to imagine how these groups could be used to promote the Great Reset agenda in 2021 and beyond, under the guise of an urgent need to solve the climate change "crisis."[418]

The blueprint for using youth engagement to support climate alarmism and socialist policies is already well established. Al Gore and other alarmists successfully piggybacked on the fame of Greta Thunberg to organize and promote massive rallies and "climate strikes" in 2019. In that year alone, *millions* of students participated in climate strikes around the world.[419]

The Global Shapers and Climate Reality Project have extensive climate activist infrastructure that will allow them to quickly organize hundreds of thousands or even millions of people in support of a Great Reset. In November 2019, the Climate Reality Project hosted more than two thousand presentations in eighty-four countries and all fifty U.S. states, reaching more than 119,000 people, as part of its "24 Hours of Reality" worldwide event.[420]

Gore and other climate activists—including groups like Greenpeace International[421]—are deeply tied to the Great Reset, but it is not because the Reset is the only, or even best, way to reduce carbon dioxide levels. As I discussed in chapter 3, even if you believe a climate crisis is happening as a result of human-created CO_2 emissions, nuclear power and other forms of energy production now in development clearly offer a more realistic and environmentally friendly path toward phasing out the use of fossil fuels. The only reason elites like Gore so desperately want to expand the use of wind and solar power is because it would demand huge new public works projects, massive amounts of government funding, and an expansion of power for large corporations and financial institutions—all of which are strategies the ruling class has been using for more than a century to transform society, going back decades before anyone ever heard of "global warming."

EXHIBIT B: JOHN KERRY

Al Gore is not the only prominent member of the ruling class or ally of Joe Biden to support the Great Reset. In addition to the long list of U.S. business leaders who have already stated publicly that they support the Great Reset,[422] there is John Kerry—the Democrats' 2004 presidential nominee, the former secretary of state during Barack Obama's second term, and one of the least inspiring speakers on the face of the planet.

In a June 2020 interview with the World Economic Forum, Kerry confessed his love for the Reset and demanded a new "social contract" that could address "climate change and inequity"—a key talking point of the WEF's Great Reset campaign.

"All the forces and pressures that were pushing us into crisis over the social contract are now exacerbated," Kerry said. "And exacerbated at a time when the world is in many ways coming apart."[423]

"What we never did," Kerry added, "was adequately address the social contract, the franchisement of human beings around the world, to be able to participate in things they can see with their smartphones everywhere but can't participate in."[424]

Kerry then argued that the United States is too politically "gridlocked," so it is going to be up to the World Economic Forum and its allies to promote the Reset on a global scale.

"This is a big moment," Kerry said, according to WEF. "The World Economic Forum—the CEO capacity of the Forum—is really going to have to play a front and center role in refining the Great Reset to deal with climate change and inequity, all of which is being laid bare as a consequence of COVID-19."[425]

Kerry mostly disappeared from the public spotlight after Donald Trump defeated Hillary Clinton in the 2016 presidential race, but beginning in 2020, Kerry managed to take on an increasingly important role within the Democratic Party.

In 2020, Kerry was named by Joe Biden and Bernie Sanders to cochair one of their Unity Task Forces, which were given the responsibility of rewriting the platforms of the Democratic Party and Biden's presidential campaign. Kerry served as cochair of the Climate Change Task Force, alongside Alexandria Ocasio-Cortez, just as the Great Reset movement was starting to gain steam.[426]

As I mentioned earlier, Kerry is a close political ally of Biden, whom Kerry endorsed early in the 2020 race.[427] In November 2020, as a reward for his loyalty, Biden named Kerry America's newest climate envoy for national security, a cabinet-level position the media often refers to as the "climate czar." It should come as no surprise, then, that some of the Great Reset's policy proposals and talking points managed to find their way into Biden's 2020 campaign platform, as I'll show in detail in exhibit C next.[428]

EXHIBIT C: JOE BIDEN'S "BUILD BACK BETTER" PLAN AND ITS TIES TO THE GREAT RESET

Biden's "Build Back Better" plan—by the way, great name, Joe— is full of the World Economic Forum's policy ideas. For example, Biden's climate and energy "Build Back Better" plan aimed to "make a $2 trillion accelerated investment, with a plan to deploy those resources over his first term, setting us on an irreversible course to meet the ambitious climate progress that science demands," by moving "ambitiously to generate clean, American-made electricity to achieve a carbon pollution-free power sector by 2035."[429]

According to Biden's website, the transition to "green" energy sources like wind and solar is necessary to stop the "existential threat of climate change."[430]

"Transforming the U.S. electricity sector—and electrifying an increasing share of the economy—represents the biggest job creation and economic opportunity engine of the 21st century," Biden's campaign website claims. "These jobs include every kind of worker from scientists to construction workers to electricity generation workers to welders to engineers. Existing iron casting and steel fabrication plants will have new customers in the solar and wind industries."[431]

These and many other parts of Biden's "Build Back Better" campaign proposals would later become core pieces in President Biden's infrastructure legislation proposed in early 2021.[432]

Boy, all this talk about massive climate infrastructure plans sure does sound familiar, doesn't it? Klaus Schwab would be so proud.

Biden's connection to Great Reset policies was made even clearer at a July 2020 campaign event in Pennsylvania, during which Biden pitched his $700 billion jobs plan while calling for an end to the "era of shareholder capitalism"—a common Reset talking point.[433]

"Let's make sure workers have power and a voice," Biden said. "It's way past time to put an end to the era of shareholder capitalism—the idea that the only responsibility a corporation has is to its shareholders. That's simply not true and it's an absolute farce. They have a responsibility to their workers, to their country. That isn't a new or radical notion." It is almost as though Biden were reading directly from a Great Reset press release written by Schwab himself.

In reality, forcing companies to put the collective before their customers and owners is absolutely a radical idea in a free society, but Joe is right that it is hardly new. The Great Reset's supporters have been loudly calling for the end of "shareholder capitalism" for a long time—in some cases for years, as I showed in detail in chapter 5.

Additionally, the very name Biden used for some of his campaign's largest jobs and energy plans—"Build Back Better"—is the exact title used for similar proposals and articles written by supporters or allies of the World Economic Forum and the Great Reset movement, with some of those writings going back several years.

In 2015, Raja Rehan Arshad, the lead disaster risk management specialist for the Global Facility for Disaster Reduction and

Recovery (GFDRR), authored an article for the World Economic Forum in which he wrote that following natural disasters, policy-makers should restore "damaged houses, hospitals, schools, and other public infrastructure to more disaster-resilient standards," a plan that "is one aspect of the 'building back better' strategy."[434]

In 2016, the World Bank and World Economic Forum published an article about climate change disasters titled "How Can We Reduce the Risk of Climate Disasters?" In the article, the author wrote, "The pressure for governments now is not to wait until a disaster strikes to 'build back better.' Instead, the urgent need is to build better now, and to thoroughly assess current risks to indus-trial infrastructure."[435]

Following the emergence of the coronavirus pandemic in 2020, WEF writers published a flurry of articles citing "building back better"—or some variation of that slogan—prior to and after Biden's decision to ramp up the marketing of his "Build Back Better" plan as a key component of his 2020 campaign.

In March 2020, two marketing heads at WEF wrote, "Business leaders have pledged to contribute their skills, networks and resources to shape the COVID-19 recovery and build back better." The statement was made in an article published on WEF's website, under the subheading "Companies Commit to Realizing a Great Reset of Capitalism."[436]

In April 2020, Maria Mendiluce, the interim CEO of the We Mean Business coalition, wrote for the World Economic Forum, "As governments develop longer-term economic stimulus packages to combat the crisis, they must be designed around the core principle of building a stronger economy that ensures the long-term health and wellbeing of citizens, job creation, tackling climate change once and for all, and building a more resilient and inclusive society."[437]

Mendiluce then wrote, "Business and government can and must work together at this extremely challenging time to lay the

foundations to build back better. Concrete government policies that send a clear signal to business will help us rebuild from
this devastating crisis in a way that delivers a healthy future for
everyone, through greater resilience and a clear pathway to a zero-
carbon future."[438]

In May 2020, the World Economic Forum posted a piece titled
"'Building Back Better'—Here's How We Can Navigate the Risks
We Face after COVID-19." In the article, writer Johnny Wood
noted, "We have looked at ways to 'build back better' and it's very
clear that investing in greener economies is going to be a huge part
of recovery efforts."[439]

In June 2020, David Victor, chairman of the Global Agenda Council
on Governance for Sustainability at the World Economic Forum—if
ever there were a quintessential Orwellian job title, *this* is it—wrote an
article for Yale's *Environment 360* website titled "Building Back Better:
Why Europe Must Lead a Global Green Recovery."[440]

On July 13, 2020, just several days after Biden said it is time
to "put an end to the era of shareholder capitalism" while pitching
his "Build Back Better" jobs plan in Pennsylvania,[441] Peter Bakker
and John Elkington authored an article for the World Economic
Forum titled "To Build Back Better, We Must Reinvent Capitalism.
Here's How."

In the article, the authors wrote,

A true recovery from COVID-19 will not be about putting
things back together the way they were: we need to "build back
better," to "reset," if we are to address the deep systemic vulnera-
bilities the pandemic has exposed. For businesses, building back
better is about much more than corporate social responsibility:
it is about truly aligning markets with the natural, social and
economic systems on which they depend. It is about building

real resilience, driving equitable and sustainable growth, and reinventing capitalism itself.[442]

Having read the articles cited here, along with numerous others using very similar language, it is hard to imagine that Joe Biden—or whoever else was really calling the shots in Biden's campaign—was not deliberately aligning his talking points and policy proposals with the Great Reset movement, especially in light of Al Gore and John Kerry's clear-cut endorsements of the Great Reset and their connection to Biden.

EXHIBIT D: JOE BIDEN'S COZY RELATIONSHIPS WITH GREAT RESET LEADERS

The evidence does not stop at Biden's campaign. Biden also has close relationships with at least three World Economic Forum board members: Al Gore, David Rubenstein, and Laurence Fink, the chairman and CEO of BlackRock.[443] And one of Vice President Kamala Harris's longtime supporters is the CEO of Salesforce, Marc Benioff, another WEF board member.[444]

Further, my coauthor of this book, Justin Haskins, reported exclusively for the Blaze in October 2020 that additional "evidence of Biden's intimate relationship with Great Reset advocates can be found in the launch of the Biden Institute, which is based at the University of Delaware."

"In 2017," Haskins continued, "when the Biden Institute first started, Biden said he wanted to model some of the new organization's activities after the World Economic Forum, and he even met with the WEF's leader and the world's biggest advocate of the Great Reset, Klaus Schwab, to help develop a plan for the future of the Institute."[445]

Joe Biden has apparently been taking advice from Schwab for years, so it really shouldn't surprise anyone that Biden has also been drinking from Klaus's Great Reset Kool-Aid. Speaking of, if Schwab ever decides to give up this whole evil genius, take-over-the-world career path he's been on for the past half century, starting a knock-off Kool-Aid brand called Klaus-Aid ought to be priority number one. The commercials showing Klaus busting through kids' walls to give them sugary drinks and teach them about the evils of free markets would practically write themselves.

EXHIBIT E: JOHN KERRY'S HONEST MOMENT

But if all that evidence is still not enough to convince you of Biden's commitment to the Great Reset—and it should be; I mean, really, what's wrong with you?—consider the following smoking-gun proof that emerged just weeks after the mainstream press declared Biden the winner of the 2020 election.[446]

At a panel discussion about the Great Reset hosted by the World Economic Forum in November 2020, John Kerry adamantly stated that Joe Biden and his administration *will* support the Great Reset, and he will do so with "greater speed and with greater intensity than a lot of people might imagine."[447]

During the panel discussion, host Børge Brende—WEF's president—asked Kerry whether the World Economic Forum's members and other Great Reset supporters are "expecting too much too soon from the new president, or is he going to deliver first day on this [sic] topics?" to which Kerry responded, "The answer to your question is, no, you're not expecting too much."[448]

Kerry then added, "And yes, it [the Great Reset] will happen. And I think it will happen with greater speed and with greater intensity than a lot of people might imagine. In effect, the citizens of the United States have just done a Great Reset. We've done a Great Reset. And it was a record level of voting."[449]

It doesn't get much clearer than that, folks.

EXHIBIT F: JOE BIDEN'S MAO AGENCY

Kerry's promise of a Biden-led American Great Reset was *not* merely talk either. Since President Biden has entered the White House, he and his administration have imposed countless policies and proposed numerous more that fit perfectly in line with the Great Reset's goals, framework, and principles. For example, consider Biden's new Made in America Office—or as I like to call it, his MAO agency. (Sometimes they really do make it too easy, don't they?)

On the surface, the Made in America agency sounds like something that might have been created by the Trump administration—other than the agency's acronym, of course. Something tells me Donald Trump wouldn't want a supposedly pro-America bureaucratic agency named after a mass-murdering communist dictator.

The stated purpose of MAO is to require that government offices spend more of their budgets working with American companies, as opposed to purchasing goods and services from businesses located overseas. This sounds like a noble goal that most Americans can get behind, but the devil is in the details.[450] When the White House announced the creation of MAO, it noted that the agency would *not* direct government agencies to do business with just any old U.S. company that offers the best product or service at the lowest price; rather, MAO would be used as a tool to advance the Biden administration's political and social agendas.

According to the White House, the order creating MAO "is deeply intertwined with the President's commitment to invest in American manufacturing, including clean energy and critical supply chains, grow good-paying union jobs, and advance racial equity. The federal government should buy from suppliers that are growing the sectors of the future and treating their workers with dignity and respect."[451]

In other words, the MAO agency's mission is to make sure that the federal government buys only from the "good" companies, meaning those businesses that reflect the values of the Biden administration. This is unquestionably a Great Reset policy proposed by the World Economic Forum's Klaus Schwab, as well as other supporters of the Reset.

As I noted earlier in the book, in Schwab's article titled "Now Is the Time for a 'Great Reset,'" published in June 2020, he wrote,

> The second component of a Great Reset agenda would ensure that investments advance shared goals, such as equality and sustainability....Rather than using these funds, as well as investments from private entities and pension funds, to fill cracks in the old system, we should use them to create a new one that is more resilient, equitable, and sustainable in the long run. This means, for example, building "green" urban infrastructure and creating incentives for industries to improve their track record on environmental, social, and governance (ESG) metrics.[452]

Biden's MAO agency is designed to do exactly what Schwab said is a core component of the Great Reset: ensure that government funds are funneled into the businesses committed to making the social and political changes desired by elites.

EXHIBIT G: BIDEN'S "30 BY 30" LAND AND WATER PLAN

In one of his first acts as president, Joe Biden released an executive order calling on government to conserve about 30 percent of all U.S.

lands and waters by 2030, a program widely referred to as "30 by 30."[453] According to the *Washington Post*, as of May 2021, "roughly 12 percent of U.S. land and 11 percent of its freshwater ecosystems enjoy some level of official protection."[454]

That means if Biden is successful in ensuring that 30 percent of all U.S. lands and waters are conserved by 2030, it would more than double the amount of land conserved in the United States, making this program one of the largest government takeovers in U.S. history.

Moving many forms of property ownership—not just land ownership—away from private individuals and farmers and into the hands of government and large corporations is viewed by many within the Great Reset movement as an imperative. In the minds of many Resetters, land under public or corporate ownership can more easily be conserved and/or utilized for the public good. Government laws can be crafted to slow or stop land use, and corporations can be discouraged or severely hindered from developing land through ESG systems. Many ESG scoring systems already include metrics for land use and consumption of resources.

It's not enough, according to many involved with the World Economic Forum and the Great Reset, to limit environmental harm; we must also "enhance ecosystems" by severely restricting and even reducing humans' existing land use.

In an article titled "What Is 'Nature Positive' and Why Is It the Key to Our Future?" published by WEF in June 2021, high-profile environmentalists and members of the World Economic Forum outlined their vision for a "nature positive" approach to policy-making and corporate management.

In the past, the mantra among a growing number of inspired leaders has been to do less harm, to reduce impact and to tread lightly across our world. Of course, this mantra remains.

But now there is a new worldview gathering pace: "nature positive." This asks: What if we go beyond damage limitation? What if our economic activities not only minimize impact, but also enhance ecosystems? ...

Nature positive is a disruptive idea. It forces us to think differently about our place in the world. It is a destination for humanity. It is a foundation for good governance, long-term stable societies and healthy economies. It is a philosophy that values our common future. And it is a new business model based on regeneration, resilience and recirculation—not destruction and pollution.[455]

What exactly do these Great Resetters have in mind when they talk about "enhancing ecosystems"?

This means governments, cities and businesses need to know what to measure. Science-based targets for a nature positive trajectory are still under intense discussion. As of today, the proposed quantitative targets are as follows: zero loss of nature from 2020 onwards, nature positive by 2030, and full recovery by 2050. An important step towards this is to aim to protect 30% of the land and ocean by 2030.[456]

Wait, conserving 30 percent of land and oceans by 2030? You mean like a "30 by 30" plan? Didn't I just read something about that somewhere?

This movement within the Great Reset to limit property ownership and centralize control of property might also explain why Reset-affiliated investment firms are buying up as much property as they can get their hands on. Fox News reported in June 2021, citing additional reporting by the *Wall Street Journal*, that "BlackRock—led by billionaire Laurence Fink—is purchasing entire neighborhoods and converting single-family homes into rentals; while in cities like Houston, investors like Fink account for one-quarter of the home purchasers."[457]

BlackRock is one of the world's powerful investment management companies, and as I mentioned earlier in this chapter and in chapter 5, its billionaire leader Laurence Fink is an ally of Joe Biden and serves as a member of the World Economic Forum's board of directors. Other Great Reset-linked businesses and financial institutions have also taken part in the buying spree, including JPMorgan Chase.[458]

Although not all people affiliated with the World Economic Forum believe that the results of this shift would be wholly positive, many do think it is an unavoidable part of elites' new economy and that the reduction of private ownership would be a mostly good development.

Danish member of Parliament Ida Auken was asked by the World Economic Forum to provide a prediction for 2030, to which Auken responded with an article titled "Welcome to 2030. I Own Nothing, Have No Privacy, and Life Has Never Been Better."[459]

In the article, Auken wrote that in her vision of 2030,

I don't own anything. I don't own a car. I don't own a house. I don't own any appliances or any clothes.

It might seem odd to you, but it makes perfect sense for us in this city [in 2030]. Everything you considered a product, has now become a service. We have access to transportation, accommodation, food and all the things we need in our daily lives. One by one all these things became free, so it ended up not making sense for us to own much.

Once in a while I get annoyed about the fact that I have no real privacy [in 2030]. Nowhere I can go and not be registered. I know that, somewhere, everything I do, think and dream of is recorded. I just hope that nobody will use it against me.

All in all, it is a good life. Much better than the path we were on, where it became so clear that we could not continue with the same model of growth. We had all these terrible things happening: lifestyle diseases, climate change, the refugee crisis, environmental degradation, completely congested cities, water pollution, air pollution, social unrest and unemployment. We lost way too many people before we realised that we could do things differently.[460]

Well, we know that the folks at the World Economic Forum think an existence in which regular people own almost nothing and have "no real privacy" is "all in all ... a good life," but is that the world you want to leave for *your* children and grandchildren? I know it's not the one I want to leave for mine, and I'm willing to bet many of you reading this book agree.

EXHIBIT H: BIDEN KILLS TRUMP'S "FAIR ACCESS" RULE

In President Trump's final days in office, his administration released what would have been an incredibly important regulation, one that had the potential to stop some of the most dangerous parts of the Great Reset in their tracks.

Trump's Fair Access Rule would have made it difficult—and in many cases, impossible—for banks to discriminate against legal businesses on the basis of the type of industry they are in, thus forcing banking institutions to focus solely on financial matters. According to the rule, "banks should conduct risk assessment of individual customers, rather than make broad-based decisions affecting whole categories or classes of customers when provisioning access to services, capital, and credit."[461]

In practice, the rule would have made it difficult for a bank to, for example, deny a gun-store owner access to a loan solely because the bank's leaders didn't think legal gun ownership was good for America. Similarly, a bank would not have been permitted to deny an oil company a loan because of concerns over CO_2 emissions.

Although the rule had been approved by the Trump administration's Office of the Comptroller of the Currency, it had not gone into effect when Biden entered the White House, so the Biden administration killed the regulation before it could be fully implemented.[462]

If Trump's Fair Access Rule had been imposed, it's unlikely the Great Reset would be gaining so much ground today within much of the banking industry, because one of the most powerful devices in the Great Reset toolbox—the use of ESG scores and other, similar metrics by banks to determine access to credit—would have been unavailable.

Biden knew how vital the Fair Access Rule would have been in slowing the Great Reset, so—unsurprisingly—he crushed it before it could take effect.

EXHIBIT I: CONGRESS FLIRTS WITH ESG

Nothing would advance the Great Reset agenda more than a new law that mandates ESG standards and reporting. In June 2021, Congress moved a step closer to imposing far-reaching ESG rules with the passage of the ESG Disclosure Simplification Act of 2021 in the U.S. House of Representatives.[463]

According to a report by the *National Law Review*, the bill (which has still not been reviewed by the Senate as of this writing, in September 2021) would "require the Securities and Exchange Commission ('SEC'), for the first time, to define, in regulations, 'ESG metrics,' for the purpose of guiding required corporate disclosures under the Securities Exchange Act of 1934 and the Securities Act of 1933, as amended."[464]

The *National Law Review* further noted that if the bill were to pass into law, then "in consent solicitation or proxy statements, issuers would be required to include '(a) a clear description of the views of the issuer about the link between ESG metrics and the long-term business strategy of the issuer; and (b) a description of any process the issuer uses to determine the impact of ESG metrics on the long-term business strategy of the issuer.'"

The legislation also would establish a Sustainable Finance Advisory Committee, which would be required to submit to the SEC within 180 days after its initial meeting "a report with recommendations on what ESG metrics issuers should be required to disclose."

The language of the bill states that the Sustainable Finance Advisory Committee's report would need to "(i) identif[y] the challenges and opportunities for investors associated with sustainable finance; and (ii) recommend policy changes to facilitate the flow of capital towards sustainable investments, in particular environmentally sustainable investments."[465]

The ESG Disclosure Simplification Act also would allow the SEC to "incorporate any internationally recognized, independent, multi-stakeholder environmental, social, and governance disclosure standards," including any standards created by the European Union, World Economic Forum, or United Nations.[466]

Although the bill is not likely to pass in the U.S. Senate with the current composition of Congress, its passage in the House and the support it received from the Biden administration should serve as a slap in the face to any doubters who think ESG mandates are not a priority for many in Washington. A wide-ranging ESG system is on the verge of becoming law in the United States—even though most Americans still have no idea what ESG metrics are.

EXHIBIT J: CALLS FOR A CREDIT SCORE TAKEOVER

In addition to attempting to pass sweeping ESG mandates, many members of Congress and nonprofit advocacy groups have called for the federal government to take over individual credit scoring, a move some prominent activists are already suggesting could be used to help Congress and federal bureaucracies reshape society. Think of it as a government-provided personal ESG score.

At the time of this writing, personal credit scores are developed by three nongovernment credit bureaus, Equifax, TransUnion, and Experian, each of which creates a unique FICO score for individuals.[467] Credit scores are based entirely on financial information that helps banks and other institutions determine how much risk is associated with various financial arrangements made with a potential customer or lendee.

The popular finance/economics website The Balance notes, "Traditionally, the FICO score is the most popular score used for important loans like home and auto loans. No matter what score you use, most models are looking for a way to predict how likely you are to pay your bills on time."[468]

The Balance further explains, "The FICO credit score looks at how much debt you have, how you've repaid in the past, and more. Scores range from 300 and 850 and are made up of the following components:" credit mix (10 percent), payment history (35 percent), current debt (30 percent), length of credit history (15 percent), and new credit (10 percent).[469]

Many members of Congress and supporters of the Great Reset want to alter the existing credit score system so it can be used to redistribute wealth and power. One of the most popular proposals involves creating a government-run credit agency—the Public Credit Registry—that would be responsible for issuing "fair" credit scores to consumers. It would be housed under the Consumer Financial Protection Bureau, the brainchild of Senator Elizabeth Warren from Massachusetts.[470]

Many of those in Congress advocating for putting government in charge of individual credit scores have said that the existing credit scoring agencies are too dysfunctional to be trusted and that a government agency would be more effective and fairer in its approach—because, you know, when you're faced with a large, irresponsive, inefficient bureaucratic system, the first group of people you turn to in order to fix the problem is the federal government, right?

Others, however, have been a little more honest about their motives. At a hearing about the possibility of overhauling the existing credit system, held in June 2021 by the U.S. House Committee on Financial Services, Representative Maxine Waters, the chair of the committee, said that the current model needs to be deconstructed because "for far too long, our credit reporting system has kept people of color and low-income persons from access to capital to start a small business; access to mortgage loans to become homeowners; and access to credit to meet financial emergencies."[471]

As her statement makes clear, in Waters's view, credit scoring reforms should center on social justice, not merely financial concerns.

At the same hearing, Chi Chi Wu, an attorney at the National Consumer Law Center, advocated for the passage of legislation creating a federal credit scoring agency, and she specifically noted that one of the benefits would be that the new agency would give novel tools to government to fix social and economic problems.

"While public agencies are not perfect, at least they would not have profit-making as their top priority," Wu said at the hearing. "They would be responsive to public pressure and government oversight. They could also be charged with developing credit scoring models to reduce the yawning racial and economic inequality in this country."[472]

Reducing "yawning racial and economic inequality" makes for a good sound bite on CNN, but the ramifications of putting the federal government in charge of credit scoring decisions would be far-reaching and deeply troubling, especially if the agency tasked with creating and managing scores is empowered with the authority to "fix" society's ills.

A Public Credit Registry could, for example, ensure that some races get lower-interest car loans than more "privileged" races. "Asians and whites already have enough cars," PCR bureaucrats could reason, "so let's make sure other racial groups get the best rates."

Similarly, a Public Credit Registry could effectively deny access to loans for some successful business owners. After all, they already have enough wealth, don't they? Let's give other people a chance.

"Oh, and you want a mortgage for a new home that you have been saving up for, for a decade? Sorry, we already have enough homeowners of *your* race in your zip code. We need greater racial equity, so you are going to have to get by with a rock-bottom credit score and sky-high mortgage rates."

These hypotheticals might sound extreme, but what else could Chi Chi possibly have had in mind when she said a government credit agency could develop "credit scoring models to reduce the yawning racial and economic inequality in this country"?

The current credit scoring industry could be improved. No doubt about that. But putting a politically motivated government bureaucracy in charge of credit scoring would create far more problems than it would solve—unless, of course, you want a total reset of the current economic system and social contract. If that's your goal, then Chi Chi's call for a government credit score makes a whole lot of sense.

EXHIBIT K: BUILDING BACK BETTER AT THE G7

In most years, watching meetings of the G7—a group of world leaders hailing from Canada, France, Germany, Italy, Japan, the United Kingdom, and the United States—is about as interesting as watching half-blurred reruns of traffic court on public-access television. But the 2021 meeting of the G7, the first such meeting featuring President Biden, caught my attention when Biden announced he and his G7 pals had agreed to launch a global infrastructure development plan that seemed nearly identical to numerous proposals I had previously heard ooze out of the mouth of Klaus Schwab and other Great Reset advocates. Biden called the initiative Build Back Better World. (Sound familiar?)

According to a statement by the White House, "Through B3W [Build Back Better World], the G7 and other like-minded partners will coordinate in mobilizing private-sector capital in four areas of focus—climate, health and health security, digital technology, and gender equity and equality—with catalytic investments from our respective development finance institutions."[473]

Huh. Those "areas of focus" sound eerily similar to the goals set forth by just about every single Great Reset document ever published.

The Build Back Better World plan, which the White House esti-mates will lead to "hundreds of billions of dollars of infrastructure investment," would not simply provide run-of-the-mill investments in roads and bridges. No, the White House says the investments will be "values-driven" and "carried out in a transparent and sustainable manner—financially, environmentally, and socially."[474] They will also, of course, be focused on battling climate change and "achieving the goals of the Paris Climate Agreement." (ESG, anyone?)

I could write a few more paragraphs further outlining how the Build Back Better World plan is overtly connected to Great Reset goals, but if you can't see that by now, you really haven't been paying attention.

COULD THE GREAT RESET REALLY HAPPEN IN AMERICA?

Toward the end of my detailed look at the Great Reset in chapter 5, I included a modified version of a question that I hear all the time from listeners and readers: "Can the Great Reset really happen in America, of all places?"

It is an important question. The United States is not China or Europe—at least not yet—so just because there are some troubling developments occurring on the other side of the world does not necessarily mean Americans are going to be forced to deal with the same problems. Despite all our issues and the near-fundamental transformation of American society that has occurred in recent years, the United States has not totally lost its soul. If it had, I wouldn't have bothered with writing this book.

But when you add up all the evidence I've outlined throughout this chapter and in chapter 5—Biden's policy platforms and statements, Biden's "Build Back Better" slogan, the massive ESG infrastructure that has already been put into place in America's banks and large corporations, attempts to have government take over America's credit scoring system, the commitments made by more than two hundred major financial institutions around the world to support ESG systems, calls in Congress for ESG mandates, the more than $100 trillion in support from investors associated with the Principles for Responsible Investment, the G7's Build Back Better World plan, and quotes promoting the Reset by powerful figures like Al Gore, John Kerry, and leaders of a seemingly endless list of activist groups, international organizations, and billion-dollar corporations in the United States—it's hard to see how any reasonable person could deny that the Great Reset has already gained significant momentum in America.

The most important question we can ask ourselves, then, is not whether the Great Reset is possible or even desired by many in the ruling class. Nor is it whether the Great Reset would be harmful to markets or individual liberty. The answers to those questions have already been determined, as this chapter and my others have proven. Rather the essential question, the one that will define the next century of American history, is, *What can we do to stop it?*

That vital question is the subject of this book's next and final chapter.

7

DERAILING THE GREAT RESET

The truth of the matter is that you always know the
right thing to do. The hard part is doing it.

—General Norman Schwarzkopf[475]

B Y ALL ACCOUNTS, THERE WAS NOTHING SPECIAL ABOUT THE train that left Zurich for Germany on April 9, 1917. As with the dozens of other train rides that occurred in the region, the machine's loud, powerful engine bellowed across Switzerland's beautiful landscape, featuring rolling hills, picturesque farmhouses, and the stunning Rhine Falls, one of Europe's largest waterfalls, as the train moved ever closer to its destination farther north.

Had you watched the train from afar, you would have thought nothing was out of the ordinary. For most bystanders, the speeding passenger train was likely a welcome departure to normalcy in an otherwise chaotic world. Although Switzerland in 1917 had managed to remain at peace, much of the rest of Europe was mired in a bloody "Great War."

By 1917, World War I had already taken the lives of millions of men, women, and children. On its own, Russia had suffered five million casualties. On all sides of the conflict, soldiers died in the most wretched of conditions—from chemical weapons or a bayonet to the chest in a frozen trench hundreds of miles from home. At the Battle of the Somme in France, more than sixty thousand British soldiers died on the battle's first day alone.[476]

But there were few soldiers on the Swiss train from Zurich, and just as few weapons of war. Many of its passengers were shabbily dressed and carried only the most basic of provisions: light clothing, blankets, books for the long journey ahead, paper and ink for writing, and limited food rations consisting of sausage, cheese, bread rolls, and hard-boiled eggs.

The train, its destination, and its passengers appeared in almost every way to be normal, yet there was nothing commonplace about this fateful trip. It was, in fact, in the most meaningful sense, *extraordinary* and world changing. The fate of hundreds of millions of people would forever be altered by the work of its passengers, and millions of lives would be lost at the hands of the train's most profound and ruthless traveler: Vladimir Ilyich Ulyanov, a man better known today by his alias, Lenin.[477]

Lenin, then in his midforties, had spent the better part of the previous two decades in exile, eventually settling in Switzerland with radicals who had been forced out of Russia and other European nations for attempting to spark an international, revolutionary socialist movement.[478]

While in Switzerland, Lenin had spent his days feverishly writing. In 1916, he authored *Imperialism, the Highest Stage of Capitalism* and started one of his most important books, *State and Revolution*—all while secretly working from across the continent to undermine the authority of Russia's czar, Nicholas II.

So in March 1917, when Lenin—who had in recent months grown disheartened and convinced that the global Marxist revolution he believed to be inevitable could be many years away—heard that Nicholas had abdicated the throne, he was nothing short of exhilarated. Czar Nicholas had been forced from power following a spontaneous revolution of the Russian people and soldiers, who had become disenfranchised over Nicholas's handling of World War I and disturbed by rumors of the growing influence in Russia's royal court of a bizarre Siberian mystic, Rasputin.[479]

When word of the czar's removal reached Lenin, he and his fellow Marxists began to tirelessly work to find a way to return to Russia. The trip was, at that time, a monumental challenge because the nations surrounding Switzerland were still at war. In the weeks prior to Lenin's departure from Zurich, Lenin and some of his closest comrades became so desperate that they approached a most unlikely potential ally, Germany, hoping that a deal could be struck between the two parties.

The German government was no friend of Lenin or his socialist compatriots, but German officials were eventually persuaded to broker a deal with him. They would allow Lenin and thirty-one other socialist revolutionaries to travel in April through Germany on their way to Russia, but only if they agreed to work toward ending Russia's involvement in the war once they arrived home. It was a remarkable and unexpected conspiracy, one that would reshape world history.

With the help of anti-socialist German officials, Lenin returned to Russia a hero among those sympathetic to his Marxist views.

Despite being a relatively small minority in Russia, the more radical Bolshevik socialists, led by Lenin, stormed the Winter Palace in Petrograd—now called Saint Petersburg—on the night of October 25, seizing power from the Russian provisional government. The provisional government was so weak and the skirmish so short that on the following morning, many citizens of Petrograd had no idea the revolution had occurred or that an entirely new nation was about to be created.

Soon thereafter Lenin's socialists took control of the Kremlin in Moscow. A secret police force, the Cheka, and prison camps were then established, and rival newspapers and political parties were eliminated.

The Bolsheviks renamed themselves "communists," both to help with branding outside of Russia, where the term "Bolshevik" was not well known, and to differentiate Lenin's revolutionaries from the other European socialists who had supported getting involved in World War I. They then negotiated a treaty with Germany to buy time while they waged a civil war in Russia with counterrevolutionary White Army forces.

World War I ended in 1918, but Russia's civil war would last until 1920, and the socialist Red Army would continue fighting in Eastern Europe into 1921, in the hope of ushering in a worldwide Marxist revolution.

On December 30, 1922, Lenin's socialists founded the Union of Soviet Socialist Republics, and over its sixty-nine-year history, tens of millions of Russians and Eastern Europeans would be murdered, exiled, or unjustly imprisoned by its ruthless government, all in the name of "equality."[480]

Although by 1917 a revolution in Russia was likely inevitable, a *Marxist socialist revolution* most certainly was not. Had the German government refused to conspire with Lenin to allow him and his comrades to travel through Germany on their way to Russia, it is entirely possible the Bolsheviks' attempt to seize power would have been derailed, and perhaps today Lenin would be only a footnote in history.

CONSPIRACY THEORIES

Lenin's historic train ride through Germany is important for a number of reasons, but perhaps the most overlooked is that it is proof that a well-timed conspiracy can bring about remarkable and dangerous change, even when such change seems highly improbable.

Americans often think the United States is too big to fail and that fringe political groups seeking revolutionary changes to our society and Constitution have little chance of success. But I am sure Czar Nicholas II felt the same way for much of his life, and I am willing to bet that most Russians at the start of 1917 did not believe that within just a few years, a band of relatively poor, shabbily dressed political exiles from Switzerland would be ruling with an iron fist over one of the world's largest nations. Yet that is exactly what happened.

Of course, this does not mean that all or even most conspiracies should be taken seriously. In recent years, ridiculous conspiracy theories covering everything from fake moon landings to shapeshifting reptilians controlling the government have become popular among some groups of Americans. And although it is tempting to laugh away sweaty rants by tinfoil hat-wearing fat guys lamenting the rise of lizard people, conspiracy theories that are not grounded in truth, and the media's decision to engage in the rampant dissemination of false information to achieve political goals, have become two of the biggest threats facing America today.

Because people do not know who to trust, we now live in a world of "alternative facts," where seemingly everything is fake—fake news, fake outrage, fake accusations. Now they even sell "turkeys" made of tofu. Is anything *real* anymore?

As a result, Americans are deeply confused and incredibly skeptical of anything that does not fit into their preexisting set of beliefs. Trust in the media is embarrassingly low. Only one-third of self-identified Republicans and less than half of independents say they trust the media.[481] Even among Democrats, who have a long list of left-leaning publications and television networks to choose from, trust in media is just 66 percent.[482]

The world's massive social media infrastructure and online publisher model have also contributed to the conspiracy theory pandemic. Most publishers and many authors earn much of their money by getting clicks on articles they produce, so the more outrageous the article, the more likely it is that the publisher and author will have a big payday. How many hundreds of millions of dollars did the media earn by churning out literally thousands of Trump-Russia collusion stories, most of which ended up being based on false information? It is probably impossible to calculate, but I can say this for certain: they made a heck of a lot more money *with* the collusion narrative than they would have made *without* it. The truth didn't matter; the money did.

Conspiracy theories, dishonest media reports, and the deep political and social divisions that have resulted from them could end up being the final nail in America's coffin. If we can't even agree on whether the stories we see in the press are true, or even what "truth" means, how can we have honest conversations about complex issues like race, religion, foreign policy, artificial intelligence, or just about anything else that actually matters?

The confusion and tribalism that have resulted from this culture of disregarding carefully cultivated truths in favor of outrage and clickbait have presented an unprecedented opportunity for supporters of the Great Reset, who use societal divisions and fear as cover for their attempts to alter nearly every part of our country. Anyone with the courage to stand up against them is labeled a conspiracy theorist and tossed aside as a lunatic. And because the mainstream press is so unwilling to expose the truth, tens of millions of Americans never hear well-documented, highly sourced facts that could shed a dramatic new light on nearly everything that they see in the news on a daily basis.

The media's constant catastrophizing and general lack of trustworthiness, mixed with the profusion of conspiracy theories—both lizard people–level ones and your run-of-the-mill "Trump is a Russian agent" garbage—have left many honest people on both sides of the aisle thinking that every claim of conspiracy is false and usually the product of political forces working to get or keep their side in power. However, as we saw with Lenin's rise to power, there's a big difference between conspiracy *theories* and conspiracy *facts*, and knowing what that difference is could prove vital for America's survival.

CONSPIRACY FACTS

How can you know whether something is a fact in a world chock-full of misinformation? If you have been listening to my radio show or reading my books for a while, you probably already know what I am about to say: the absolutely most important rule to follow is that you must *do your own homework*. Do not believe something just because your favorite media personality or news outlet said it. Even well-meaning, honest people can make mistakes or misunderstand something they have seen, read, or heard.

Above all else, doing your own homework requires going directly to primary sources, whenever possible, and then examining quotes and data in the proper context. As you probably can imagine, I get a lot of suggestions, tips, and ideas for stories from listeners, friends, and generally top-notch reporters and sources. But you wouldn't believe how many hundreds of times I have *heard* that something is true only to find out later that when seen in context, that "jaw-dropping" quote or "incredible" piece of evidence means something completely different from what many others had interpreted it to mean.

In addition to doing your own homework by going straight to the original sources, it is also vital that you spend time reading news and commentary from sources with which you do not agree, whether they be on the right or the left. People are often surprised to hear that I read the *New York Times*. Of course, there are a lot of opinion pieces and biased news articles in the *Times* that I do not agree with. You should never assume that what you're reading in any media outlet is true, without first verifying the information. With that said, the *Times* is still one of the world's most influential news outlets, and its staff has done some truly remarkable reporting over the years, so I am not going to throw the baby out with the bathwater, no matter how ugly the little guy is.

If you do your own homework, go straight to the original sources, and read everything you can get your hands on, I am confident you'll see that the warnings I have outlined throughout this book are real and that if we don't work together to stop the spread of the Great Reset, it will soon become our reality.

FIGHTING BACK

I know I often come off as a doom-and-gloom kind of person. Watching the news sixteen hours a day will do that to you. But the truth is, I am often filled with great hope for this nation's future.

People are living longer, healthier lives than ever before because of the wonders of capitalism. The internet has provided people with access to information that was hidden from view in generations past, when most families got their news and information from one of three network television stations and their local newspaper.

Prior to the coronavirus, America's economy was booming, thanks in large part to conservative principles like reducing regulations and taxes, and everyone—including African Americans, Hispanics, and women—was benefiting at levels we have never seen before. And perhaps most important, rising through the ranks is a new generation of young thinkers, speakers, and activists who I am confident will passionately advocate for individual liberty for decades to come, long after guys like me retire.

There are reasons to be hopeful, but there also plenty of reasons to be deeply concerned. When I look at what has happened in the United States over the past couple of years, I feel like a stranger in my own country. Rioting, looting, burned-down police stations, expenditures that are trillions of dollars more than we can afford, economic shutdowns, social distancing requirements, trillion-dollar bailouts of billion-dollar corporations, tyrannical state governments—is this who we are now?

Americans are at a crossroads. We must make a choice. We have to decide whether we are going to go the way of China and twenty-first century fascism or pursue the promise of our forefathers, who bled on fields, deserts, beaches, and mountains—both at home and in faraway lands—trying to guarantee the continued existence of this grand experiment in human freedom.

The United States has faced challenges and crossroads before, and they have come in many forms. But I am not sure that the country has ever experienced anything quite like the Great Reset.

Never before have so many Americans been as eager as they are today to give away their freedom to global elites. Never before have so many powerful U.S. business interests worked with such vigor to betray their country in pursuit of a lucrative new crony deal. Never before have American politicians and activist groups so openly demanded that more power be given to the ruling class and been met by the media, Hollywood, and academic institutions with joy and excitement.

We have an important, world-changing opportunity to change course and embrace the principles of individual freedom and respect for all people, regardless of race, religion, or gender. But make no mistake about it, time is running out. If we fail now, our country might never recover. The forces at work are so powerful, well funded, and devoted to their cause that reversing the Reset might be virtually impossible if it is fully brought into existence.

Throughout the remainder of this chapter, I will discuss several strategies for derailing the Great Reset movement, and in the process, stopping twenty-first century fascism and saving our republic. This list is not meant to be exhaustive, nor will it provide readers with all-encompassing information about each topic. It is, however, a good place to start and offers a solid foundation for building a movement to fight back against the Great Reset and other, similar movements pushed by elites, both now and in the future.

LIVE NOT BY LIES

The struggle against the Great Reset begins when you stand unwaveringly for the truth, no matter where it takes you. Don't allow the shackles of political loyalty to restrict you. Become a slave to the truth. Stand up against all those who would have you support or even tolerate lies.

The primary reason Germany succumbed to the Nazis in the wake of World War I is that there were too few good people willing to push back against the dishonest fearmongering and mythology propagated by Hitler and his supporters. Many of the German people had already forgotten the truths of their forefathers by the time men like Dietrich Bonhoeffer attempted to build a mass resistance movement against the Nazis.

We cannot wait for such a dire situation to act. We must earnestly, passionately, and peacefully resist *now*, before it's too late.

One of the best treatises ever written on the importance of the truth was by Soviet dissident Aleksandr Solzhenitsyn. On February 12, 1974, one day before being exiled from the Soviet Union, Solzhenitsyn published a powerful essay titled "Live Not by Lies."

In this highly influential work, Solzhenitsyn identified the Communist government's most vulnerable point as its lies. He insisted that if the Russian people could merely gather the will to reject "a daily participation in deceit," the Communist Party's stranglehold on society would not last.

And therein we find, neglected by us, the simplest, the most accessible key to our liberation: a personal nonparticipation in lies! Even if all is covered by lies, even if all is under their rule, let us resist in the smallest way: Let their rule hold not through me!

And this is the way to break out of the imaginary encirclement of our inertness, the easiest way for us and the most devastating for the lies. For when people renounce lies, lies simply cease to exist. Like parasites, they can only survive when attached to a person.

We are not called upon to step out onto the square and shout out the truth, to say out loud what we think—this is scary, we are not ready. But let us at least refuse to say what we do not think![483]

After inspiring the Soviet people to reject lies in their everyday lives, he then provided a blueprint for living as an "honest man," one that could serve as a model for our own resistance against the ruling class.

According to Solzhenitsyn, the honest man

> Will not write, sign, nor publish in any way, a single line distorting, so far as he can see, the truth;

> Will not utter such a line in private or in public conversation, nor read it from a crib sheet, nor speak it in the role of educator, canvasser, teacher, actor;

> Will not in painting, sculpture, photograph, technology, or music depict, support, or broadcast a single false thought, a single distortion of the truth as he discerns it;

> Will not cite in writing or in speech a single "guiding" quote for gratification, insurance, for his success at work, unless he fully shares the cited thought and believes that it fits the context precisely;

> Will not be forced to a demonstration or a rally if it runs counter to his desire and his will; will not take up and raise a banner or slogan in which he does not fully believe;

> Will not raise a hand in vote for a proposal which he does not sincerely support; will not vote openly or in secret ballot for a candidate whom he deems dubious or unworthy;

> Will not be impelled to a meeting where a forced and distorted discussion is expected to take place;

> Will at once walk out from a session, meeting, lecture, play, or film as soon as he hears the speaker utter a lie, ideological drivel, or shameless propaganda;

Will not subscribe to, nor buy in retail, a newspaper or journal that distorts or hides the underlying facts.[484]

Solzhenitsyn's plan for resistance was simple yet powerful. Not everyone has the courage to protest an authoritarian regime openly, but by refusing to participate in lies, the people could severely reduce the Communist Party's power and influence.

The same is true today. No matter who you are or how uncomfortable you feel with pushing back against the Great Reset openly, you don't have to participate in those particularly damning and dishonest parts of our society and economy. By refusing to be a part of elites' lies, you remove much of the power that the ruling class has over your life and the lives of your family members.

A UNITED FRONT

One of the most important ways we can stop the Great Reset is to educate the people in our lives about what is really going on. But that cannot happen unless we know how other people think and why they believe the things they do.

Reading and listening to what different media outlets are reporting is a great place to start, because it provides an important opportunity to learn how to communicate with friends, neighbors, and family members who rely on media sources you may not trust to get their news and commentary.

Further, many of the people with whom you discuss the Great Reset are not going to believe you if you start a conversation with crazy-sounding warnings about faraway European billionaires meeting in secret in Davos. But most of the people you know *will* be interested to hear about what's going on with their banks, plans to eliminate all gasoline-powered cars, radical "diversity" initiatives and racial employment quotas, ESG scores applied to their own personal investment accounts, and proposals for a federal jobs guarantee and universal basic income. The key to talking to others about the Great Reset is to find the issues *they* care about the most and start your conversation there.

The Great Reset is so much bigger than any one political party or ideological group. Conservatives cannot stop the Great Reset on their own. Neither can independents nor the liberals who truly care about protecting free speech and individual rights. We must work together by finding common ground upon which we can all stand firmly united, in the same way Americans of all political persuasions in the past have worked together to help those suffering in the wake of natural disasters and to fight against foreign threats and the racial bigotry of the Jim Crow-era South.

There are still many honest, kindhearted Americans on both sides of the political aisle who recognize the immense dangers posed by large tech companies, cancel culture, and massive, powerful, international corporations and financial institutions. Some of these people even work in Big Tech, Hollywood, and legacy media outlets. They do not want the Great Reset any more than I do. But few of us on the right have taken the steps necessary to reach out to them and to others on the left in order to develop a coalition capable of taking on the grave threats facing all of us.

For those of you skeptical of reaching across the aisle, consider that a December 2020 survey of likely voters conducted by Rasmussen Reports and the Heartland Institute found that the majority of voters reject the core concepts that serve as the foundation of the Great Reset.[485]

When asked, "What should be the highest priority for business in the United States?" the overwhelming majority of respondents—a whopping 84 percent—said businesses should focus on earning profits, "providing good benefits and pay to employees," or offering consumers "high quality products and services at the lowest prices."

Only 6 percent of respondents said "climate change" should be the highest priority, and just 3 percent answered with "using business resources to pursue social justice causes."

Perhaps even more telling, when asked, "How influential should international institutions like the United Nations, World Economic Forum, and International Monetary Fund be in creating regulations governing United States businesses?" only 9 percent answered with "very influential."

As these results show, many of the most important policies demanded by supporters of the Great Reset are wildly unpopular, and polling shows that the more Americans of every political persuasion learn about the Reset, the more they want nothing to do with it.[486]

We must put aside our differences and focus on the principles that unite most Americans, and in the process end the toxic us-versus-them culture that pervades nearly every part of our society today—just as we have done innumerable times throughout American history. One of the most recent examples is the fight against the Obama administration's Common Core national curriculum standards. Had parents of every political persuasion not worked together to push back against that top-down approach to education, Common Core would have prevailed, and parents forever would have lost control over what their children learn. Also, most American children would have been taught to think that 2 + 7 = big blue square.

Believe me, no one knows better than I do how difficult it is to put political differences aside, especially after everything that has happened over the past decade. But we are out of options. If we work together, it is possible to stop the Great Reset from taking hold in America. But if we allow our pride and partisanship to distract us from the greater threats at hand, our country will not survive the dark days ahead.

COMMUNITY FIRST

One of the defining characteristics of the modern era is that so few Americans know—and I mean really *know*—their neighbors. Think about it. How many of your ten closest neighbors can you name? (And no, "guy with the terrible toupee" and "woman with the yappy dog" don't count.) Do you know what your neighbors do for a living? Their hobbies? Skills? In a time of crisis, how many of your neighbors could you comfortably ask for help?

What about your local community? Do you know local law enforcement? Could you name your local sheriff, even if your life depended on it? (And someday it might.) How about local store owners? How often do you purchase goods and services from small businesses in town, as opposed to large corporate chains? Do you bank with one of the "big guys" like Chase, Bank of America, or Wells Fargo, or do you have accounts with local banks or credit unions?

Americans used to depend on their neighbors, local businesses, and churches, but now we rely almost entirely on gigantic corporations to fulfill our needs—even though we know that many of them couldn't care less about our values, desires, or even consumer preferences. And as I've shown throughout this book, many large corporations and banks are selling out the American people in order to appease other elites, fill their coffers full of cash, and attain more power for themselves and their corrupt allies in government.

We cannot continue to hand our wealth over to people working to undermine everything we believe in, simply because Amazon's two-day shipping is a convenient luxury. We need to learn about our neighbors and local community businesses and officials and then support them whenever possible.

You should try to limit your debt as much as possible, but if you do need a loan, borrow locally with a small regional bank or credit union. Meet your local bankers in person. Ask them questions about environmental, social, and governance scores, and find out how much of your money they keep locally on hand versus sending to other institutions or lending out. Find out what their relationship is to the Federal Reserve.

Discover which people in your town or city have essential skills like welding, plumbing, automotive repair, tech knowledge, and farming, and develop skills of your own that you can use to trade with others.

Reject money from the federal government at every opportunity, especially federal loans for college and business activities. Those dollars can and will be used against you—or at the very least, to control your behavior.

We also must become active members of our communities. Join the local school board or PTA. If your children don't attend a local school, start a homeschooling association. If you're religious, find a church and become an active member. Join a civic group, club, or other organization that will help you build local relationships. If your area doesn't already have a farmers' market, start one.

If you're politically active, don't spend all your time and money on congressional and presidential elections. Work with others to ensure that your local sheriff and district attorney are committed to defending the Constitution. Learn about your state's attorney general. If he or she isn't fighting tirelessly to defend your liberties, find someone who will. In the coming decades, state and local officials could be your biggest defenders.

I know that all of this is going to require a lot of work and that it would be much easier to continue living as we have for the past two decades. But make no mistake about it, Great Reset elites know that too. They are hoping for apathy and laziness, because if everyone takes the easiest route imaginable, elites' efforts will march on unimpeded, and they will get significantly richer and more powerful at our expense.

Living locally is not the easiest or cheapest thing to do, but it's one of the most important steps you can take to separate yourself from the corrupt Great Reset system that now dominates many of our lives.

REGULATORY CHANGES

Perhaps the quickest way to derail the Great Reset in the United States would be for the federal government to issue regulatory changes that would make it illegal for banks and financial institutions to make lending decisions based on anything other than financial concerns, a move that would gut the Great Reset's ESG system.

Interestingly, in the final weeks of the Trump presidency, his administration's Office of the Comptroller of the Currency issued a rule aimed at doing just that, which it titled Fair Access to Financial Services. As Benjamin Zycher noted for *Real Clear Markets*, the rule required that:

> large banks and federal savings associations make lending decisions based upon "individualized, quantitative risk-based analysis and management of customer risk." Translation: The lenders are not to make such decisions on the basis of the political unpopularity . . . of certain businesses, obvious examples of which are producers of fossil fuels or firearms, operators of for-profit colleges or private prisons, and payday lenders, and perhaps others engaged in entirely legal business activities.[487]

Trump's Fair Access to Financial Services rule would have stopped much of the Great Reset from happening in the United States—or at the very least, would have made it much less likely to occur. I say "would have" because one of the first moves made by the Biden administration in early 2021 was to halt the rule's implementation.[488]

Given Biden's affinity for the Great Reset, his decision to stop Trump's regulatory change should not come as a surprise. It is yet another clear signal that Biden plans to continue moving the ESG ball down the field as quickly as he can. However, this does not mean that a future administration—even a Democratic one—would be unwilling to reinstate the Fair Access to Financial Services rule. It wouldn't be a permanent solution, of course, because like all executive actions, the rule could easily be overturned again in the future, but it would be a good place to start.

A decision by Congress to codify such a rule into law would be a much better, longer-term strategy for stopping the Reset, but that isn't likely to occur until at least 2025.

DEFUND GLOBALISM

Although the United Nations has a long track record of attacking U.S. interests and allies, especially Israel, Americans continue to spend huge amounts of money supporting U.N. agencies. The United States pays for roughly one-fifth of the United Nations's total budget, about $10 billion per year—the most, by far, of any country in the world.[489] Much of the money distributed to the United Nations goes toward humanitarian efforts, a noble cause, but significant funding also ends up paying for other U.N. expenses, such as administrative costs and the cost of developing and promoting a global Great Reset of capitalism.

Much of the funding from the United States comes from "mandatory" payments. These required payments fund specific U.N. agencies like the World Health Organization.[490] Instead of forking over this taxpayer money to be parceled out by U.N. bureaucrats, the United States should consider voluntarily allocating its funding to specific agencies like the World Food Program or other worthwhile endeavors.

Switching to a voluntary payment model would turn up the heat on the United Nations and its agencies. If additional U.S. funding were at stake, these agencies would be more likely to operate effectively and efficiently. For far too long, these agencies have been allowed to operate like the massive, bloated, ineffective global bureaucracies they are.

The United States should also demand a new, extensive audit of the United Nations—and I am not talking about some internal investigation from the U.N. Board of Auditors. We need a U.S.-led, bipartisan examination of how Americans' money is being spent. After all, as noted previously, Americans are footing one-fifth of the bill, so shouldn't they have the right to make sure the money is not being wasted on corruption, bridges to nowhere, or a third espresso machine for John Q. Globalist's office?

Further, rather than continue to passively bankroll ruling-class causes, the United States should demand that the United Nations reverse course on its many leftist campaigns or risk losing American funding for projects that don't provide direct humanitarian aid or clearly benefit U.S. national security. And the same threat should be made to other international organizations that are backing the Great Reset while also relying on the generosity of Americans, like the International Monetary Fund, which remains one of the biggest supporters of the Great Reset. According to a 2018 report, U.S. commitments to the IMF total $155 billion, the largest of any of the IMF's 189 members.[491]

If the United Nations and other international groups refuse to clean up their act, the United States should build more coalitions outside of the United Nations and its allies—ones not devoted to elitist principles and globalism and not riddled with corruption—and redirect funding to those groups instead. This endeavor would be costly and time-consuming, but it would almost certainly prove to be worth the effort.

A BALANCED BUDGET

Over the past two decades, the idea of a balanced federal budget has gone from being a reality to being a near impossibility. The U.S. national debt will almost certainly approach or surpass $29 trillion by the time this book finds its way into your hands, and it could be as high as $30 trillion, depending on just how many more government giveaways Congress approves over the next several months.

Americans have been desensitized to Congress's reckless spending, but I think that is because they have not been thinking about it in the proper context. As I discussed in chapter 4, the massive money printing operations that have occurred over the past twenty years not only pose grave economic risks like hyperinflation and economic stagnation but have become a tool with which supporters of the Great Reset can manipulate and control nearly every aspect of society—from the food you eat to the car you drive to the composition of your house. For that reason, modern monetary theory is, in so many ways, the heart of twenty-first century fascism.

Without modern monetary theory or some other similar system of massive money printing, the Great Reset and comparable schemes would be impossible or require severe violence, which has become much more difficult for governments to resort to in our modern age. This means that a balanced budget is important not only for maintaining economic security but also for ensuring that Americans remain free.

The primary problem is that Congress and presidents have few incentives to rein in spending. Other than a few voices of reason in Washington, D.C., most people in government—Democrats and Republicans alike—are much more interested in buying votes, appeasing special interests, and engaging in cronyism than in being fiscally responsible.

How can the American people force their government to act with fiscal restraint? Modern monetary theory is fascistic poison, and the only antidote is a balanced budget amendment or some other constitutional amendment that puts strict limits on spending.

You might be wondering, "Glenn, if we can't even get members of Congress to pass a balanced budget—or on many occasions, any budget at all—how are we going to push them to pass a new amendment that would forever limit their spending powers?"

Great question. We can't.

When it comes to controlling spending, Congress is likely a lost cause. The political advantages to endless money printing will always outweigh the long-term health of the economy and the possibility of a dangerous expansion of government. Fortunately, though, the American people do not need Congress to pass a balanced budget amendment.

The U.S. Constitution provides two ways to pass new amendments. The first, as I just alluded to, is through Congress. If two-thirds of both houses of Congress agree on a constitutional amendment—fat chance, I know—it will become law once three-fourths of the states, either by convention or by a vote in the state legislature, ratify the proposed amendment.[492]

The second, lesser-known way to approve new amendments is through an Article V convention. According to Article V of the Constitution, if two-thirds of the states, currently thirty-four states, agree to call a convention for proposing amendments, state legislators can then take the role normally held by Congress and write new amendments to the Constitution. Once approved by the state legislatures, the proposed amendment must still be ratified by three-fourths of states.[493]

At first glance, this might sound like an insurmountable hill for the American public to climb, but over the past few decades, a movement to call an Article V convention has gained significant traction throughout much of the country. You might be shocked to learn that, according to constitutional law scholar Robert Natelson, as of 2018, "at least 27 state legislatures have valid applications outstanding for a convention to propose a balanced budget amendment." That's just seven shy of the number required to call a convention.[494]

Even more incredible, some constitutional historians and legal analysts, including Natelson, argue that the number of state applications could actually be as high as thirty-three, because "at least six states without BBA applications have outstanding applications calling for a plenary convention."[495] A plenary convention is a call for an open-ended amendments convention that is not restricted to a single issue, like a balanced budget amendment. Natelson and others say that history and legal precedent suggest that open-ended convention applications can be added to more-specific applications like those calling for a balanced budget, putting the country just a single state away from an amendments convention that could pass a federal budget requirement.

The passage of an amendment to control federal spending would render modern monetary theory useless and slow the rapid growth that the U.S. government has had during the past two decades. And the best part is, Congress could do very little to stop it if the states were to gain the required number of applications.

Some state lawmakers, including many conservatives in states that you would expect to be in favor of a balanced budget amendment, have opposed this important movement over concerns of a "runaway convention." They fear that if there is an Article V convention, the entire Constitution could be rewritten in one fell swoop, giving the Far Left the opportunity it needs to finally cut down parts of the Constitution it has long opposed, such as the Second Amendment.

However, legal experts generally agree that such fears are unfounded. As the Convention of States organization notes, "Article V includes numerous safeguards that protect the U.S. Constitution and ensure that only widely approved amendments are adopted. The strongest safeguard? Any amendment proposed by the Convention goes through the exact same ratification process as amendments proposed by Congress. It must be approved by 38 states. That means if only 13 states vote no, the answer is no. It doesn't get much safer than that!"[496]

Although it has received little media attention, the balanced budget amendment movement has earned the support of countless well-respected current and former conservative government officials like Senator Tom Coburn, Governor Scott Walker, and Senator Rand Paul.

Without a constitutional mandate to limit government spending, it seems highly unlikely, and perhaps even impossible, that future Congresses and presidential administrations would choose to restrain their spending to such great lengths that they would reverse the current trend toward modern monetary theory. That makes a balanced budget amendment an essential part of any plan to derail the Great Reset in the United States.

OTHER CONSTITUTIONAL REFORMS

Time for a history pop quiz. How many amendments to the U.S. Constitution were passed by Congress in 1789 as part of the Bill of Rights?

If you guessed ten, then congratulations; you clearly paid attention in your high school history class. Unfortunately for you, though, your high school history class was wrong. Congress actually approved twelve amendments to the Constitution in the Bill of Rights, but only ten were ratified by the required three-fourths of states soon after the amendments were sent to the states, which is why most Americans think of the Bill of Rights as including only ten amendments.[497]

The original Second Amendment had nothing to do with gun rights; rather, it concerned the compensation awarded to members of Congress. Although three-fourths of states did not initially agree to ratify this amendment, it would eventually receive ratification two hundred years later, in 1992, as the Twenty-Seventh Amendment.

The original First Amendment, often called "Article the First" by historians, has never been ratified by three-fourths of the states, but it came very close in the 1790s. Although very few Americans know anything about Article the First, had it been ratified, it would have had a remarkable impact on the future of the nation.

The purpose of Article the First was to ensure that the House of Representatives provided adequate representation for the citizens of the United States. The fear among many of the Founding Fathers was that Congress could someday transform into an oligarchy, in which a handful of the richest and most powerful would lord over a massive country of diverse people. (Sound familiar?)

To combat this problem, the Founders proposed putting a limit on the population size of congressional districts, so that as America's population grew, the House of Representatives would grow along with it. The big question facing the Founders, though, was, just how large should the cap be?

Following numerous debates on the issue, Congress settled on 40,000 Americans per district, but at the request of George Washington, who had earlier in 1789 began his first term as president, Congress reduced the cap to 30,000 per district. Washington's concern was that House districts greater than 30,000 would be too large for representatives to fairly represent.[498] Incredibly, it was the only request Washington made at the convention to establish the Bill of Rights.

Under Article the First, the cap would, over time, increase until it topped out at one representative for every 50,000 people. But because Article the First was never ratified—likely because of a scribal error that would have made the amendment unworkable in the draft of the Bill of Rights submitted to the states in 1789[499]— Congress was given the power to set its own caps on House representation.

Over time, members of the House realized that the fewer people in Congress, the more power each member would have. So over the course of the nineteenth century, the size of congressional districts steadily increased, until, in 1929, Congress passed the Permanent Apportionment Act, which fixed the total number of House members at 435.[500] At present, the size of the House remains at 435, despite there being 200 million more Americans today than there were in 1929.

Because of Congress's unwillingness to expand the size of the House of Representatives, the average population of a House district is now greater than 750,000, more than twenty-four times larger than what George Washington had suggested in 1789. If the United States had adopted a correctly written Article the First, there would be roughly 6,600 representatives serving in the U.S. House today, transforming how Congress operates.[501]

I know that the thought of sending six thousand more politicians to Washington, D.C., sounds like a gut-wrenching idea, but before dismissing the notion, consider the following reasons why, when it comes to the size of Congress, bigger might very well be better.

1. Adding thousands of members to the House would substantially shrink the size of the average congressional district. In numerous cases, small cities and individual neighborhoods in large cities would have their own member of Congress. This would make it much easier for regular folks to run for office.

2. Smaller district sizes would limit the impact of special interest groups and corporations without the need for laws controlling free speech, because it would no longer require a fortune to win elections. Running for the House would be comparable to trying to win a mayoral election in many small cities.

3. Smaller districts would allow citizens to more easily hold politicians accountable, not only because it would be less difficult for others to run for Congress but also because congressional representatives would, in a very literal sense, be neighbors with their constituents and thus less likely to screw them over every chance they got, as so many in Congress do today.

4. Because regular Americans, including many in the middle and working classes, would be given the opportunity to become members of Congress under Washington's model, it's far less likely Congress would ever be willing to adopt globalist proposals put forward by groups like the World Economic Forum and international governing bodies, making international authoritarian movements like the Great Reset much less influential in the United States.

5. The Founding Fathers strongly believed that limiting the population size of congressional districts was important. It was only a century later, when corrupt politicians were running things, that a permanent cap on House representation was imposed on the American people. Who do you trust: George Washington or our power-hungry oligarchs in Congress?

Of course, ratifying a corrected Article the First, or passing an entirely new version of it and then ratifying it, would be very difficult to achieve outside of an Article V convention like the one described in this chapter, but either is possible if given enough time. And it's worth remembering that congressional representation can be changed at any time by law. With enough pressure from Americans, Congress could be forced to expand the size of the House without ever needing a new constitutional amendment.

Other constitutional amendments also could be used to reform Congress and limit the power of the ruling class in America, such as term limits for members of the House and Senate (an idea already supported by more than 80 percent of Americans[502]), a strict limit on income taxes, and a repeal of the Seventeenth Amendment, which established the direct election of U.S. senators and, in the process, took from state legislatures their ability to check the power of the federal government.[503]

EDUCATION FREEDOM

New constitutional amendments would, on their own, substantially move the country toward stopping the rise of authoritarianism and twenty-first century fascism, but in the long run the only way to slow the growing power of global elites is to reform America's educational systems, which have over the past century been hijacked by establishment progressives. A necessary place to begin is with K–12 education.

There is no doubt that U.S. education is dominated by Democrat-leaning teachers. In 2017, the Education Week Research Center conducted a nationwide survey of 1,122 educators, including teachers, "school leaders," and "district leaders." Of those surveyed, only one-quarter identified as registered Republicans, about the same proportion who said they voted for Donald Trump in the

2016 general election.[504] By comparison, 41 percent of educators said they identify as Democrats, and 50 percent claimed to have voted for Hillary Clinton in 2016.

Bias among teachers unions, which hold a massive amount of political power in national, state, and local elections, is even stronger. During the 2018 election cycle, teachers unions donated more than $30 million to candidates and political or ideological organizations, with 96 percent of that money going to liberals.[505] Further, about 97 percent of the $43 million in donations made by teachers unions in the 2020 election cycle were given to Democrats and liberal groups. It doesn't get more overtly biased than that.[506]

I have no doubt that many teachers affiliated with the Democratic Party are just as antiestablishment and disinterested in the Great Reset as I am, but it is just as certain that a large segment of teachers—especially self-identified Democrats—are devoted to expanding international institutions promoting the values of ruling-class elites.

This bias undoubtedly spills over into the curriculum. Students are inundated with rhetoric about the "existential threat" of climate change, myths about free markets, and Howard Zinn lies about the history of America. These lessons are meant to turn our youth against the United States, the Bill of Rights, and capitalism—the economic system that has made America the world's most powerful, prosperous nation and has liberated hundreds of millions of people from poverty, slavery, and tyranny.

The only way to ensure that America's children are being taught the values that parents on the left and right want to pass along to their children is to empower parents with education savings accounts (ESAs) that would allow them to send their kids to any K–12 school of their choice, whether it be a public school, a private school, or a home school. Scholars have been advocating for such ESAs for decades, but cowardly politicians in both parties, fearing backlash from teachers unions, have largely failed to act, even though numerous surveys show that school choice programs are popular among virtually every demographic.

A survey of people likely to vote in the 2018 elections, published by the American Federation for Children and conducted by polling firm Beck Research (no relation), found overwhelming and bipartisan support for school choice. Three-quarters of all respondents said they favor education savings accounts, including 70 percent of Democrats, 78 percent of independents, 81 percent of Republicans, 87 percent of Hispanics, and 73 percent of African Americans.[507]

Not only would giving parents education freedom be wildly popular across the political spectrum and allow parents to remove their kids from schools promoting elitist ideologies, but it would also dramatically improve educational outcomes and better prepare students for work or higher education.

In 2019, EdChoice, a nonpartisan think tank, reviewed more than 140 empirical studies of U.S. school choice programs and determined that the vast majority of the reports showed that parent satisfaction, civic values, and racial/ethnic integration all improved with the presence of school choice.[508] Further, of the twenty-six studies examined that considered school choice's effect on test scores in public schools, twenty-four revealed that school choice programs improve test scores, and only one showed that a school choice program had a negative effect on outcomes.[509]

In light of all these figures, it is astounding that the ruling class has managed to keep parents from having access to school choice for as long as it has.

SAVING OUR REPUBLIC

If books could save the world, I would have saved it long ago—well, either me, Tom Clancy, or Sue Grafton. (My money is on Sue.) But books cannot save the world. Individuals and families can—people like you.

Even the Bible, the greatest, most influential book on the planet, is useless without people to preach and explain the gospel. As Paul wrote in the tenth chapter of Romans, "How, then, can they call on the one they have not believed in? And how can they believe in the one of whom they have not heard? And how can they hear without someone preaching to them? And how can anyone preach unless they are sent? As it is written: 'How beautiful are the feet of those who bring good news!'" (vv. 14–15 NIV)—or in the case of the Great Reset, the bad news.[510]

The forces behind the Great Reset are powerful. Some of the richest, most well-connected men and women on the planet are lining up to take away your freedom and to alter the American way of life forever. If we do not push back against them, they will succeed. No one can win this battle on their own. Not me, not you—no one. But if those of us who are committed to preserving the freedoms that Americans have long enjoyed devote themselves to the cause of liberty, we will not fail.

You might be thinking, "I have nothing to offer. These problems are so much bigger than I am. How can I make a difference?" If we're going to survive the Great Reset and rebuild our country, we *must change* our way of thinking and our attitudes about the challenges ahead. We must find the strength to become happy warriors, and we can no longer allow ourselves to believe the big lie that there's nothing we can do in our own personal lives to move the needle. You are *not* too small to help change the world.

The history of America has been shaped by ordinary men and women refusing to back down when forced to confront seemingly overwhelming odds. From sit-ins at segregated lunch counters to the beaches of Normandy, when Americans stand for the truth and against authoritarianism, they win.

I've seen this firsthand more times than I can count, but one of the most powerful experiences in my life occurred in the summer of 2021. When President Biden's disastrous handling of the withdrawal of U.S. soldiers in Afghanistan led to a collapse of the Afghan government and a nationwide takeover by the Taliban, my audience raised more than $30 million for the Nazarene Fund to rescue thousands of vulnerable Afghans, including numerous people marked for death. The Biden administration's State Department not only left Americans and Afghans to die but inexplicably resisted our rescue efforts at every turn.

Government officials and massive corporations did not save those thousands of men, women, and children in Afghanistan; military veterans, devoted nonprofit workers, and everyday Americans watching and listening to my television and radio shows did. I can't think of better proof for the claim that you don't need to be a politician or the head of a multibillion-dollar corporation to make a real impact in the world.

As I noted at the start of this chapter, perhaps the most important thing anyone can do is to sound the alarm about the dangers of the Great Reset by talking to others about these problems in relatable terms. In so many ways, you are better equipped to do that than people with gigantic microphones and large social media followings.

I know it is hard to believe, because I am such a likable guy, but there are a lot—and I mean, *a lot*—of people out there who don't exactly think highly of me, to say the least. (And since this is my book, I'm sticking with "the least.") But I am willing to bet there are many people who might not listen to me but know and respect you, people who will take seriously your opinions and warnings because *they trust you.*

This book offers a wealth of information that you can use to help show others how to recognize the Great Reset for what it really is—a globalist, authoritarian scheme to manipulate virtually every industrialized society on earth—but please do not stop learning about the twenty-first century brand of fascism promoted by supporters of the Great Reset when you close this book.

Take the time needed to do your own homework and conduct your own research into each of the ideas I have discussed here, and then make and share your discoveries with others. Find neighbors concerned that America is sliding toward authoritarianism and organize yourselves for the fight ahead. Stay informed by supporting pro-liberty voices, researchers, and investigative reporters like those who work with me daily at Blaze Media. Teach your children the values that built America into the remarkable place it is today: respect for others, honor, humility, compassion, a commitment to freedom for *all* people, and faith. Hold your elected representatives accountable when they fail to pursue those ideals.

After the U.S. Constitution was signed by members of Congress in 1787, Elizabeth Powel, a prominent society figure in Philadelphia and the wife of the city's mayor, asked Benjamin Franklin, "Well, Doctor, what have we got: a republic or a monarchy?" to which Franklin replied, "A republic—if you can keep it."[511]

Let's keep our republic, by fighting back against the Great Reset and every other attempt by elites in America and abroad to seize our liberties in favor of their promises of benevolent rule and smiley-face fascism. We owe it to ourselves, to those who came before us, and to the generations of Americans not yet born, who will someday remember and thank us for not throwing away our freedoms—and their future.

ENDNOTES

Preface

1 Thomas Jefferson to Peter Carr, August 10, 1787, quoted in "Jefferson Quotes & Family Letters," Thomas Jefferson Foundation, US Library of Congress, accessed September 26, 2021, https://tjrs.monticello.org/letter/1297.

Chapter 1: A Brave Terrifying New World

2 See Michael Tadeo, "New Study: 10.3 Million U.S. Jobs Supported by Natural Gas & Oil in 2015," American Petroleum Institute, August 1, 2017, https://www.api.org/news-policy-and-issues/news/2017/08/01/10-3-million-us-jobs-supported-by-natura.

3 Paul Driessen, "Protecting the Environment from the Green New Deal," *Policy Brief*, The Heartland Institute, December 2019, https://www.heartland.org/_template-assets/documents/publications/EnviHarmsPB.pdf.

4 Driessen, "Protecting the Environment."

5 See CAGW Staff, "California's $100 Billion Nightmare High-Speed Rail Project," Citizens Against Government Waste, July 1, 2020, https://www.cagw.org/thewastewatcher/californias-100-billion-nightmare-high-speed-rail-project.

6 For what to expect in the United States, see national debt and GDP of Japan from 1995 to 2019. Data, "GDP (Current US$)—Japan," The World Bank, accessed March 14, 2021, https://data.worldbank.org/indicator/

NY.GDP.MKTP.CD?locations=JP.

7   See "Climate Change Takes Center Stage at the SEC," Perkins Coie, March 8, 2021, https://www.perkinscoie.com/en/news-insights/climate-change-takes-center-stage-at-the-sec.html.

8   Federica Russo, "Politics in the Boardroom: The Role of Chinese Communist Party Committees," *The Diplomat*, December 24, 2019, https://thediplomat.com/2019/12/politics-in-the-boardroom-the-role-of-chinese-communist-party-committees.

9   See Ceri Parker, "8 Predictions for the World in 2030," World Economic Forum, November 12, 2016, https://www.weforum.org/agenda/2016/11/8-predictions-for-the-world-in-2030/.

10 See, for example, Arnoud Boot et al., "What Is Really New in Fintech," *IMFBlog*, International Monetary Fund, December 17, 2020, https://blogs.imf.org/2020/12/17/what-is-really-new-in-fintech.

11 Under Joe Biden's higher education plan, this is likely to occur. See Justin Haskins and Chris Talgo, "Haskins & Talgo: Biden Plan for Free Public College Tuition Could Doom Most Private Colleges," Fox News, July 19, 2020, https://www.foxnews.com/opinion/biden-free-college-justin-haskins-chris-talgo.

12 Bernie Sanders, "A Thurgood Marshall Plan for Public Education," Friends of Bernie Sanders, accessed September 22, 2021, https://berniesanders.com/issues/reinvest-in-public-education.

13 Klaus Schwab, "Now Is the Time for a 'Great Reset,'" World Economic Forum, June 3, 2020, https://www.weforum.org/agenda/2020/06/now-is-the-time-for-a-great-reset.

14 Schwab, "Now Is the Time for a 'Great Reset.'"

15 "About: The Great Reset: A Unique Twin Summit to Begin 2021," World Economic Forum, accessed July 14, 2020. Website has since been removed by World Economic Forum but remains available at Wayback Machine, https://web.archive.org/web/20200919193837/https://www.weforum.org/great-reset/about.

16 Kate Whiting, "How the World Can 'Reset' Itself After COVID-19—According to These Experts," World Economic Forum, June 3, 2020, https://www.weforum.org/agenda/2020/06/covid19-great-reset-gita-gopinath-jennifer-morgan-sharan-burrow-climate.

17 Whiting, "How the World Can 'Reset.'"

18   Whiting, "How the World Can 'Reset.'"

19   Whiting, "How the World Can 'Reset.'" Emphasis in quote added by the authors.

20   "About: The Great Reset," World Economic Forum.

21   NBC News, "Al Gore Talks Climate Crisis: 'This Is the Time for a Great Reset,'" TODAY Show, June 19, 2020, streaming video, 7:02, https://www.today.com/video/al-gore-talks-climate-crisis-this-is-the-time-for-a-great-reset-85439045592, quoted in Justin Haskins, "Al Gore Joins Global Elites Calling for Eco-Socialist 'Great Reset' Proposal," Stopping Socialism, June 22, 2020, https://stoppingsocialism.com/2020/06/al-gore-great-reset.2.

22   Anna Bruce-Lockhart and Ross Chainey, "'Normal Wasn't Working'—John Kerry, Phillip Atiba Goff and Others on the New Social Contract Post-COVID," World Economic Forum, June 24, 2020, https://www.weforum.org/agenda/2020/06/great-reset-social-contract-john-kerry-phillip-goff.

23   "About: The Great Reset," World Economic Forum.

24   Schwab, "Now Is the Time for a 'Great Reset.'"

25   See, for example, "Zhu Min—Profile Contributor," World Economic Forum, accessed March 19, 2021, https://www.weforum.org/agenda/authors/min-zhu.

26   See, for example, Brian Flood, "Amazon Slammed after Banning Books It Says Frames Transgenderism as Mental Illness," Fox News, March 13, 2021, https://www.foxnews.com/media/amazon-bans-books-that-frame-transgender-and-other-sexual-identities-as-mental-illnesses.

27   Among many citations, see Jordan Novet, "Parler's De-Platforming Shows the Exceptional Power of Cloud Providers Like Amazon," CNBC, January 16, 2021, https://www.cnbc.com/2021/01/16/how-parler-deplatforming-shows-power-of-cloud-providers.html.

28   Flood, "Amazon Slammed after Banning Books."

Chapter 2: Never Let a Global Pandemic Go to Waste

29   Viveca Novak, "Bum Rap for Rahm," FactCheck.org, January 13, 2011, https://www.factcheck.org/2011/01/bum-rap-for-rahm.

30   See, for example, Billie Thomson, "The Coronavirus Vigilantes: Chinese Villagers Dig Up Roads and Arm Themselves with Spears to Prevent Wuhan Residents from Escaping into Their Communities," *Daily Mail*, January 29, 2020, https://www.dailymail.co.uk/news/article-7941947/

How-Chinese-villages-coronavirus-epicentre-stop-Hubei-residents-fleeing-land.html.

31   Alice Miranda Ollstein, "Coronavirus Quarantine, Travel Ban Could Backfire, Experts Fear," *Politico*, February 4, 2020, https://www.politico.com/news/2020/02/04/coronavirus-quaratine-travel-110750.

32   Rosie Spinks, "Who Says It's Not Safe to Travel to China?," *New York Times*, February 5, 2020, https://www.nytimes.com/2020/02/05/opinion/china-travel-coronavirus.html.

33   Megan Thielking, "Health Experts Warn China Travel Ban Will Hinder Coronavirus Response," *STAT*, January 31, 2020, https://www.statnews.com/2020/01/31/as-far-right-calls-for-china-travel-ban-health-experts-warn-coronavirus-response-would-suffer/.

34   Zachary Stieber, "New York City Mayor Threatens to 'Permanently' Close Places of Worship That Resist Shutdown Order," *The Epoch Times*, March 30, 2020, https://www.theepochtimes.com/new-york-city-mayor-threatens-to-permanently-close-places-of-worship-that-resist-shutdown-order_3290771.html.

35   OregonLive Politics Team, "Read Oregon Gov. Kate Brown's New Executive Order," *The Oregonian*, updated March 23, 2020, https://www.oregonlive.com/coronavirus/2020/03/read-oregon-gov-kate-browns-new-executive-order.html.

36   MyNorthwest Staff, "Gov. Inslee Issues 'Stay at Home' Proclamation for Washington State," MyNorthwest, March 24, 2020, https://mynorthwest.com/1782819/inslee-washington-stay-at-home-order/.

37   See "Responses to the COVID-19 Pandemic," Prison Policy Initiative, updated July 14, 2020, https://www.prisonpolicy.org/virus/virusresponse.html.

38   Lisa Bartley, "Few of 3,500 California State Prisoners Released Early Were Tested for COVID-19," KABC-TV, April 25, 2020, https://abc7.com/prison-jail-inmate-newsom/6127979.

39   Lee DeVito, "Violating Michigan's Stay-at-Home Order Is Now a $1,000 Fine," *Detroit Metro Times*, April 3, 2020, https://www.metrotimes.com/news-hits/archives/2020/04/03/violating-michigans-stay-at-home-order-is-now-a-1000-fine.

40   Jim Geraghty, "Rhode Island's Governor Sends the National Guard Out in a Door-to-Door Search for New Yorkers," *National Review*, March 30,

2020, https://www.nationalreview.com/corner/rhode-islands-governor-sends-the-national-guard-out-in-a-door-to-door-search-for-new-yorkers.

41 See Alan Reynolds, "How One Model Simulated 2.2 Million U.S. Deaths from COVID-19," Cato Institute, April 21, 2020, https://www.cato.org/blog/how-one-model-simulated-22-million-us-deaths-covid-19.

42 World Health Organization, "WHO Coronavirus (COVID-19) Dashboard," United Nations, last accessed September 22, 2021, https://covid19.who.int.

43 Christine Ferretti, "Whitmer Expects Short-Term Extension of Stay-at-Home Order," *Detroit News*, updated April 22, 2020, https://www.detroitnews.com/story/news/local/michigan/2020/04/22/whitmer-expects-short-term-extension-stay-home-order-covid-19/3006012001.

44 Caleb Parke, "New York Pastor Threatened with $1,000 Fine for Holding Drive-in Church Service," Fox News, May 19, 2020, https://www.foxnews.com/us/coronavirus-new-york-church-police-drive-in-service.

45 Mike Suriani, "Mississippi Churchgoers Fined $500 while Attending Drive-in Service," WREG-TV, April 10, 2020, https://wreg.com/news/coronavirus/mississippi-churchgoers-fined-500-while-attending-drive-in-service.

46 "Kentucky Couple under House Arrest After Testing Positive for COVID-19, Refusing to Quarantine," KMOV, July 19, 2020, https://www.kmov.com/news/kentucky-couple-under-house-arrest-after-testing-positive-for-covid-19-refusing-to-quarantine/article_7924c1b2-c9d8-11ea-982e-8f88f63760aa.html.

47 "Kentucky Couple," KMOV.

48 "Kentucky Couple," KMOV.

49 Data from the US Bureau of Labor Statistics, accessed July 23, 2020, bls.gov.

50 See "Dow Jones Industrial Average," *Trading Economics*, accessed July 23, 2020, https://tradingeconomics.com/united-states/stock-market.

51 See St. Louis Federal Reserve, "Median Sales Price of Houses Sold for the United States," FRED, updated April 23, 2020, https://fred.stlouisfed.org/series/MSPUS, citing data from the US Census Bureau.

52 US Bureau of Labor Statistics, bls.gov.

53 US Bureau of Labor Statistics, bls.gov.

54 Jeff Cox, "Another 2.1 Million File Jobless Claims, but Total Unemployed

Shrinks," CNBC, May 28, 2020, https://www.cnbc.com/2020/05/28/weekly-jobless-claims.html.

55 US Bureau of Labor Statistics, bls.gov.

56 Megan Henney, "Most Small Businesses Requested PPP Coronavirus Relief: Here's How Many Received Loans," Fox Business, May 22, 2020, https://www.foxbusiness.com/small-business/most-small-businesses-applied-for-coronavirus-relief-through-ppp-heres-how-many-received-the-cash.

57 Amanda Macias, "Nearly 90% of the US Navy Hospital Ship in New York Is Empty amid Coronavirus Fight," CNBC, April 17, 2020, https://www.cnbc.com/2020/04/17/nearly-90percent-of-the-us-navy-hospital-ship-in-new-york-is-empty-amid-coronavirus-fight.html.

58 Event 201, "About the Event 201 Exercise," Center for Health Security, accessed August 20, 2020, https://www.centerforhealthsecurity.org/event201/about.

59 Mike Lillis and Scott Wong, "House Democrats Eyeing Much Broader Phase 3 Stimulus," The Hill, March 19, 2020, https://thehill.com/homenews/house/488543-house-democrats-eyeing-much-broader-phase-3-stimulus.

60 Lillis and Wong, "House Democrats." Emphasis in the quote added by the authors.

61 Lillis and Wong, "House Democrats."

62 Andrew Mark Miller, "Top Democrat Says Coronavirus Relief Package a 'Tremendous Opportunity to Restructure Things to Fit Our Vision': Report," Washington Examiner, March 24, 2020, https://www.washingtonexaminer.com/news/report-clyburn-says-coronavirus-relief-package-a-tremendous-opportunity-to-restructure-things-to-fit-our-vision.

63 Brooke Singman, "Rand Paul Says GOP Lunch Was Like Meeting with 'Bernie Bros,' Blasts Party on Spending," Fox News, July 22, 2020, https://www.foxnews.com/politics/rand-paul-gop-lunch-meeting-bernie-bros.

64 Singman, "Rand Paul."

65 Tara Siegel Bernard and Ron Lieber, "F.A.Q. on Stimulus Checks, Unemployment and the Coronavirus Plan," New York Times, June 25, 2020, https://www.nytimes.com/article/coronavirus-stimulus-package-questions-answers.html.

66 Some individuals and couples earning more than the income limits

described here received stimulus money as well. The amount varied based on income and eventually phased out entirely.

67   Lorie Konish, "159 Million Stimulus Checks Have Been Sent. What to Do If You Still Haven't Received Yours," CNBC, June 4, 2020, https://www.cnbc.com/2020/06/04/irs-has-sent-159-million-stimulus-checks-how-to-get-your-1200.html.

68   Bernard and Lieber, "F.A.Q."

69   Jacob Pramuk, "Biden Signs $1.9 Trillion Covid Relief Bill, Clearing Way for Stimulus Checks, Vaccine Aid," CNBC, March 11, 2021, https://www.cnbc.com/2021/03/11/biden-1point9-trillion-covid-relief-package-thursday-afternoon.html.

70   See Amelia Thomson-DeVeaux, "Many Americans Are Getting More Money From Unemployment Than They Were From Their Jobs," *FiveThirtyEight*, ABC News, May 15, 2020, https://fivethirtyeight.com/features/many-americans-are-getting-more-money-from-unemployment-than-they-were-from-their-jobs.

71   Thomson-DeVeaux, "Many Americans Are Getting More Money."

72   Jeff Stein, Andrew Van Dam, and Eli Rosenberg, "White House Signals Openness to Unemployment Compromise as Crucial Deadline Looms for 30 Million Americans," *Washington Post*, July 14, 2020, https://www.washingtonpost.com/business/2020/07/14/unemployment-benefits-expiring-coronavirus.

73   Pramuk, "Biden Signs $1.9 Trillion Covid Relief Bill."

74   Jonathan Ingram, Nicholas Horton, and Sam Adolphsen, "Extra COVID-19 Medicaid Funds Come at a High Cost to States," Foundation for Government Accountability, April 8, 2020, https://thefga.org/research/covid-19-medicaid-funds.

75   Ingram, Horton, and Adolphsen, "Extra COVID-19 Medicaid Funds."

76   Ingram, Horton, and Adolphsen, "Extra COVID-19 Medicaid Funds."

77   Carol Roth, *The War on Small Business: How the Government Used the Pandemic to Crush the Backbone of America* (New York: Broadside Books, 2021).

78   Roth, *War on Small Business.*

79   See "United States Government Debt: 1942–2020," Trading Economics, accessed July 24, 2020, https://tradingeconomics.com/united-states/government-debt.

80   Chris Edwards, "Crisis May Add $6 Trillion to Federal Debt," *Cato at Liberty*, Cato Institute, April 21, 2020, https://www.cato.org/blog/crisis-may-add-6-trillion-federal-debt.

81   See "United States Government Debt: 1942–2020," Trading Economics.

82   "Credit and Liquidity Programs and the Balance Sheet," Board of Governors of the Federal Reserve System, accessed August 18, 2020, https://www.federalreserve.gov/monetarypolicy/bst_recenttrends.htm.

83   Manoj Singh, "Understanding the Federal Reserve Balance Sheet," Investopedia, May 11, 2020, https://www.investopedia.com/articles/economics/10/understanding-the-fed-balance-sheet.asp.

84   "Credit and Liquidity Programs," Board of Governors of the Federal Reserve System.

85   Bill Dudley, "The Fed's Risky Business Is Worth It," *Bloomberg*, June 23, 2020, https://www.bloomberg.com/opinion/articles/2020-06-23/coronavirus-fed-risk-with-10-trillion-balance-sheet-is-worth-it.

86   Michael P. Regan and Katherine Greifeld, "Like It or Not, a Modern Monetary Theory Experiment Is Underway," *Bloomberg*, August 14, 2020, https://www.bloomberg.com/news/articles/2020-08-14/like-it-or-not-a-modern-monetary-theory-experiment-is-underway.

87   Regan and Greifeld, "Like It or Not."

88   Sergei Klebnikov, "Trump Criticizes Federal Reserve at Davos for Holding Back U.S. Economy," *Forbes*, January 21, 2020, https://www.forbes.com/sites/sergeiklebnikov/2020/01/21/trump-criticizes-federal-reserve-at-davos-for-holding-back-us-economy/#577c32319ebd.

89   Paul Conner, "Trump: Federal Reserve Holding US Economy Back," Fox Business, October 29, 2019, https://www.foxbusiness.com/markets/trump-federal-reserve-holding-economy-back.

90   Stephanie Kelton, "Paul Krugman Asked Me about Modern Monetary Theory. Here Are 4 Answers," Stephanie Kelton (website), accessed August 20, 2020, https://stephaniekelton.com/paul-krugman-asked-me-about-modern-monetary-theory-here-are-4-answers.

91   "The Great Reset," World Economic Forum, accessed July 24, 2020, https://www.weforum.org/great-reset.

92   "The Great Reset," World Economic Forum.

93   Chloe Taylor, "Coronavirus Crisis Presents a 'Golden Opportunity' to Reboot the Economy, Prince Charles Says," CNBC, June 3, 2020, https://

www.cnbc.com/2020/06/03/prince-charles-covid-19-a-golden-oppor-tunity-to-reboot-the-economy.html.

94   "The Great Reset: About," World Economic Forum, June 3, 2020, https://web.archive.org/web/20200919193837/https://www.weforum.org/great-reset/about.

95   "The Great Reset: About," World Economic Forum.

96   Kate Whiting, "How the World Can 'Reset' Itself After COVID-19—According to These Experts," World Economic Forum, June 3, 2020, https://www.weforum.org/agenda/2020/06/covid19-great-reset-gita-gopinath-jennifer-morgan-sharan-burrow-climate.

97   "Kristalina Georgieva: Greener, Smarter, Fairer," World Economic Forum, June 3, 2020, https://www.weforum.org/great-reset/live-updates/week-ending-june-7#greenest-recovery-ever-ma-jun-china-green-finance-committee.

98   Robert E. Moritz, "To Reinvent the Future, We Must All Work Together," World Economic Forum, July 17, 2020, https://www.weforum.org/agenda/2020/07/to-reinvent-the-future-we-must-all-work-together.

99   Moritz, "To Reinvent the Future."

100   Taylor, "Coronavirus Crisis Presents a 'Golden Opportunity.'"

101   Whiting, "How the World Can 'Reset' Itself After COVID-19."

Chapter 3: Climate Change: The Catalyst for a "New World Order"

102   Nandita Bose, "Biden Tours Flood-Hit Areas; Calls Climate Change 'Existential Threat,'" Reuters, September 7, 2021, https://www.reuters.com/world/us/biden-renews-focus-domestic-issues-with-tour-new-york-area-flood-damage-2021-09-07.

103   See Glenn Beck, "Eco-Socialism and Climate Change," chap. 8 in *Arguing with Socialists* (New York: Threshold Editions, 2020).

104   "Total Wildland Fires and Acres (1926–2019)," National Interagency Fire Center, accessed September 20, 2019, https://www.nifc.gov/fireInfo/fireInfo_stats_totalFires.html.

105   P. J. Klotzbach et al., "Continental U.S. Hurricane Landfall Frequency and Associated Damage Observations and Future Risks," *Bulletin of the American Meteorological Society* 99, no. 7, 1359–77, https://journals.ametsoc.org/doi/pdf/10.1175/BAMS-D-17-0184.1.

106   Food and Agriculture Organization, "World Food Situation," United

Nations, accessed July 28, 2020, http://www.fao.org/worldfoodsituation/csdb/en.

107 "Record Global Cereal Production Forecast Boosts Stock-to-Use Ratio to a Twenty-Year High," World Food Situation, Food and Agriculture Organization of the United Nations, accessed July 28, 2020, http://www.fao.org/worldfoodsituation/csdb/en.

108 Kelsey Piper, "Is Climate Change an 'Existential Threat'—Or Just a Catastrophic One?," Vox, June 28, 2019, https://www.vox.com/future-perfect/2019/6/13/18660548/climate-change-human-civilization-existential-risk.

109 Joe Biden @JoeBiden, "Climate Change Poses an Existential Threat," Twitter, January 27, 2020, https://twitter.com/joebiden/status/1221880050951176192.

110 Katrina vanden Heuvel, "Media Must Put the Existential Threat of Climate Change Front and Center," The Washington Post, September 22, 2020, https://www.washingtonpost.com/opinions/2020/09/22/media-must-put-existential-threat-climate-change-front-center.

111 Daniel Kraemer, "Greta Thunberg: Who Is the Climate Campaigner and What Are Her Aims?," BBC, February 28, 2020, https://www.bbc.com/news/world-europe-49918719.

112 Kraemer, "Greta Thunberg."

113 Elizabeth Weise, "'How Dare You?' Read Greta Thunberg's Emotional Climate Change Speech to UN and World Leaders," USA Today, September 24, 2019, https://www.usatoday.com/story/news/2019/09/23/greta-thunberg-tells-un-summit-youth-not-forgive-climate-inaction/2421335001.

114 Weise, "'How Dare You?'"

115 Weise, "'How Dare You?'"

116 Ghostbusters, directed by Ivan Reitman (Columbia-Delphi Productions, 1984). Performances by Bill Murray, Dan Aykroyd, and Harold Ramis.

117 See full survey results at Matthew Smith, "New YouGov Study of 30,000 People in 28 Countries and Regions Uncovers Noticeable Differences in Attitudes Between East and West," YouGov, September 15, 2019, https://yougov.co.uk/topics/science/articles-reports/2019/09/15/international-poll-most-expect-feel-impact-climate.

118 Smith, "New YouGov Study."

119 Thomas Reuters Foundation, "One in Five UK Children Report Night-mares About Climate Change," Reuters, March 2, 2020, https://www. reuters.com/article/climate-change-children/one-in-five-uk-children-report-nightmares-about-climate-change-idUSL1N2AV1FF.

120 Thomas Reuters Foundation, "One in Five UK Children Report Night-mares."

121 Victoria Knight, "'Climate Grief': Fears About the Planet's Future Weigh on Americans' Mental Health," Kaiser Health News, July 18, 2019, https:// khn.org/news/climate-grief-fears-about-the-planets-future-weigh-on-americans-mental-health.

122 Knight, "'Climate Grief.'"

123 Knight, "'Climate Grief.'"

124 Ayanna Runcie, "Support Group Helps to Deal with Psychological Effects of Climate Change," CBS News, August 29, 2019, https://www.cbsnews. com/news/the-good-grief-network-support-group-helps-to-deal-with-psychological-effects-of-climate-change.

125 "What is the Good Grief Network?," Good Grief Network, accessed July 29, 2020, https://www.goodgriefnetwork.org/about.

126 Runcie, "Support Group."

127 Susan Clayton et al., *Mental Health and Our Changing Climate: Impacts, Implications, and Guidance*, American Psychological Association, March 2017, https://www.apa.org/news/press/releases/2017/03/mental-health-climate.pdf.

128 Jessica Colarossi, "Feeling Stressed About the Environment? You're Not Alone," *The Brink*, Boston University, April 22, 2019, http://www.bu.edu/articles/2019/climate-grief.

129 Umair Irfan, "We Need to Talk About the Ethics of Having Children in a Warming World," Vox, March 11, 2020, https://www.vox.com/2019/3/11/18256166/climate-change-having-kids.

130 Eliza Relman and Walt Hickey, "More Than a Third of Millennials Share Rep. Alexandria Ocasio-Cortez's Worry About Having Kids while the Threat of Climate Change Looms," *Business Insider*, March 4, 2019, https://www.businessinsider.com/millennials-americans-worry-about-kids-children-climate-change-poll-2019-3?r=US&IR=T.

131 Claire Cain Miller, "Americans Are Having Fewer Babies. They Told Us Why," *New York Times*, July 5, 2018, https://www.nytimes.com/2018/07/

05/upshot/americans-are-having-fewer-babies-they-told-us-why.html.

132 "About Us," Extinction Rebellion, accessed August 18, 2020, https://
extinctionrebellion.uk/the-truth/about-us.

133 Mattha Busby, "Extinction Rebellion Protesters Spray Fake Blood on to
Treasury," *The Guardian*, October 3, 2019, https://www.theguardian.com/
environment/2019/oct/03/extinction-rebellion-protesters-spray-fake-
blood-treasury-london.

134 Jessie Yeung and Eliza Mackintosh, "Angry Commuters Drag Extinction
Rebellion Protesters off Trains during London Travel Disruption," CNN,
October 17, 2019, https://www.cnn.com/2019/10/17/uk/extinction-
rebellion-london-intl-hnk/index.html.

135 "Extinction Rebellion Protesters Glue Themselves to Door of Bank," Dutch
News, October 8, 2019, https://www.dutchnews.nl/news/2019/10/
extinction-rebellion-protesters-glue-themselves-to-door-of-bank

136 David Wallace-Wells, "The Uninhabitable Earth," *New York Magazine*,
July 10, 2017, https://nymag.com/intelligencer/2017/07/climate-change-
earth-too-hot-for-humans.html.

137 Wallace-Wells, "Uninhabitable Earth."

138 Wallace-Wells, "Uninhabitable Earth."

139 Jen Christensen, "250,000 Deaths a Year from Climate Change Is a 'Conservative Estimate,' Research Says," CNN, January 16, 2019, https://www.cnn.
com/2019/01/16/health/climate-change-health-emergency-study/index.
html.

140 Tedros Adhanom Ghebreyesus, "Climate Change Is Already Killing Us,"
Foreign Affairs, September 23, 2019, https://www.foreignaffairs.com/
articles/2019-09-23/climate-change-already-killing-us.

141 Adhanom Ghebreyesus, "Climate Change."

142 Matt Simon, "How the Climate Crisis Is Killing Us, in 9 Alarming Charts,"
Wired, November 13, 2019, https://www.wired.com/story/how-the-
climate-crisis-is-killing-us.

143 Doyle Rice, "Climate Change Could Zap Clouds, Bake the Earth Even
More," *USA Today*, February 25, 2019, https://www.usatoday.com/story/
news/nation/2019/02/25/global-warming-could-zap-earths-clouds-bake-
us-even-more/2980788002.

144 Sarah Knapton, "BBC Staff Told to Stop Inviting Cranks on to Science
Programmes," *The Telegraph*, July 4, 2014, https://www.telegraph.co.uk/

culture/tvandradio/bbc/10944629/BBC-staff-told-to-stop-inviting-cranks-on-to-science-programmes.html.

145 Aaron Rupar, "CNN Urges People to Ignore Climate Change Deniers They Regularly Feature on TV," Vox, December 11, 2018, https://www.vox.com/2018/12/11/18136551/cnn-climate-change-debunk.

146 Ian Schwartz, "Chuck Todd: 'We're Not Going to Give Time to Climate Deniers,'" RealClear Politics, January 2, 2019, https://www.realclearpolitics.com/video/2019/01/02/chuck_todd_im_not_going_to_give_time_to_climate_deniers.html.

147 See Mark Perry, "There Is No Climate Emergency, Say 500 Experts in Letter to the United Nations," American Enterprise Institute, October 1, 2019, https://www.aei.org/carpe-diem/there-is-no-climate-emergency-say-500-experts-in-letter-to-the-united-nations.

148 Perry, "There Is No Climate Emergency."

149 Perry, "There Is No Climate Emergency."

150 Roger Bezdek et al., Climate Change Reconsidered II: Fossil Fuels (Arlington Heights, IL: Nongovernmental Panel on Climate Change, 2019), http://climatechangereconsidered.org/climate-change-reconsidered-ii-fossil-fuels.

151 George Getze, "Dire Famine Forecast by 1975," Salt Lake Tribune, November 17, 1967, quoted by Myron Ebell and Steven Milloy, "Wrong Again: 50 Years of Failed Eco-Pocalyptic Predictions," Competitive Enterprise Institute, September 18, 2019, https://cei.org/blog/wrong-again-50-years-failed-eco-pocalyptic-predictions.

152 Getze, "Dire Famine Forecast by 1975."

153 Getze, "Dire Famine Forecast by 1975."

154 See Myron Ebell and Steven Milloy, "Wrong Again: 50 Years of Failed Eco-Pocalyptic Predictions," Competitive Enterprise Institute, September 18, 2019, https://cei.org/blog/wrong-again-50-years-failed-eco-pocalyptic-predictions.

155 Ebell and Milloy, "Wrong Again."

156 Ebell and Milloy, "Wrong Again."

157 Anthony Tucker, "Space Satellites Show New Ice Age Coming Fast," The Guardian, January 29, 1974, quoted in Ebell and Milloy, "Wrong Again."

158 "Another Ice Age?," TIME, June 24, 1974, quoted in Ebell and Milloy, "Wrong Again."

159 "Another Ice Age?," TIME.

160 Antonio Gasparrini et al., "Mortality Risk Attributable to High and Low Ambient Temperature: A Multicountry Observational Study," *The Lancet* 386, no. 9991 (July 2015), 369–75, https://www.thelancet.com/journals/lancet/article/PIIS0140-6736(14)62114-0/fulltext.

161 Suzy Hansen, "Stormy Weather," *Salon*, October 23, 2001, https://web.archive.org/web/20110202162233/https:/www.salon.com/books/int/2001/10/23/weather.

162 Seth Borenstein, "NASA Scientist: 'We're Toast,'" Associated Press, June 24, 2008, quoted in Ebell and Milloy, "Wrong Again."

163 "Rising Seas Could Obliterate Nations: U.N. Officials," Associated Press, June 30, 1989, https://www.newspapers.com/image/247922164/?terms=global%2Bwarming%2Bnoel%2Bbrown.

164 "Rising Seas Could Obliterate Nations," Associated Press.

165 "Key Findings of the Pentagon," *The Guardian*, February 22, 2004, https://www.theguardian.com/environment/2004/feb/22/usnews.theobserver1?CMP=share_btn_link.

166 "Key Findings," *The Guardian*.

167 "Acton Research: Lord Acton Quote Archive," Acton Institute, accessed July 31, 2020, https://www.acton.org/research/lord-acton-quote-archive.

168 "What Is U.S. Electricity Generation by Energy Source?," US Energy Information Administration, accessed July 31, 2020, https://www.eia.gov/tools/faqs/faq.php?id=427&t=3.

169 "What Is U.S. Electricity Generation by Energy Source?," US Energy Information Administration.

170 Michael Shellenberger, "Unreliable Nature of Solar and Wind Makes Electricity More Expensive, New Study Finds," *Forbes*, April 22, 2019, https://www.forbes.com/sites/michaelshellenberger/2019/04/22/unreliable-nature-of-solar-and-wind-makes-electricity-much-more-expensive-major-new-study-finds/#60c6cedf4f59. Emphasis appearing in this quote is in the original text.

171 "What's the Lifespan for a Nuclear Reactor? Much Longer Than You Might Think," US Office of Nuclear Energy, April 16, 2020, https://www.energy.gov/ne/articles/whats-lifespan-nuclear-reactor-much-longer-you-might-think.

172 Isaac Orr, "Every Wind Turbine and Solar Panel Built Today Will Be Scrap Metal by 2050," Center of the American Experiment, June 26, 2019,

https://www.americanexperiment.org/2019/06/every-wind-turbine-solar-panel-built-today-will-scrap-metal-2050/.

173 Orr, "Every Wind Turbine and Solar Panel."

174 Orr, "Every Wind Turbine and Solar Panel."

175 Orr, "Every Wind Turbine and Solar Panel."

176 Isaac Orr, "Biden's New Energy Plan Is Terrible," Center of the American Experiment, July 16, 2020, https://www.americanexperiment.org/2020/07/bidens-new-energy-plan-is-terrible.

177 See "The Complete Case for Nuclear," Environmental Progress, accessed July 31, 2020, https://environmentalprogress.org/the-complete-case-for-nuclear.

178 Paul Driessen, "Protecting the Environment from the Green New Deal," *Policy Brief*, Heartland Institute, December 2019, https://www.heartland.org/_template-assets/documents/publications/EnviHarmsPB.pdf.

179 Driessen, "Protecting the Environment."

180 Michael Shellenberger, "If Solar Panels Are So Clean, Why Do They Produce so Much Toxic Waste?," *Forbes*, May 23, 2018, https://www.forbes.com/sites/michaelshellenberger/2018/05/23/if-solar-panels-are-so-clean-why-do-they-produce-so-much-toxic-waste/#404c9a1121cc.

181 Christina Stella, "Unfurling the Waste Problem Caused by Wind Energy," NPR, September 10, 2019, https://www.npr.org/2019/09/10/759376113/unfurling-the-waste-problem-caused-by-wind-energy.

182 Michael Shellenberger, "Why Renewables Can't Save the Planet," *Quillette*, February 27, 2019, https://quillette.com/2019/02/27/why-renewables-cant-save-the-planet.

183 Michael Shellenberger, "Stop Letting Your Ridiculous Fears of Nuclear Waste Kill the Planet," *Forbes*, June 19, 2018, https://www.forbes.com/sites/michaelshellenberger/2018/06/19/stop-letting-your-ridiculous-fears-of-nuclear-waste-kill-the-planet/#55589ab8562e.

184 Shellenberger, "Stop Letting Your Ridiculous Fears."

185 See Hannah Ritchie, "What Was the Death Toll from Chernobyl and Fukushima?," *Our World in Data*, July 24, 2017, https://ourworldindata.org/what-was-the-death-toll-from-chernobyl-and-fukushima.

186 Ritchie, "What Was the Death Toll?"

187 See "Top 15 Nuclear Generating Countries," Nuclear Energy Institute, accessed July 31, 2020, https://www.nei.org/resources/statistics/

top-15-nuclear-generating-countries.

188 "Top 15 Nuclear Generating Countries," Nuclear Energy Institute.

189 Mark P. Mills, "The 'New Energy Economy': An Exercise in Magical Thinking," Manhattan Institute, March 26, 2019, https://www.manhattan-institute.org/green-energy-revolution-near-impossible.

190 Ariel Cohen, "Rolls-Royce Reignites the Race to Build Mini-Nuclear Power Plants," Forbes, February 21, 2020, https://www.forbes.com/sites/arielcohen/2020/02/21/rolls-royce-reignites-the-race-to-build-mini-nuclear-power-plants/#3d8cb4187aab.

191 Cohen, "Rolls-Royce Reignites the Race."

192 Jason Reed, "Nuclear Energy Is Almost Here," RealClear Energy, August 10, 2020, https://www.realclearenergy.org/articles/2020/08/10/nuclear_energy_is_almost_here_501542.html.

193 Kate Whiting, "How the World Can 'Reset' Itself After COVID-19— According to These Experts," World Economic Forum, June 3, 2020, https://www.weforum.org/agenda/2020/06/covid19-great-reset-gita-gopinath-jennifer-morgan-sharan-burrow-climate.

194 Whiting, "How the World Can 'Reset' Itself."

195 Whiting, "How the World Can 'Reset' Itself."

196 Whiting, "How the World Can 'Reset' Itself."

197 See "António Guterres: Equal, Inclusive, Sustainable," The Great Reset, World Economic Forum, June 3, 2020, https://www.weforum.org/great-reset/live-updates/week-ending-june-7#greenest-recovery-ever-ma-jun-china-green-finance-committee.

198 James Shaw, "The Covid-19 Crisis Creates a Chance to Reset Economies on a Sustainable Footing," The Guardian, April 22, 2020, https://www.theguardian.com/world/commentisfree/2020/apr/23/covid-19-crisis-reset-economies-sustainable-footing.

199 Shaw, "Covid-19 Crisis Creates a Chance to Reset."

200 Chloe Taylor, "Coronavirus Crisis Presents a 'Golden Opportunity' to Reboot the Economy, Prince Charles Says," CNBC, June 3, 2020, https://www.cnbc.com/2020/06/03/prince-charles-covid-19-a-golden-oppor-tunity-to-reboot-the-economy.html.

201 Taylor, "Coronavirus Crisis Presents a 'Golden Opportunity.'"

202 "The Great Reset: A Unique Twin Summit to Begin 2021," World Economic Forum, June 3, 2020, https://www.weforum.org/press/2020/

06/the-great-reset-a-unique-twin-summit-to-begin-2021.

203   "'Our House is on Fire': Greta Thunberg, 16, Urges Leaders to Act on Climate," *The Guardian*, January 25, 2019, https://www.theguardian.com/ environment/2019/jan/25/our-house-is-on-fire-greta-thunberg16-urges-leaders-to-act-on-climate.

Chapter 4: Modern Monetary Theory: Fuel for a Global Economic Takeover

204   Thomas Jefferson, letter to John Taylor, May 28, 1816, Founders Online, National Archives, accessed September 23, 2021, https://founders. archives.gov/documents/Jefferson/03-10-02-0053.

205   Murray Rothbard, *The Case Against the Fed* (Auburn, AL: Mises Institute, 1994), https://mises.org/library/case-against-fed-0/html/c/306.

206   Jacob Goldstein and Robert Smith, "A Locked Door, a Secret Meeting and the Birth of the Fed," NPR, December 23, 2013, https://www.npr. org/sections/money/2013/12/23/256326325/a-locked-door-a-secret-meeting-and-the-birth-of-the-fed.

207   "A History of Central Banking in the United States," Federal Reserve Bank of Minneapolis, accessed August 8, 2020, https://www.minneapolisfed. org/about-us/our-history/history-of-central-banking.

208   "History of Central Banking," Federal Reserve Bank of Minneapolis.

209   Rothbard, *Case Against the Fed*.

210   Rothbard, *Case Against the Fed*.

211   Amy Goldstein, "Why Vermont's Single-Payer Effort Failed and What Democrats Can Learn from It," *The Washington Post*, April 29, 2019, https://www.washingtonpost.com/national/health-science/why-vermonts-single-payer-effort-failed-and-what-democrats-can-learn-from-it/2019/ 04/29/c9789018-3ab8-11e9-a2cd-307b06d0257b_story.html.

212   Goldstein, "Why Vermont's Single-Payer Effort Failed."

213   Douglas Holtz-Eakin et al., "The Green New Deal: Scope, Scale, and Implications," American Action Forum, February 25, 2019, https://www. americanactionforum.org/research/the-green-new-deal-scope-scale-and-implications.

214   Jim Chappelow, "Economics: Overview, Types, and Economic Indicators," Investopedia, accessed August 10, 2020, https://www.investopedia.com/ terms/e/economics.asp.

215   David Brennan, "Alexandria Ocasio-Cortez to Heckler: Conflict Happens

'Under a Scarcity Mindset. This Should Not Be the Fight,'" *Newsweek*, March 18, 2019, https://www.newsweek.com/alexandria-ocasio-cortez-scarcity-conflict-education-town-hall-college-1365949.

216 Stephanie Kelton, "About Stephanie Kelton," Stephanie Kelton (website), accessed July 29, 2020, https://stephaniekelton.com/about.

217 Stephanie Kelton, "About the Deficit Myth," Stephanie Kelton (website), accessed July 29, 2020, https://stephaniekelton.com/book.

218 Peter Kirsanow, "President Obama Calls His Own Actions Irresponsible and Unpatriotic," *National Review*, August 24, 2011, https://www.national-review.com/corner/president-obama-calls-his-own-actions-irresponsible-and-unpatriotic-peter-kirsanow.

219 Jordan Malter, "Bernie Sanders' 2016 Economic Advisor Stephanie Kelton on Modern Monetary Theory and the 2020 Race,"CNBC, March 2, 2019, https://www.cnbc.com/2019/03/01/bernie-sanders-economic-advisor-stephanie-kelton-on-mmt-and-2020-race.html.

220 "U.S. National Debt Clock: Real Time," accessed August 11, 2020, https://www.usdebtclock.org.

221 Malter, "Bernie Sanders."

222 Malter, "Bernie Sanders."

223 Matthew Klein, "Everything You Need to Know About Modern Monetary Theory," *Barron's*, June 7, 2019, https://www.barrons.com/articles/modern-monetary-theory-51559956914.

224 Stephanie Kelton, *The Deficit Myth: Modern Monetary Theory and the Birth of the People's Economy* (New York: PublicAffairs, 2019).

225 Kelton, *Deficit Myth*.

226 Jake Frankenfield, "Cryptocurrency," Investopedia, May 5, 2020, https://www.investopedia.com/terms/c/cryptocurrency.asp.

227 Felix Richter, "The Rise of E-Commerce in the United States," Statista, January 16, 2020, https://www.statista.com/chart/14011/e-commerce-share-of-total-retail-sales.

228 Kelton, *Deficit Myth*.

229 Kelton, *Deficit Myth*.

230 L. Randall Wray, "Response to Doug Henwood's Trolling in Jacobin," *New Economic Perspectives*, February 25, 2019, http://neweconomicperspectives.org/2019/02/response-to-doug-henwoods-trolling-in-jacobin.html.

231 Pavlina Tcherneva, "MMT Is Already Happening," *Jacobin*, February 27,

2019, https://jacobinmag.com/2019/02/mmt-modern-monetary-theory-doug-henwood-overton-window.

232 Janelle Cammenga, "How High Are Cigarette Taxes in Your State?," Tax Foundation, April 10, 2019, https://taxfoundation.org/2019-state-cigarette-tax-rankings.

233 Kelton, *Deficit Myth.*

234 Steve H. Hanke and Alex K. F. Kwok, "On the Measurement of Zimbabwe's Hyperinflation," *Cato Journal* 29, no. 2 (Spring/Summer 2009), https://www.cato.org/sites/cato.org/files/serials/files/cato-journal/2009/5/cj29n2-8.pdf.

235 "Hyperinflation in Zimbabwe," in *Globalization and Monetary Policy Institute 2011 Annual Report,* Federal Reserve Bank of Dallas, 2011, https://www.dallasfed.org/~/media/documents/institute/annual/2011/annual11b.pdf.

236 Richard Best, "How the U.S. Dollar Became the World's Reserve Currency," Investopedia, October 1, 2019, https://www.investopedia.com/articles/forex-currencies/092316/how-us-dollar-became-worlds-reserve-currency.asp.

237 L. Randall Wray, "Helicopter Ben—How Modern Money Theory Responds to Hyperinflation Hyperventilators," *Naked Capitalism,* September 7, 2011, https://www.nakedcapitalism.com/2011/09/randy-wray-helicopter-ben-%E2%80%93-how-modern-money-theory-responds-to-hyperinflation-hyperventilators.html.

238 Malter, "Bernie Sanders."

239 "CBO's Failed Obamacare Enrollment Projections," White House, June 20, 2017, https://www.whitehouse.gov/articles/cbos-failed-obamacare-enrollment-projections.

240 Malter, "Bernie Sanders."

241 Beatrice Di Caro, "The Great Reset: Building Future Resilience to Global Risks," World Economic Forum, November 17, 2020, https://www.weforum.org/agenda/2020/11/the-great-reset-building-future-resilience-to-global-risks.

242 John Ainger and Liz McCormick, "Goldman Warns the Dollar's Grip on Global Markets Might Be Over," *Bloomberg,* July 28, 2020, https://www.bloomberg.com/news/articles/2020-07-28/goldman-warns-dollar-s-role-as-world-reserve-currency-is-at-risk.

243 Adam Hayes, "IMF Special Drawing Rights," Investopedia, June 25, 2019, https://www.investopedia.com/articles/forex/040215/what-are-imf-special-drawing-rights.asp.

244 "Mark Carney," World Economic Forum, accessed January 15, 2021, https://www.weforum.org/agenda/authors/mark-carney.

245 Phillip Inman, "Mark Carney: Dollar Is Too Dominant and Could Be Replaced by Digital Currency," The Guardian, August 23, 2019, https://www.theguardian.com/business/2019/aug/23/mark-carney-dollar-dominant-replaced-digital-currency.

246 Phillip Inman, "Mark Carney Clears the Path for New Digital Currency Providers," The Guardian, June 20, 2019, https://www.theguardian.com/business/2019/jun/20/mark-carney-bank-of-england-lend-digital-business-sme-cryptocurrency.

247 "About the Jackson Hole Economic Policy Symposium," Federal Reserve Bank of Kansas City, https://www.kansascityfed.org/publications/research/escp/jackson-hole.

248 Inman, "Mark Carney."

249 "Governing the Coin: World Economic Forum Announces Global Consortium for Digital Currency Governance," World Economic Forum, January 24, 2020, https://www.weforum.org/press/2020/01/governing-the-coin-world-economic-forum-announces-global-consortium-for-digital-currency-governance.

250 Dashveenjit Kaur, "'Digital Dollar' Is Now a High Priority Project for the US," TechHQ, March 1, 2021, https://techhq.com/2021/03/digital-dollar-is-now-a-high-priority-project-for-the-us.

251 Kaur, "'Digital Dollar.'"

252 Rakesh Sharma, "IMF Chief Suggests IMFCoin Cryptocurrency as Possibility," Investopedia, June 25, 2019, https://www.investopedia.com/news/imf-chief-suggests-imfcoin-cryptocurrency-possibility.

253 Jackie Wattles, "George Soros Has Given $18 Billion to His Pro-Democracy Foundation," CNN Money, CNN, October 17, 2017, https://money.cnn.com/2017/10/17/news/george-soros-18-billion-open-society-foundations/index.html.

254 Stefan Kanfer, "Connoisseur of Chaos," City Journal (Winter 2017), https://www.city-journal.org/html/connoisseur-chaos-14954.html.

255 Daniel Bessner, "The George Soros Philosophy—And Its Fatal Flaw," The

Guardian, July 6, 2018, https://www.theguardian.com/news/2018/jul/06/the-george-soros-philosophy-and-its-fatal-flaw.

256 Bessner, "George Soros Philosophy."

257 Bessner, "George Soros Philosophy."

258 Bessner, "George Soros Philosophy."

259 George Soros, *The Age of Fallibility* (New York: PublicAffairs, 2007).

260 Malter, "Bernie Sanders."

261 Martin Fackler, "Japan's Big-Works Stimulus Is Lesson," *New York Times*, February 5, 2009, https://www.nytimes.com/2009/02/06/world/asia/06japan.html.

262 "GDP (Current US$)—Japan, United States," World Bank, accessed August 7, 2020, https://data.worldbank.org/indicator/NY.GDP.MKTP.CD?Locations=JP-US.

263 James Freeman, "Obama's Stimulus, Five Years Later," *Wall Street Journal*, February 17, 2014, https://www.wsj.com/articles/obama8217s-stimulus-five-years-later-1392640078.

264 Kelton, *Deficit Myth.*

265 Justin Haskins, "Biden's Socialists—Look Who the So-Called Moderate Has Added to His Campaign," Fox News, May 25, 2020, https://www.foxnews.com/opinion/biden-socialists-bernie-sanders-aoc-no-moderate-justin-haskins.

266 George Sorors, "Remarks Delivered at the World Economic Forum," George Sorors (website), January 23, 2020, https://www.georgesoros.com/2020/01/23/remarks-delivered-at-the-world-economic-forum-3.

267 Elizabeth Redden, "Open Society University Network Launched With $1 Billion Gift," Insider HigherEd, February 4, 2020, https://www.inside-highered.com/news/2020/02/04/amid-authoritarian-resurgence-george-soros-pledges-1-billion-toward-new-university.

268 "Bard College and Partners Establish Global Network to Transform Higher Education," Bard College, January 28, 2020, https://www.bard.edu/news/bard-college-and-partners-establish-global-network-to-transform-higher-education-2020-01-28.

269 Levy Economics Institute, "Scholars," Bard College, accessed September 20, 2020, http://www.levyinstitute.org/scholars/?Order=K.

270 "About the Great Reset: A Unique Twin Summit to Begin 2021," World Economic Forum, accessed July 14, 2020, https://web.archive.org/

web/20200919193837/https://www.weforum.org/great-reset/about.

271 Kate Whiting, "How the World Can 'Reset' Itself After COVID-19—
According to These Experts," World Economic Forum, June 3, 2020,
https://www.weforum.org/agenda/2020/06/covid19-great-reset-gita-
gopinath-jennifer-morgan-sharan-burrow-climate.

Chapter 5: The Great Reset: Building a Twenty-First Century Fascism Machine

272 "'Normal Wasn't Working'—John Kerry, Phillip Atiba Goff and Others
on the New Social Contract Post-COVID," World Economic Forum, June
24, 2020, https://www.weforum.org/agenda/2020/06/great-reset-social-
contract-john-kerry-phillip-goff.

273 Klaus Schwab, "Now Is the Time for a 'Great Reset,'" World Economic
Forum, June 3, 2020, https://www.weforum.org/agenda/2020/06/now-is-
the-time-for-a-great-reset.

274 Schwab, "Now Is the Time for a 'Great Reset.'"

275 Christopher Alessi, "'Collective Action'—Restarting the Global Economy
Amid a Great Reset," World Economic Forum, June 10, 2020, https://
www.weforum.org/agenda/2020/06/covid-great-reset-gillian-tett-abiy-
ahmed.

276 See Ben Zimmer, "Who First Put 'Lipstick on a Pig,'" *Slate*, September 10,
2008, https://slate.com/news-and-politics/2008/09/where-does-the-
expression-lipstick-on-a-pig-come-from.html. (Yes, I, Glenn Beck, really
did just cite an article by *Slate*. Deal with it.)

277 Schwab, "Now Is the Time for a 'Great Reset.'"

278 Schwab, "Now Is the Time for a 'Great Reset.'"

279 Schwab, "Now Is the Time for a 'Great Reset.'"

280 Schwab, "Now Is the Time for a 'Great Reset.'"

281 Schwab, "Now Is the Time for a 'Great Reset.'"

282 Schwab, "Now Is the Time for a 'Great Reset.'"

283 Kate Whiting, "How the World Can 'Reset' Itself After COVID-19—
According to These Experts," World Economic Forum, June 3, 2020,
https://www.weforum.org/agenda/2020/06/covid19-great-reset-gita-
gopinath-jennifer-morgan-sharan-burrow-climate.

284 Whiting, "How the World Can 'Reset.'"

285 Whiting, "How the World Can 'Reset.'"

286 ITUC Campaign Brief, "A Global Social Protection Fund Is Possible,"

International Trade Union Confederation, June 29, 2020, https://www.
ituc-csi.org/global-social-protection-fund.

287 ITUC Campaign Brief, "A Global Social Protection Fund Is Possible."

288 Kristalina Georgieva, "Remarks to World Economic Forum," speech given
to the World Economic Forum, June 3, 2020, https://www.imf.org/en/
News/Articles/2020/06/03/sp060320-remarks-to-world-economic-
forum-the-great-reset.

289 Georgieva, "Remarks to World Economic Forum."

290 Georgieva, "Remarks to World Economic Forum."

291 Georgieva, "Remarks to World Economic Forum."

292 David D. Kirkpatrick and Benjamin Mueller, "U.K. Backs Off Medical
Rationing Plan as Coronavirus Rages," New York Times, April 3, 2020,
https://www.nytimes.com/2020/04/03/world/europe/britain-corona-
virus-triage.html.

293 Kirkpatrick and Mueller, "U.K. Backs Off."

294 Guy Standing, "Coronavirus Has Shown Us Why We Urgently Need to
Make a Basic Income a Reality," World Economic Forum, April 13, 2020,
https://www.weforum.org/agenda/2020/04/coronavirus-made-basic-
income-vital.

295 Kanni Wignaraja and Balazs Horvath, "Universal Basic Income is the
Answer to the Inequalities Exposed by COVID-19," World Economic
Forum, April 17, 2020, https://www.weforum.org/agenda/2020/04/
covid-19-universal-basic-income-social-inequality.

296 "The Great Reset: A Unique Twin Summit to Begin 2021," World
Economic Forum, June 3, 2020, https://www.weforum.org/great-reset/
about.

297 Martina Larkin, "The European Green Deal Must be at the Heart of the
COVID-19 Recovery," World Economic Forum, May 14, 2020, https://
www.weforum.org/agenda/2020/05/the-european-green-deal-must-be-at-
the-heart-of-the-covid-19-recovery.

298 Larkin, "European Green Deal."

299 Sandrine Dixson-Decleve, Hans Joachim Schellnhuber, and Kate Raworth,
"Could COVID-19 Give Rise to a Greener Global Future?," World
Economic Forum and Project Syndicate, March 25, 2020, https://www.
weforum.org/agenda/2020/03/a-green-reboot-after-the-pandemic.

300 Dixson-Decleve, Schnellnhuber, and Raworth, "Could COVID-19 Give

Rise to a Greener Global Future?"

301   Dixson-Decleve, Schnellnhuber, and Raworth, "Could COVID-19 Give
      Rise to a Greener Global Future?"

302   "The Great Reset," World Economic Forum.

303   Schwab, "Now Is the Time for a 'Great Reset.'"

304   "The Great Reset," World Economic Forum.

305   Feike Sijbesma, "We Need Multilateral Cooperation and a Reset to Recover
      Better," World Economic Forum, July 21, 2020, https://www.weforum.org/
      agenda/2020/07/multilateral-cooperation-reset-recover-better.

306   Schwab, "Now Is the Time for a 'Great Reset.'"

307   Merriam-Webster's Dictionary, s.v. "stakeholder," accessed August 5, 2020,
      https://www.merriam-webster.com/dictionary/stakeholder.

308   Sijbesma, "We Need Multilateral Cooperation."

309   "Stakeholder Capitalism: A Manifesto for a Cohesive and Sustainable
      World," World Economic Forum, January 14, 2020, https://www.weforum.
      org/press/2020/01/stakeholder-capitalism-a-manifesto-for-a-cohesive-
      and-sustainable-world.

310   Sijbesma, "We Need Multilateral Cooperation."

311   "Transforming Our World: The 2030 Agenda for Sustainable Devel-
      opment," United Nations, September 2015, https://sustainabledevel-
      opment.un.org/post2015/transformingourworld.

312   "Transforming Our World," United Nations.

313   "Transforming Our World," United Nations.

314   "Transforming Our World," United Nations.

315   Klaus Schwab, "Davos Manifesto 2020: The Universal Purpose of a
      Company in the Fourth Industrial Revolution," World Economic Forum,
      December 2, 2019, https://www.weforum.org/agenda/2019/12/davos-
      manifesto-2020-the-universal-purpose-of-a-company-in-the-fourth-indus-
      trial-revolution.

316   Schwab, "Davos Manifesto 2020."

317   Jonathan Walter et al., Toward Common Metrics and Consistent Reporting
      of Sustainable Value Creation (Geneva: World Economic Forum, 2020),
      http://www3.weforum.org/docs/WEF_IBC_Measuring_Stakeholder_
      Capitalism_Report_2020.pdf.

318   Walter et al., Toward Common Metrics.

319   Walter et al., Toward Common Metrics.

320 Walter et al., *Toward Common Metrics*.

321 Elisabeth Andvig, "Corporations Must Help Shape a Better World—or Risk Being Left Behind," World Economic Forum, May 24, 2020, https:// www.weforum.org/agenda/2019/05/corporations-businesses-better-world-human-rights-corruption-environmental-social-responsibilities.

322 Christopher Flavelle, "Climate Change Poses 'Systemic Threat' to the Economy, Big Investors Warn," *New York Times*, July 21, 2020, https:// www.nytimes.com/2020/07/21/climate/investors-climate-threat-regulators.html.

323 Flavelle, "Climate Change Poses 'Systemic Threat.'"

324 Ceri Parker, "End Fossil Fuel Subsidies and Reset the Economy for a Better World—IMF Head," World Economic Forum, June 3, 2020, https://www. weforum.org/agenda/2020/06/end-fossil-fuel-subsidies-economy-imf-georgieva-great-reset-climate.

325 Perkins Coie, "Climate Change Takes Center Stage at the SEC," Perkins Coie (website), March 8, 2021, https://www.perkinscoie.com/en/news-insights/climate-change-takes-center-stage-at-the-sec.html.

326 Bill Dudley, "The Federal Reserve Takes Climate Change Seriously," *Bloomberg*, August 23, 2021, https://www.bloomberg.com/opinion/ articles/2021-08-23/the-federal-reserve-takes-climate-change-seriously.

327 Justin Haskins, "How the European Union Could Soon Force America into the 'Great Reset' Trap," Townhall, June 21, 2021, https://townhall.com/ columnists/justinhaskins/2021/06/21/how-the-european-union-could-soon-force-america-into-the-great-reset-trap-n2591253.

328 Alex Bevan et al., "EU Signals New Mandatory ESG Due Diligence for Companies Operating in EU," Shearman and Sterling, April 2021, https:// www.shearman.com/Perspectives/2021/04/New-Mandatory-Human-Rights-Environmental-and-Governance-Due-Diligence-for-Companies-in-EU-Market.

329 European Union: European Parliament, *European Parliament Resolution on Corporate Due Diligence and Corporate Accountability*, 10 March 2021, P9_TA(2021)0073, accessed October 4, 2021, https://www.europarl.europa. eu/doceo/document/TA-9-2021-0073_EN.pdf.

330 European Union: *European Parliament Resolution on Corporate Due Diligence*.

331 Klaus Schwab, "What Kind of Capitalism Do We Want?," *TIME*,

December 2, 2019, https://time.com/5742066/klaus-schwab-stakeholder-capitalism-davos.

332 Schwab, "Now Is the Time for a 'Great Reset.'"

333 Tolullah Oni, "How COVID Has Revealed the Need for a Rethink in Urban Planning," World Economic Forum, July 20, 2020, https://www.weforum.org/agenda/2020/07/marshall-plan-health-cities-future-environment-urban.

334 Oni, "How COVID Has Revealed the Need for a Rethink."

335 Whiting, "How the World Can 'Reset.'"

336 Whiting, "How the World Can 'Reset.'"

337 Jennifer Rankin, "Link Climate Pledges to €26bn Airline Bailout, Say Europe's Greens," The Guardian, April 30, 2020, https://www.theguardian.com/business/2020/apr/30/link-climate-pledges-to-26bn-airline-bailout-say-europes-greens-environment.

338 Bank of America, "Bank of America Announces Actions to Achieve Net Zero Greenhouse Gas Emissions before 2050," Yahoo!Finance, February 11, 2021, https://finance.yahoo.com/news/bank-america-announces-actions-achieve-141500511.html.

339 Jane Fraser, "Citi's Commitment to Net Zero by 2050," Citi, March 1, 2021, https://blog.citigroup.com/2021/03/citis-commitment-to-net-zero-by-2050.

340 Fraser, "Citi's Commitment to Net Zero."

341 Iain Murray, "Has Operation Choke Point Ended?," Blaze Media, October 24, 2014, https://www.theblaze.com/contributions/has-operation-choke-point-ended.

342 Murray, "Has Operation Choke Point Ended?"

343 Victoria Guida, "Justice Department to End Obama-Era 'Operation Choke Point,'" Politico, August 17, 2017, https://www.politico.com/story/2017/08/17/trump-reverses-obama-operation-chokepoint-241767.

344 "Financial Institutions Taking Action," accessed March 18, 2021, https://carbonaccountingfinancials.com/financial-institutions-taking-action.

345 "One Year On: Coalition of Signatory Banks, Civil Society Shares Progress Implementing the UN Principles for Responsible Banking," UN Environment Programme Finance Initiative, September 2020, https://www.unepfi.org/news/industries/banking/one-year-on-coalition-of-signatory-banks-civil-society-shares-progress-implementing-the-un-

principles-for-responsible-banking.

346 "One Year On," UN Environment Programme Finance Initiative.

347 "The Great Reset," World Economic Forum.

348 "About the PRI," Principles for Responsible Investment, accessed January 12, 2021, https://www.unpri.org/pri/about-the-pri.

349 "About the PRI," Principles for Responsible Investment.

350 "About the PRI," Principles for Responsible Investment.

351 "What Is the Inevitable Policy Response?" Principles of Responsible Investment, accessed January 13, 2021, https://www.unpri.org/inevitable-policy-response/what-is-the-inevitable-policy-response/4787.article.

352 "What Is the Inevitable Policy Response?" Principles of Responsible Investment.

353 Lucian Bebchuk and Scott Hirst, "The Specter of the Giant Three," *Boston University Law Review* 99, no. 721 (2019), https://scholarship.law.bu.edu/cgi/viewcontent.cgi?article=1601&context=faculty_scholarship.

354 Bebchuk and Hirst, "Specter of the Giant Three."

355 Bebchuk and Hirst, "Specter of the Giant Three."

356 Tim Lemke, "The 10 Largest Investment Management Companies Worldwide," The Balance, last updated August 6, 2021, https://www.thebalance.com/which-firms-have-the-most-assets-under-management-4173923.

357 Thomas Mitterling, Nirai Tomass, and Kelsey Wu, "The Decline and Recovery of Consumer Spending in the US," Brookings Institution, December 14, 2020, https://www.brookings.edu/blog/future-development/2020/12/14/the-decline-and-recovery-of-consumer-spending-in-the-us.

358 "Leadership and Governance," World Economic Forum, accessed September 26, 2021, https://www.weforum.org/about/leadership-and-governance.

359 Amy Whyte, "State Street to Turn Up the Heat on All-Male Boards," *Institutional Investor*, September 27, 2018, https://www.institutionalinvestor.com/article/b1b4fh28ys3mr9/State-Street-to-Turn-Up-the-Heat-on-All-Male-Boards.

360 Whyte, "State Street to Turn Up the Head."

361 "Signatory Directory," Principles for Responsible Investment, accessed September 26, 2021, https://www.unpri.org/signatories/

signatory-resources/signatory-directory.

362 Sophie Alexander, Sonali Basak, and Steven Arons, "Deutsche Bank, Signature Cutting Ties with Trump after Riots," *Bloomberg*, updated January 12, 2021, https://www.bloomberg.com/news/articles/2021-01-12/trump-s-long-favored-banks-pull-back-amid-fallout-from-d-c-riot.

363 Alexander, Basak, and Arons, "Deutsche Bank."

364 Constance Grady, "Josh Hawley's Book Deal Cancellation Comes after a Year of Social Debates in Publishing," Vox, January 11, 2021, https://www.vox.com/culture/22218971/josh-hawley-tyranny-of-big-tech-simon-schuster-publishing-controversy.

365 See Eshe Nelson, "There's a New S&P 500 Index Without All the Bad Stuff," *Quartz*, May 20, 2020, https://qz.com/1621860/a-new-sp-500-index-promotes-esg-investing.

366 Bank of America, "Bank of America Announces Actions."

367 Amanda Lee, "What Is China's Social Credit System and Why Is It Controversial?," *South China Morning Post*, August 9, 2020, https://www.scmp.com/economy/china-economy/article/3096090/what-chinas-social-credit-system-and-why-it-controversial.

368 Lee, "What Is China's Social Credit System?"

369 Klaus Schwab, "Now Is the Time for a 'Great Reset,'" World Economic Forum, June 3, 2020, https://www.weforum.org/agenda/2020/06/now-is-the-time-for-a-great-reset. Emphasis in the quote added by the authors.

370 David Sangokoya, "Social Justice, Inclusion and Sustainable Development Need a 'Great Reset.' Here Are 3 Key Steps We Can Take," World Economic Forum, October 8, 2020, https://www.weforum.org/agenda/2020/10/social-justice-inclusion-and-sustainable-development-need-a-great-reset-here-are-3-key-steps.

371 Sangokoya, "Social Justice."

372 Sangokoya, "Social Justice."

373 "Global Alliance for Responsible Media (GARM)," World Economic Forum, accessed January 13, 2021, https://www.weforum.org/projects/global-alliance-for-responsible-media-garm.

374 Hadas Gold, Ya Chun Wang, and Benjamin Berteau, "French Parliament Passes Law Requiring Social Media Companies Delete Certain Content Within an Hour," CNN, updated May 14, 2020, https://www.cnn.com/2020/05/13/tech/french-hate-speech-social-media-law/index.html.

375 Gold, Wang, and Berteau, "French Parliament Passes Law."

376 Gold, Wang, and Berteau, "French Parliament Passes Law."

377 Gold, Wang, and Berteau, "French Parliament Passes Law."

378 Aurelien Breeden, "French Court Strikes Down Most of Online Hate Speech Law," *New York Times,* June 18, 2020, https://www.nytimes.com/2020/06/18/world/europe/france-internet-hate-speech-regulation.html.

379 Andre Oboler, "How Technology Can Be Used to Combat Online Hate Speech," World Economic Forum, March 13, 2018, https://www.weforum.org/agenda/2018/03/technology-and-regulation-must-work-in-concert-to-combat-hate-speech-online.

380 Tristan Justice, "Reddit Bans Massive r/DonaldTrump Subreddit Page," *The Federalist,* January 8, 2021, https://thefederalist.com/2021/01/08/reddit-bans-massive-r-donaldtrump-subreddit-page.

381 Joy Pullmann, "Big Corporate Uses Capitol Riots to Push Communist-Style Social Credit System on Americans," *The Federalist,* January 11, 2021, https://thefederalist.com/2021/01/11/big-corporate-uses-capitol-riots-to-push-communist-style-social-credit-system-on-americans.

382 Chris Pandolfo, "Exclusive: Facebook Permanently Bans Retailer PatrioticMe from Advertising Pro-America Products," Blaze Media, January 12, 2021, https://www.theblaze.com/news/facebook-bans-retailer-pro-america-products.

383 Pandolfo, "Exclusive: Facebook Permanently Bans Retailer Patriotic Me."

384 Jordan Davidson, "The Biggest Gun Forum on the Planet Was Just Kicked off the Internet without Explanation," *The Federalist,* January 12, 2021, https://thefederalist.com/2021/01/12/the-biggest-gun-forum-on-the-planet-was-just-kicked-off-the-internet-without-explanation.

385 Erin Powell, "Alumni Want DU to Disavow Parler, the Right-Wing App Created by Two Grads," 9News, January 12, 2021, https://www.9news.com/article/news/local/next/parler-university-of-denver-alumni-app/73-1cd77a97-fff0-4bcd-ab88-de430c53f342.

386 Deepa Bharath, "Social Media Platform Parler Wins Over Millions as Some Raise Red Flags about the Site," *Daily Bulletin,* updated November 21, 2020, https://www.dailybulletin.com/2020/11/20/social-media-platform-parler-wins-over-millions-as-some-raise-red-flags-about-the-site.

387 Jonathan Shieber, "Parler Jumps to No. 1 on App Store after Facebook and Twitter Ban Trump," TechCrunch, January 9, 2021, https://techcrunch.

com/2021/01/09/parler-jumps-to-no-1-on-app-store-after-facebook-and-twitter-bans.

388 Jack Nicas and Davey Alba, "Amazon, Apple and Google Cut Off Parler, an App that Drew Trump Supporters," *New York Times*, January 13, 2021, https://www.nytimes.com/2021/01/09/technology/apple-google-parler.

389 Nicas and Alba, "Amazon, Apple and Google."

390 Audrey Courty, "Parler: What You Need to Know About the 'Free Speech' Twitter Alternative," The Conversation, July 13, 2020, https://theconversation.com/parler-what-you-need-to-know-about-the-free-speech-twitter-alternative-142268.

391 Courty, "Parler."

392 Marina Watts, "Parler, the Ted Cruz–Approved 'Free Speech' App, Is Already Banning Users," *Newsweek*, June 30, 2020, https://www.newsweek.com/parler-ted-cruz-approved-free-speech-app-already-banning-users-1514358.

393 Danielle Abril, "Conservative Social Media Darling Parler Discovers that Free Speech Is Messy," *Fortune*, July 1, 2020, https://fortune.com/2020/07/01/what-is-parler-conservative-free-speech-misinformation-hate-speech-john-matze.

394 Rachel Lerman, "The Conservative Alternative to Twitter Wants to be a Place for Free Speech for All. It Turns Out, Rules Still Apply," *Washington Post*, July 15, 2020, https://www.washingtonpost.com/technology/2020/07/15/parler-conservative-twitter-alternative.

395 Joseph A. Wulfsohn, "Twitter Bans Trump, but Iranian Ayatollah, Louis Farrakhan, Chinese Propagandists Still Active," Fox News, January 9, 2021, https://www.foxnews.com/media/twitter-permanently-bans-trumps-but-iranian-ayatollah-louis-farrakhan-chinese-propagandists-still-active.

396 Jacob Taylor, "Rep. Waters Calls for Harassing Admin Officials in Public, Trump Calls Her 'Low IQ,'" NBC News, June 25, 2018, https://www.nbcnews.com/politics/politics-news/rep-waters-draws-criticism-saying-trump-officials-should-be-harassed-n886311.

397 Joseph Wulfsohn, "CNN's Chris Cuomo Blasted for Suggesting Protesters Don't Have to Be 'Peaceful,'" Fox News, June 3, 2020, https://www.foxnews.com/media/cnns-chris-cuomo-blasted-for-suggesting-protesters-dont-have-to-be-peaceful.

398 See *Marsh v. Alabama*, 326 U.S. 501 (1946), https://supreme.justia.com/

cases/federal/us/326/501.

399 Richard Threlfall et al., *The Time Has Come: The KPMG Survey of Sustainability Reporting 2020* (Amstelveen, Netherlands: KPMG, 2020), https://assets.kpmg/content/dam/kpmg/xx/pdf/2020/11/the-time-has-come.pdf.

400 Moody's ESG Solutions, "Moody's Launches First-of-Its-Kind ESG Score Predictor to Provide Transparency on ESG Risk for Millions of SMEs Worldwide," BusinessWire, press release, July 13, 2021, https://www.businesswire.com/news/home/20210713005792/en/Moodys-Launches-First-of-Its-Kind-ESG-Score-Predictor-to-Provide-Transparency-on-ESG-Risk-for-Millions-of-SMEs-Worldwide.

Chapter 6: Joe Biden and the Great Reset of America

401 Institute of Medicine Forum on Microbial Threats; S.L. Knobler et al., eds., *The Threat of Pandemic Influenza: Are We Ready?* (Washington, DC: National Academies Press, 2005), https://www.ncbi.nlm.nih.gov/books/NBK22148.

402 "Great Depression History," HISTORY, last updated February 28, 2020, https://www.history.com/topics/great-depression/great-depression-history.

403 "Immigrants in the Progressive Era," Library of Congress, accessed July 15, 2021, https://www.loc.gov/classroom-materials/united-states-history-primary-source-timeline/progressive-era-to-new-era-1900-1929/immigrants-in-progressive-era/.

404 Ronald Sullivan, "Stuart Chase, 97; Coined Phrase 'A New Deal,'" *New York Times*, November 17, 1985, https://www.nytimes.com/1985/11/17/nyregion/stuart-chase-97-coined-phrase-a-new-dea.html.

405 Sullivan, "Stuart Chase."

406 Stuart Chase, *The Road We Are Traveling, 1914–1942* (New York: Twentieth Century Fund, 1942).

407 Chase, *Road We Are Traveling.*

408 Chase, *Road We Are Traveling.*

409 Chase, *Road We Are Traveling*, 95–96.

410 Chase, *Road We Are Traveling.*

411 Chase, *Road We Are Traveling*, 102.

412 Chloe Taylor, "Coronavirus Crisis Presents a 'Golden Opportunity' to

Reboot the Economy, Prince Charles Says," CNBC, June 3, 2020, https://www.cnbc.com/2020/06/03/prince-charles-covid-19-a-golden-opportunity-to-reboot-the-economy.html.

413 Chase, *Road We Are Traveling.*

414 NBC News, "Al Gore Talks Climate Crisis: 'This Is the Time for a Great Reset,'" TODAY Show, June 19, 2020, streaming video, 7:02, https://www.today.com/video/al-gore-talks-climate-crisis-this-is-the-time-for-a-great-reset-85439045592, quoted in Justin Haskins, "Al Gore Joins Global Elites Calling for Eco-Socialist 'Great Reset' Proposal," Stopping Socialism, June 22, 2020, https://stoppingsocialism.com/2020/06/al-gore-great-reset.

415 "World Economic Forum Appoints New Members to Board of Trustees," World Economic Forum, September 2, 2020, https://www.weforum.org/press/2020/09/world-economic-forum-appoints-new-members-to-board-of-trustees-3b4f679708.

416 *2019 Annual Report,* Climate Reality Project, accessed August 6, 2020, https://www.climaterealityproject.org/2019-annual-report.

417 "The Great Reset: A Unique Twin Summit to Begin 2021," World Economic Forum, June 3, 2020, https://web.archive.org/web/20200919193837/https://www.weforum.org/great-reset/about.

418 "Great Reset," World Economic Forum.

419 "Greta Thunberg: Who is She and What Does She Want?," BBC News, February 28, 2020, https://www.bbc.com/news/world-europe-49918719; see also "Youth Climate Strikes: Speak Up to Save the World," Climate Reality Project, September 17, 2019, https://www.climaterealityproject.org/blog/youth-climate-strikes-speak-save-world; and *2019 Annual Report,* Climate Reality Project.

420 *2019 Annual Report,* Climate Reality Project.

421 Kate Whiting, "How the World Can 'Reset' Itself after COVID-19—According to These Experts," World Economic Forum, June 3, 2020, https://www.weforum.org/agenda/2020/06/covid19-great-reset-gita-gopinath-jennifer-morgan-sharan-burrow-climate.

422 See chapter 5.

423 "'Normal Wasn't Working'—John Kerry, Phillip Atiba Goff and Others on the New Social Contract Post-COVID," World Economic Forum, June 24, 2020, https://www.weforum.org/agenda/2020/06/great-reset-social-contract-john-kerry-phillip-goff.

424 "'Normal Wasn't Working,'" World Economic Forum.

425 "'Normal Wasn't Working,'" World Economic Forum.

426 Quint Forgey, "Biden, Sanders Name Leaders of Their 'Unity Task Forces'—Including AOC," *Politico*, May 13, 2020, https://www.politico.com/news/2020/05/13/biden-sanders-unity-task-forces-leaders-aoc-254456.

427 Forgey, "Biden, Sanders Name Leaders."

428 Ellen Knickmeyer, "Biden Names Climate Statesman John Kerry as Climate Envoy," Associated Press, November 23, 2020, https://apnews.com/article/joe-biden-climate-climate-change-john-kerry-national-security-ee05316df77b8d532921a2e299388a62\.

429 Joe Biden, "The Biden Plan to Build a Modern, Sustainable Infrastructure and an Equitable Clean Energy Future," Joe Biden (website), accessed August 8, 2020, https://joebiden.com/clean-energy.

430 Biden, "The Biden Plan."

431 Biden, "The Biden Plan."

432 Emma Newburger, "Here's How Biden's $2 Trillion Infrastructure Plan Addresses Climate Change," CNBC, March 31, 2021, https://www.cnbc.com/2021/03/31/biden-infrastructure-plan-spending-on-climate-change-clean-energy.html.

433 Jonathan Easley, "Biden Strikes Populist Tone in Blistering Rebuke of Trump, Wall Street," *The Hill*, July 9, 2020, https://thehill.com/homenews/campaign/506634-biden-strikes-populist-tone-in-blistering-economic-rebuke-of-trump-wall.

434 Raja Rehan Arshad, "How Would Your Country Recover from Disaster?," World Economic Forum, March 17, 2020, https://www.weforum.org/agenda/2015/03/how-would-your-country-recover-from-disaster.

435 Etienne Kechichian, "How Can We Reduce the Risk of Climate Disasters?," World Economic Forum, March 1, 2016, https://www.weforum.org/agenda/2016/03/how-can-we-reduce-the-risk-of-climate-disasters; Etienne Kechichian, "Build It Better: Climate Competitive Industries and Resilience," *World Bank Blogs*, World Bank, February 22, 2016, https://blogs.worldbank.org/psd/build-it-better-climate-competitive-industries-and-resilience.

436 Katie Clift and Alexander Court, "How Are Companies Responding to the Coronavirus Crisis?," World Economic Forum, March 23, 2020, https://

www.weforum.org/agenda/2020/03/how-are-companies-responding-to-the-coronavirus-crisis-d15bed6137.

437 Maria Mendiluce, "How to Build Back Better after COVID-19," World Economic Forum, April 3, 2020, https://www.weforum.org/agenda/2020/04/how-to-build-back-better-after-covid-19.

438 Mendiluce, "How to Build Back Better."

439 Johnny Wood, "'Building Back Better'—Here's How We Can Navigate the Risks We Face After COVID-19," World Economic Forum, May 20, 2020, https://www.weforum.org/agenda/2020/05/covid-19-risks-outlook-saadia-zahidi.

440 David Victor, "Building Back Better: Why Europe Must Lead a Global Green Recovery," *Environment 360*, Yale University, June 11, 2020, https://e360.yale.edu/features/building-back-better-why-europe-must-lead-a-global-green-recovery.

441 Easley, "Biden Strikes Populist Tone."

442 Peter Bakker and John Elkington, "To Build Back Better, We Must Reinvent Capitalism. Here's How," World Economic Forum, July 13, 2020, https://www.weforum.org/agenda/2020/07/to-build-back-better-we-must-reinvent-capitalism-heres-how.

443 See Justin Haskins, "Joe Biden Has Deep Ties to the Radical 'Great Reset' Movement and Its Globalist Leaders," Blaze Media, October 26, 2020, https://www.theblaze.com/op-ed/joe-biden-ties-great-reset.

444 Haskins, "Joe Biden Has Deep Ties."

445 Haskins, "Joe Biden Has Deep Ties."

446 Justin Haskins, "John Kerry Reveals Biden's Devotion to Radical 'Great Reset' Movement," *The Hill*, December 3, 2020, https://thehill.com/opinion/energy-environment/528482-john-kerry-reveals-bidens-devotion-to-radical-great-reset-movement.

447 Haskins, "John Kerry Reveals."

448 Haskins, "John Kerry Reveals."

449 Haskins, "John Kerry Reveals."

450 Justin Haskins, "Biden's Made in America Order—Here's What Part of America He's Talking About," Fox News, February 14, 2021, https://www.foxnews.com/opinion/biden-made-america-order-social-justice-justin-haskiins.

451 "President Biden to Sign Executive Order Strengthening Buy American

Provisions, Ensuring Future of America Is Made in America by All of America's Workers," White House, January 25, 2021, https://www. whitehouse.gov/briefing-room/statements-releases/2021/01/25/ president-biden-to-sign-executive-order-strengthening-buy-american- provisions-ensuring-future-of-america-is-made-in-america-by-all-of- americas-workers.

452 Klaus Schwab, "Now Is the Time for a 'Great Reset,'" World Economic Forum, June 3, 2020, https://www.weforum.org/agenda/2020/06/now-is- the-time-for-a-great-reset.

453 Josh Lederman, "Biden's Land Conservation Program to Rely on Voluntary, Local Efforts," NBC News, May 6, 2021, https://www.nbcnews.com/ politics/politics-news/bidens-land-conservation-program-rely-voluntary- local-efforts-rcna846.

454 Sarah Kaplan and Juliet Eilperin, "A Narrow Path for Biden's Ambitious Land Conservation Plan," *Washington Post*, May 6, 2021, https://www. washingtonpost.com/climate-environment/2021/05/06/biden-conser- vation-30x30.

455 Dominic Kailash Nath Waughray et al., "What Is 'Nature Positive' and Why Is It the Key to Our Future?," World Economic Forum, June 23, 2021, https://www.weforum.org/agenda/2021/06/what-is-nature-positive-and- why-is-it-the-key-to-our-future.

456 Waughray et al., "What Is 'Nature Positive'?"

457 Charles Creitz, "BlackRock, Other Investment Firms 'Killing the Dream' of Home Ownership, Journalist Says," Fox News, June 12, 2021, https:// www.foxnews.com/media/blackrock-investment-firms-killing-dream- home-ownership.

458 Ryan Dezember, "If You Sell a House These Days, the Buyer Might be a Pension Fund," *Wall Street Journal*, April 4, 2021, https://www.wsj.com/ articles/if-you-sell-a-house-these-days-the-buyer-might-be-a-pension- fund-11617544801.

459 Ida Auken, "Welcome to 2030. I Own Nothing, Have No Privacy, and Life Has Never Been Better," World Economic Forum, November 11, 2016, https://web.archive.org/web/20200920085124/https://www.weforum. org/agenda/2016/11/shopping-i-can-t-really-remember-what-that-is/.

460 Auken, "Welcome to 2030."

461 Sonny Mazzone, "Biden Administration Suspends Rule Protecting

Businesses from Banking Discrimination," *Reason*, February 2, 2021, https://reason.com/2021/02/11/biden-administration-suspends-rule-protecting-businesses-from-banking-discrimination.

462 Mazzone, "Biden Administration."

463 Richard Friedman, E. Suchman, and Neil Popovic, "House Passes Bill Requiring SEC to Define Mandatory ESG Metrics," *National Law Review*, June 23, 2021, https://www.natlawreview.com/article/house-passes-bill-requiring-sec-to-define-mandatory-esg-metrics.

464 Friedman, Suchman, and Popovic, "House Passes Bill."

465 Friedman, Suchman, and Popovic, "House Passes Bill."

466 Friedman, Suchman, and Popovic, "House Passes Bill."

467 Justin Pritchard, "How Credit Scores Work and What They Say About You," *The Balance*, updated March 16, 2020, https://www.thebalance.com/how-credit-scores-work-315541.

468 Pritchard, "How Credit Scores Work."

469 Pritchard, "How Credit Scores Work."

470 Adam S. Minsky, "New Bills Would Reshape Credit Reporting for Private Student Loan Borrowers and Other Consumers," *Forbes*, July 8, 2021, https://www.forbes.com/sites/adamminsky/2021/07/08/new-bills-would-reshape-credit-reporting-for-private-student-loan-borrowers-and-other-consumers/?sh=6fbe45e5191c.

471 Jayme Deerwester, "Congress Considers Credit-Reporting Overhaul, Including Putting Government in Charge of Scores," *USA Today*, July 2, 2021, https://www.usatoday.com/story/money/personalfinance/2021/07/02/congress-credit-score-overhaul-proposal-act/46965135.

472 Deerwester, "Congress Considers Credit-Reporting Overhaul."

473 "FACT SHEET: President Biden and G7 Leaders Launch Build Back Better World (B3W) Partnership," White House, June 12, 2021, https://www.whitehouse.gov/briefing-room/statements-releases/2021/06/12/fact-sheet-president-biden-and-g7-leaders-launch-build-back-better-world-b3w-partnership.

474 "FACT SHEET: President Biden," White House.

Chapter 7: Derailing the Great Reset

475 Nina Strochlic, "Gen. Norman Schwarzkopf's Best Quotes," *The Daily Beast*, last updated July 14, 2017, https://www.thedailybeast.com/

gen-norman-schwarzkopfs-best-quotes.

476 Brian Dunleavy, "Life in the Trenches of World War I," HISTORY, updated January 6, 2020, https://www.history.com/news/life-in-the-trenches-of-world-war-i.

477 For a detailed description of Lenin's train ride and its implications, see Catherine Merridale, *Lenin on the Train* (New York: Metropolitan Books, 2017).

478 History.com Editors, "April 16: Lenin Returns to Russia from Exile," HISTORY, updated April 14, 2021, https://www.history.com/this-day-in-history/lenin-returns-to-russia-from-exile.

479 See Vejas Gabriel Liulevicius, "World War I as a Revolutionary Opportunity," in *The Rise of Communism: From Marx to Lenin*, The Great Courses, 2019, https://www.thegreatcourses.com/courses/the-rise-of-communism-from-marx-to-lenin.html.

480 Liulevicius, "World War I."

481 Sara Fischer, "Only 33% of Republicans Trust the Media," Axios, February 25, 2020, https://www.axios.com/republicans-democrats-media-trust-a8e5da5c-637c-4d22-bbd1-47915f748699.html.

482 Fischer, "Only 33%."

483 Aleksandr Solzhenitsyn, "Live Not by Lies," February 12, 1974, Aleksandr Solzhenitsyn Center, https://www.solzhenitsyncenter.org/live-not-by-lies.

484 Solzhenitsyn, "Live Not by Lies."

485 "Toplines—The Heartland Institute: Great Reset of Global Economy—December 6–7, 2020," Rasmussen Reports, December 2020, https://www.rasmussenreports.com/public_content/politics/partner_surveys/toplines_the_heartland_institute_great_reset_of_global_economy_december_6_7_2020.

486 "Great Reset of Global Economy," Rasmussen Reports.

487 Benjamin Zycher, "With Politicized Lending, Biden Aims to Revive 'Operation Choke Point,'" RealClear Markets, February 17, 2021, https://www.realclearmarkets.com/articles/2021/02/17/with_politicized_lending_biden_aims_to_revive_operation_choke_point_660612.html.

488 Zycher, "Biden Aims to Revive."

489 Amanda Shendruk, "A Simple Guide to Exactly How the United Nations Is Funded," *Quartz*, September 24, 2019, https://qz.com/1712054/who-funds-the-united-nations.

490 Shendruk, "Simple Guide."

491 Gordan Gray and Thomas Wade, "U.S. Participation in the International Monetary Fund (IMF): A Primer," American Action Forum, October 23, 2018, https://www.americanactionforum.org/insight/u-s-participation-in-the-international-monetary-fund-imf-a-primer.

492 Robert G. Natelson, "Counting to Two Thirds: How Close Are We to a Convention for Proposing Amendments to the Constitution?," Federalist Society Review 19 (May 9, 2018), https://fedsoc.org/commentary/publications/counting-to-two-thirds-how-close-are-we-to-a-convention-for-proposing-amendments-to-the-constitution.

493 Natelson, "Counting to Two Thirds."

494 Natelson, "Counting to Two Thirds."

495 Natelson, "Counting to Two Thirds."

496 "Is It Safe? Absolutely," Convention of States, accessed August 18, 2020, https://conventionofstates.com.

497 "Bill of Rights," National Archives, accessed August 19, 2020, https://www.archives.gov/legislative/features/bor.

498 See Jonah Goldberg, "George Will Called Me An Idiot," National Review, January 15, 2001, https://www.nationalreview.com/2001/01/george-will-called-me-idiot-jonah-goldberg.

499 See Justin Haskins, "Did This New Jersey Lawyer Discover a Lost Constitutional Amendment?," Blaze Media, November 2, 2015, https://www.theblaze.com/contributions/did-this-new-jersey-lawyer-discover-a-lost-constitutional-amendment.

500 Office of the Historian, "The Permanent Apportionment Act of 1929," United States House of Representatives: History, Art & Archives, accessed August 19, 2020, https://history.house.gov/Historical-Highlights/1901-1950/The-Permanent-Apportionment-Act-of-1929.

501 America's current estimated population is 330 million. When divided by 50,000, the cap that would be in place today—had a correctly written Article the First been ratified into law—is 6,600.

502 See, for example, John McLaughlin & Brittany Davin, "Voters Overwhelmingly Support Term Limits for Congress," McLaughlin and Associates, February 8, 2018, https://mclaughlinonline.com/2018/02/08/ma-poll-voters-overwhelmingly-support-term-limits-for-congress.

503 For other proposed amendments to the US Constitution, see Mark Levin,

The Liberty Amendments: Restoring the American Republic (New York: Threshold Editions, 2014).

504 Alyson Klein, "Survey: Educators' Political Leanings, Who They Voted For, Where They Stand on Key Issues," *Education Week*, December 12, 2017, https://www.edweek.org/ew/articles/2017/12/13/survey-paints-political-portrait-of-americas-k-12.html.

505 "Teachers Unions," Open Secrets: Following the Money in Politics, accessed August 19, 2020, https://www.opensecrets.org/industries/indus.php?cycle=2020&ind=l1300.

506 "Teachers Unions," Open Secrets.

507 See "Fourth Annual School Choice Survey Research Results," Beck Research, January 18, 2018, https://www.federationforchildren.org/wp-content/uploads/2018/01/1-18-18-AFC-2018-National-School-Choice-Release-Memo.pdf.

508 Andrew D. Catt et al., *The 123s of School Choice: What the Research Says about Private School Choice Programs in America* (Indianapolis, IN: EdChoice, 2019), accessed August 19, 2020, https://www.edchoice.org/wp-content/uploads/2019/04/123s-of-School-Choice.pdf.

509 Catt et al., *123s of School Choice.*

510 From the letter of St. Paul to the Romans (10:14–15 NIV 2011), available at Bible Hub, last accessed September 23, 2021, https://biblehub.com/niv/romans/10.htm.

511 Gillian Brockell, "'A Republic, If You Can Keep It': Did Ben Franklin Really Say Impeachment Day's Favorite Quote?," *Washington Post*, December 18, 2019, https://www.washingtonpost.com/history/2019/12/18/republic-if-you-can-keep-it-did-ben-franklin-really-say-impeachment-days-favorite-quote.

ABOUT THE AUTHORS

GLENN BECK, RADIO AND TELEVISION HOST AND FOUNDER of TheBlaze.com, has written thirteen #1 bestselling books and is one of the few authors in history to have had #1 national bestsellers in the fiction, nonfiction, self-help, and children's picture book genres. His recent fiction works include the thrillers *Agenda 21*, *The Overton Window*, and its sequel, *The Eye of Moloch*; his many nonfiction titles include *Miracles and Massacres*, *Being George Washington*, *Dreamers and Deceivers*, and *Arguing with Socialists*. For more information about Glenn Beck, his books, television show, podcasts, and live events, visit GlennBeck.com.

JUSTIN HASKINS IS THE DIRECTOR OF THE STOPPING Socialism Center at The Heartland Institute, where he also serves as the organization's editorial director. Haskins is the editor-in-chief of StoppingSocialism.com and a prolific writer. His opinion and analysis articles are regularly published by FoxNews.com, *The Hill*, *Newsweek*, and *Washington Examiner*. Haskins has also appeared on hundreds of radio and television shows and his work has been featured by *The Wall Street Journal*, *Chicago Tribune*, and the White House. For more information about Justin Haskins, visit Heartland.org.